Teacher's Resource Guide
for use with

Architecture

Residential Drawing and Design

by

Clois E. Kicklighter
Dean, School of Technology
and Professor of Construction Technology
Indiana State University
Terre Haute, Indiana

Joan C. Kicklighter, C.H.E.
Co-author of *Residential Housing*
Terre Haute, Indiana

South Holland, Illinois
THE GOODHEART-WILLCOX COMPANY, INC.
Publishers

CONTENTS

INTRODUCTION 5
THE TEXTBOOK 5
    Learning Objectives 6
    Text Body 6
    New Terms 6
    Review Questions 6
    Suggested Activities 6
    Reference Section 6
    Glossary 7
    Index 7

THE WORKBOOK 7
    Questions 7
    Problems/Activities 7

THE TEACHER'S RESOURCE GUIDE 7
COURSE CONTENT 7
TEACHING METHODS 8
    Importance of Planning 9
    Motivation 9
    Student Participation 9
    Create Enthusiasm and Excitement 9
    Problem Solving 10
    Keeping Current 10
VARYING STUDENT ABILITIES 10
    Identifying Students with Special Needs 10
    Mainstreaming the Special Needs Student 11
    Teaching Students with Special Needs 11
    Identifying Gifted Students 12
    Teaching Gifted Students 12
ADDITIONAL STUDENT EXPERIENCES 13
    Architecture and Construction Resources 13
    Field Trips 22
    Student Organizations 22
    Summer Work Experience 23
EVALUATION 23
CHAPTER RESOURCES 24
    Objectives 25
    Displays 25
    Instructional Materials 25
    Teaching Strategy 25
    Transparency/Duplicating Masters 25
    Chapter Exam 25

		Resource Guide	Text	Work-book
1	The World of Architecture	27	7	7
2	Basic House Design	31	25	9
3	Primary Considerations	37	37	15
4	Drawing Instruments and Techniques	43	49	21
5	Room Planning, Sleeping Area	55	73	31
6	Room Planning, Living Area	63	89	41
7	Room Planning, Service Area	73	127	53
8	Plot Plans	93	151	63
9	Footings, Foundations, and Concrete	105	161	75
10	The Foundation Plan	117	183	87
11	Sill and Floor Construction	123	193	93
12	Wall and Ceiling Construction	133	209	101
13	Doors and Windows	143	223	107
14	Stairs	153	253	117
15	Fireplaces and Chimneys	163	265	125
16	The Floor Plan	171	283	135
17	Roof Designs	179	301	145
18	Elevations	191	319	157
19	Residential Electrical	199	331	165
20	The Electrical Plan	209	343	173
21	Residential Plumbing	217	349	179
22	The Plumbing Plan	227	359	185
23	Residential Climate Control	233	367	191
24	Climate Control Plan	243	387	197
25	Solar Space Heating	249	395	201
26	Earth Sheltered Dwellings	259	405	207
27	Dome Structures	265	413	213
28	Modular Applications	269	421	217
29	Perspective Drawings	275	429	221
30	Presentation Drawings	287	453	233
31	Architectural Models	291	471	239
32	Material and Tradework Specifications	295	481	243
33	Estimating Building Cost	299	489	245
34	Computer Applications	303	497	251
35	Introduction to Computer-Aided Drafting and Design	307	509	255
36	CADD Software	315	523	261
37	CADD Commands and Functions	325	539	267
38	Architectural CADD Applications	335	555	277
39	Career Opportunities	343	581	283
	Reference Section		587	
	Glossary		637	
	Index		649	

INTRODUCTION

ARCHITECTURE, Residential Drawing and Design provides a complete textbook, workbook, and teacher's resource guide package for use in beginning architectural drawing and design. The package includes comprehensive coverage of design fundamentals and procedures used to represent design ideas using traditional, as well as state-of-the-art technology. The package also helps students to solve problems related to the design of structures. The package also helps to reinforce the topics discussed and assist the student in becoming proficient in illustrating residential designs in proper form.

The ARCHITECTURE, Residential Drawing and Design textbook supplies key knowledge required for designing most types of residential structures. It also includes information in regard to making drawings employing traditional methods as well as CADD systems. Clear and concise drawings illustrate current drafting standards which are consistent with the skills required by modern design and construction firms. The textbook also serves as a resource for design and building principles and techniques. It can also be used to assist in developing the skills required to convey design ideas in an intelligent and precise manner as required in the field.

The subject matter of the textbook is presented in a systematic arrangement. It includes step-by-step instructions written in understandable language. The textbook is completely illustrated with quality photographs and drawings. The functional use of color is used throughout to create interest and add clarity.

Each textbook chapter is enhanced with corresponding chapters in the workbook and resource guide. Various types of questions, problems, and activities are included to reinforce the material presented in the textbook upon completion of each chapter. In addition, teaching strategies and test masters are provided in the Teacher's Resource Guide for each chapter to assist the instructor with the topics presented. The student will gain a thorough understanding of architectural drawing and design and residential construction practices after utilizing all the materials in the package.

THE TEXTBOOK

The textbook contains 39 chapters dealing with all phases of architectural drawing and design. Two chapters discuss house styles and basic house designs, while another deals with factors to be considered when evaluating home sites. Traditional and computer-aided design and drafting equipment is presented and illustrated. Three chapters are devoted to planning activity areas for efficient use of space. Materials and construction methods are discussed followed by detailed instructions for drawing each of the different architectural plans — Plot Plans, Foundation Plans, Floor Plans, Elevations, Electrical Plans, Plumbing Plans, Climate Control Plans, and Presentations. Various systems (floors, walls, and roof) and elements (doors and windows, stairs, and fireplaces) of the residential structure are presented in detail and are fully illustrated. Several types of climate control systems are discussed. Methods of presenting architectural designs through pictorial drawing, illustration, and models are covered in depth. Innovations in architecture, such as earth sheltered dwellings, solar heating systems, and dome structures are also included. The influence of building costs, modular applications, building codes, and zoning regulations with respect to the site and design are presented.

This edition of the textbook has been completely revised. A comprehensive discussion of CADD hardware and software selection, CADD commands and functions, and architectural applications has been added. The last chapter of the book identifies a broad range of careers related to architecture and construction.

The textbook has been designed to develop an awareness of the types and styles of housing and factors to be considered when selecting a style. It is intended to help the student make wise choices when selecting materials, methods of construction, and developing the skills necessary to communicate these decisions through architectural drawings. A comprehensive reference section and glossary are provided in the back of the textbook to serve as a resource and define terms relevant to the subject. Each chapter is divided into various parts — learning objectives, text body, review questions, and suggested activities.

LEARNING OBJECTIVES

Learning objectives are listed at the beginning of each chapter. Students should use the objectives as a preview to the content of each chapter. They can also be used as a review after completing the chapter to determine if the major concepts of the chapter have been learned.

TEXT BODY

The text body is separated into main headings and subheadings. The main headings define the major concepts included in the chapter content. The subheadings further define the organization of material within each main concept. The content areas are presented in a logical sequence that aids in learning the material and builds a foundation for further learning.

NEW TERMS

New terms appear in bold type when initially discussed. An explanation of the term is also included at that time. The student is immediately made aware that the term is new and he/she should become familiar with the definition.

REVIEW QUESTIONS

Review questions appear at the end of each chapter. They may be used by students to determine their understanding of the subject matter covered in the chapter. A variety of multiple choice, completion, and short answer questions are used to help assess the student's knowledge. The review questions may also be used as assigned homework, or selected questions may be used as a quiz to be given over the material presented.

SUGGESTED ACTIVITIES

The suggested activities at the end of each chapter enable the student to learn more about different aspects of construction and architectural design and drawing. They are designed to provide hands-on experiences or to research further designs, construction materials, elements, and methods. More specifically, the suggested activities provide opportunities to:
- Study local building codes and regulations.
- Assemble a collection of various styles and designs of residential architecture.

- Interview practitioners in the field.
- Assemble manufacturers' literature.
- Secure speakers for the class.
- Write letters to secure information.
- Design a variety of architectural plans.
- Build scale models.
- Prepare bulletin board illustrations.
- Lead class discussions.
- Participate in a CADD demonstration.
- Evaluate software.
- Evaluate a site.
- Participate in field trips.
- Evaluate home styles in the community.
- Perform a survey.
- Write a report.
- Plan and execute a fund-raising event.
- Evaluate existing plans to meet specific requirements.
- Develop a materials list.
- Measure actual construction.
- Test building elements.
- Plan for a restoration.
- Prepare schematics.
- Secure estimates.
- Compare systems.
- Determine labor rates.
- Make detail drawings.
- Evaluate use of materials.
- Visit a building site.
- Photograph construction features.
- Examine cut-away models.
- Redesign a house plan.
- Prepare specifications.
- Study magazines in the field.
- Use the library to locate manufacturers.
- Participate in a group project.
- Perform calculations.
- Evaluate construction techniques.
- Plan furniture arrangements.
- Prepare charts and reports.
- Perform historical research.
- Make a rendering.

REFERENCE SECTION

The comprehensive reference section includes a wide variety of resources commonly used in the field of architecture. The reference section includes the following, plus much more: a complete list of symbols used in the field of architecture, standard sizes and designs of cabinetry and windows, grades of lumber, design data for roof and floor trusses, floor and ceiling joist and beam span data, resistivity of heat loss of common building materials, steel beam data, weights and measures conversion table, weights of building materials, brick and block courses, plywood grades, asphalt products, welded wire fabric, gypsum wallboard applications, reinforcing bars, recommended footcandle levels, abbreviations. One of the great strengths of this textbook is the material covered in this section. Not only is it an excellent source of information for the student, but also for the professional.

GLOSSARY

The glossary comprises a complete alphabetical listing of terms commonly used in architecture. Terms new to the field are also included. Each entry consists of the term printed in bold type followed by its definition.

INDEX

The index contains a thorough listing of the topics presented in the text body. Each topic is followed by page numbers indicating where the topic is discussed.

THE WORKBOOK

The workbook is designed to assist the student in mastering the subject matter presented in the textbook through the questions and problems/activities. It is also intended to aid in developing skill in representing ideas in acceptable form. The workbook enables the instructor to determine how the student is progressing. It is also designed for the student to use as a study guide. Students can measure their own progress by completing each of the questions and problems/activities and then verifying the answers. The workbook includes many examples of construction drawings which serve as models of professional-quality work.

The workbook is arranged to correspond to the chapters of the textbook. An instructor can use each workbook chapter to review the information or test comprehension of the major concepts in the textbook. The questions are comprehensive and include multiple choice, short answer/listing, completion, matching, and calculations.

The problems/activities enable the student to perform many of the same problem-solving tasks that would be performed as a professional. They are designed to create student interest. Typical problems/activities include preparing a notebook, gathering materials, identifying parts or features, and completing or making drawings. Some answers will be individual responses that require evaluation based on a set of principles rather than specific responses.

QUESTIONS

The student is expected to complete the questions in the workbook after careful study of the material presented in the textbook. Several types of questions

are given to determine the student's understanding of the information presented in the chapter. The student should read each question carefully and then proceed to answer it. Spaces are given for recording the appropriate answers.

PROBLEMS/ACTIVITIES

The problems enable a student to gain experience and practice in further refining the techniques presented in the textbook. They are designed to give the student experience in using traditional and computer-aided design drafting equipment. A variety of problems is included to meet the needs of students with varying abilities.

The activities encourage student exploration of community resources such as local building departments, building materials centers, architectural firms, and construction companies. The students are also exposed to the many mechanical and electrical systems and building practices currently used in residential construction. In addition, the activities require the student to develop design ideas and collect building material samples for use in the classroom.

THE TEACHER'S RESOURCE GUIDE

The Teacher's Resource Guide is invaluable for use with the ARCHITECTURE, Residential Drawing and Design textbook and workbook. It provides plans and methods for teaching architectural design and drawing, recommendations for working with students of various abilities, including those with special needs, activities to expand the student's experience outside the classroom, tools for evaluating student progress, and resources for further study.

Each chapter contains specific suggestions for teaching the contents of the textbook. Also included in each chapter are objectives, displays, references to textbook and workbook pages, teaching strategies, and a chapter exam. In addition, the TRG contains answers to review questions in the textbook, review questions and problem/activities in the workbook, and each chapter exam.

COURSE CONTENT

The ARCHITECTURE, Residential Drawing and Design package—Teacher's Resource Guide, textbook, and workbook—provides sufficient information for two years of study in architectural drafting and design. For example, the first year course could include the following chapters directly related to the production of a set of standard residential construction drawings:
1. The World of Architecture
2. Basic House Design

3. Primary Considerations
4. Drawing Instruments and Techniques
5. Room Planning, Sleeping Area
6. Room Planning, Living Area
7. Room Planning, Service Area
8. Plot Plans
9. Footings, Foundations, and Concrete
10. The Foundation Plan
11. Sill and Floor Construction
12. Wall and Ceiling Construction
13. Doors and Windows
14. Stairs
15. Fireplaces and Chimneys
16. The Floor Plan
17. Roof Designs
18. Elevations
19. Residential Electrical
20. The Electrical Plan
21. Residential Plumbing
22. The Plumbing Plan
23. Residential Climate Control
24. Climate Control Plan

The second year course would deal with the following chapters:

25. Solar Space Heating
26. Earth Sheltered Dwellings
27. Dome Structures
28. Modular Applications
29. Perspective Drawings
30. Presentation Drawings
31. Architectural Models
32. Material and Tradework Specifications
33. Estimating Building Cost
34. Computer Applications
35. Introduction to Computer-Aided Drafting and Design
36. CADD Software
37. CADD Commands and Functions
38. Architectural CADD Applications
39. Careers

Chapters 35 through 38 are designed for use with a micro-CADD system, but could be discussed in a typical classroom situation even though computers were not available.

TEACHING METHODS

A variety of teaching methods or techniques should be used to create and maintain student interest. Techniques include lectures, problem-solving activities, overhead transparencies, group discussions, demonstrations, and movies or videos. Several types of techniques should be utilized to ensure student understanding since students learn from a variety of methods. The appropriate method for each specific situation is based on experience and standard practice.

The primary tool used in teaching, in most instances, will be the textbook. It not only provides material for use in the classroom, but also has reference material for use outside the classroom. The workbook is also an important aid in teaching, serving to reinforce textbook understanding. The lectures, group discussions, and demonstrations supplemented with overhead transparencies, slides or photos, and movies or videos help to provide variety in learning and maintain interest in the topic being presented.

The Teacher's Resource Guide details suggestions for integrating these methods to obtain optimum results. It helps you to maintain a balance by combining lectures with activities and problems. The TRG describes displays that may be used to create interest in the materials being presented.

The teaching strategy presented in the Teacher's Resource Guide follows the content and organization presented in the textbook. The textbook is arranged in an appropriate learning sequence. For example, things which must be understood to construct a floor plan are presented prior to the chapter on floor plans. The teaching strategy also provides an organized step-by-step procedure for teaching the content of each chapter. It integrates displays, handout materials, suggested activities in the textbook, and workbook problems into a cohesive lesson plan. For example, the review questions in the textbook will be assigned after the material has been presented from the textbook. The students are to first answer the review questions without the use of the textbook. They may then refer to the textbook for any questions that they do not know. The teacher will then discuss the answers with the students. The answers to the review questions in the textbook, therefore, provide for interaction and discussion to occur. Next, the students will be expected to answer the review questions in the workbook and check their own answers. This is then followed up by a chapter exam.

An important element of this teaching strategy is that the teacher returns assignments promptly and with comments. Another inherent part of the teaching strategy is that the teacher is expected to spend an appropriate amount of time collecting materials for the chapter, preparing bulletin board materials, making drawings to illustrate proper procedures, and being familiar with the ARCHITECTURE package in preparation for teaching the material contained in each chapter.

At the beginning of the course, the students should be encouraged to do a cursive study of the book to become familiar with it. Have them review the units to be covered during the course as well as the reference section, glossary, and index. This procedure results in less time needed and greater ease in finding information. This leaves valuable class time for instruction and other learning activities. During the course, the students will find it necessary to review sections and materials previously studied to assure understanding of concepts. The students will need to perform a number of the activities and problems outside the classroom due to the limited amount of instruction time and the vast amount of subject matter provided in the textbook.

IMPORTANCE OF PLANNING

Have a plan for teaching the course. It is important to determine the goals and objectives of the course from the start. Goals and objectives provide structure as well as direction for the course. Planning is also critical when developing units, as well as when carrying out lesson plans. Conscientious planning is necessary in order for the class to run smoothly and allow students to accomplish as much as possible. Your job as an instructor will be simpler and easier if you plan your work. You will make more efficient use of your time enabling you to accomplish more and allowing your teaching to be more effective.

MOTIVATION

Motivation is any factor that starts an individual toward a goal and then sustains him/her until that goal is realized. The instructor should constantly motivate students until they realize their goals. Research indicates that motivated students are never bored and they are motivated to learn.

All instructors should be conscious of student motivation even though laboratory courses, such as architectural drawing, are generally of interest to most students. Instructional strategies in your presentation of topics can be used to create interest in learning. Use a variety of teaching techniques to stimulate interest. Stand while lecturing and using the chalkboard or overhead projector rather than sitting at your desk. Move about the classroom to communicate with the students at their workstations to offer advice and encouragement. Keep the students informed of their progress. Encourage them to research topics in which they have an interest. Be interested in your students and get to know them as individuals. They will be more comfortable and receptive to learning if the teacher is friendly. Students need attention and recognition. They also need approval from their peers and people of authority. The instructor should use praise and encouragement freely to help provide motivation for his/her students.

Objectives provide a basis for motivation. When students determine what their goals and objectives are, then they become motivated to attain them. The instructor can be instrumental in helping students realize their objectives and provide motivation to help them achieve their goals.

STUDENT PARTICIPATION

Encourage student participation. Students who are actively involved in class activities generally learn better and are more successful. Try to predict where failure might occur in the learning process. Put forth extra effort to help your students avoid failure and feel successful. They will have a more positive attitude toward learning if they feel successful. Let your students know that you are there to help and that you have confidence in them. The extra amount of attention that you give them will inspire them to work harder to achieve success. Plan techniques that permit your students to achieve as much as possible. Encourage them to strive for higher levels of accomplishment.

Share the latest research and developments in the field with the class and encourage your students to read publications related to architecture. Suggest that students choose an area in which they have an interest, learn more about it, and share it with the class. For example, if a student is interested in the restoration of older homes, assign the task of library research for articles and photographs of restoration projects. Have the student seek out companies manufacturing products used in restoration and obtain their product literature. Determine whether there are builders in the local area who specialize in restoration and determine if there are older homes currently under restoration. Sharing the information with the class, and possibly arranging a field trip to see the restoration in progress, would complete the task.

CREATE ENTHUSIASM AND EXCITEMENT

Enthusiasm is contagious. When an instructor is enthusiastic about the subject, the students will also be enthusiastic. It sets the stage for learning and helps to maintain the student's interest in the subject throughout the class time. Showing enthusiasm is a positive way of keeping student morale at a high level and results in better recall of the material studied.

Create excitement in the classroom. This can be accomplished by incorporating a wide range of learning techniques and hands-on activities. Attractive bulletin board displays with drawings or designs from the chapter being studied can stimulate excitement. Meet the needs of your students, for example, by showing them that the drawing techniques currently being practiced can be applied to drawing plot plans, floor plans, elevations, etc. When the students view the activities and problems as meaningful (rather than busy work), the learning experience will be more exciting.

PROBLEM SOLVING

Problem solving is fundamental to student learning. In all probability, it is the key element responsible for student success. Problem solving is a technique that the student can use to carry out research, develop projects, or write a paper. The instructor can help students develop problem-solving abilities by utilizing methods which are conducive to teaching problem solving. The instructor should develop exercises in problem solving to serve two purposes: (1) to enable the student to develop the art of reasoning, and (2) to provide the student practical knowledge or skill valuable in life. The steps required in the problem-solving process are:
1. Identifying and explaining the problem.
2. Gathering information.
3. Developing a plan for examining the facts.
4. Analyzing the facts to determine solutions.
5. Evaluate the results.

It is the instructor's responsibility to determine if the students understand the procedure and can apply it to different problem-solving situations. The laboratory and the community provide excellent opportunities for students to practice their knowledge of problem solving. The instructor can help students move from abstract to actual situations of problem-solving by using realistic problems. Students should be given the opportunity to work individually or in groups to discuss and formulate ideas, construct models for testing theories, and to simulate actual situations. The problem-solving ability is not only needed by the students now but will be invaluable to them for the remainder of their lives. Students can expect to encounter endless situations requiring experience in problem solving and decision making regardless of their ultimate walks in life.

KEEPING CURRENT

The instructor should maintain a current status with the field of architecture and construction in order to challenge and lead students. Read the latest journals and other publications to learn about new building codes and construction techniques. Periodically visit the local building materials center and collect brochures on the latest building materials on the market. Visit consruction sites to determine building materials and construction techniques currently used in your locality. Keep abreast of new designs and identify examples of these new designs in your area. Be aware of the latest computer equipment on the market with architectural applications. Make as many of these sources as possible available to the students in your classroom.

VARYING STUDENT ABILITIES

The students in your classroom possess a wide range of skills. Some have a great deal of drawing skill, while others have limited skill. Some have decided to make architectural drawing and design a career choice, while others are merely interested in the exploratory aspect.

The students in your classroom also possess a variety of abilities. There may be students with special needs who have mental or physical impairments. There may also be students who are gifted and possess the potential to exceed the limits of the course. You must challenge students along the entire range of abilities.

IDENTIFYING STUDENTS WITH SPECIAL NEEDS

Generally, students with special needs will be identified before enrolling in architectural drawing and design classes. This identification is usually performed by school personnel specifically trained to evaluate learning problems. However, there may be instances in which these students have been enrolled in classes without identification. The responsibility then rests with the instructor to identify any students who require special help.

A number of symptoms often occur in students with special needs and may include disturbances in intellectual, conceptual, motor, and social behavior. Many of these students are diagnosed early on in their educational years, while some remain undetected. Therefore, it is necessary that the instructor be aware of the behaviors commonly exhibited by special needs students. (Keep in mind that an occasional incident probably does not indicate that a student should be labeled as having special needs.) Behaviors typically found in students having special needs include:
- Short attention span.
- Attendance problems.
- Below-grade level ability in reading, writing, and mathematics.
- Low self-concept.
- Incorrect social behavior.
- Lack of eye-hand coordination.
- Frequent disruptive behavior.
- Poor peer relationships.
- Lack of class participation.
- Poorly motivated.
- Hearing, sight, or speech impairments.
- Repeatedly fails to do homework.

This is only a partial listing of behaviors found in special needs students. If you have a student who exhibits several of these behaviors, discuss your observations with the student's counselor. If the student is displaying these behaviors in other classes, then further diagnostic testing should be requested.

After the student's specific learning disabilities are determined, then the instructor can proceed to modify the teaching techniques to meet the student's needs.

MAINSTREAMING THE SPECIAL NEEDS STUDENT

Mainstreaming is in essence placing of special needs students in the regular classroom. With the passing of the Federal Education of All Handicapped Children Act of 1975, all handicapped children should have available a free education in a relatively unrestricted environment which is suitable to their needs. Many schools have taken the necessary steps to better educate the special needs students.

Prior to the passing of the act, students were taught entirely by teachers trained to work with handicapped students in resource classrooms set aside for these students. These teachers often lacked the specialized training to teach in areas such as architecture. In most cases, the rooms were not equipped with facilities required in the instruction of this particular subject. Mainstreaming the special needs students into the regular classroom enables these students to experience and investigate a greater variety of subjects. Whenever possible special needs students are placed in regular classrooms and receive assistance from special education teachers or aides. Some special needs students are mainstreamed into a number of regular classes and spend the remaining time in the resource room, while others are totally mainstreamed into regular classes.

Architecture teachers will have more opportunities to work with special needs students as more schools participate in mainstreaming. As a teacher, it may be necessary to adapt your teaching practices to enable these students to develop the required skills. Special needs students have a desire to be successful just as the majority of students in architectural classes. It is imperative that the teacher informs these students that high standard expectations are just as applicable to them as the remainder of the class. These high expectations and a great deal of encouragement result in the students putting forth extra effort to meet these goals and achieve success. Special needs students can be successful in architecture classes. In architecture, the students study and learn the subject matter in the textbook and then apply this knowledge to generate drawings. Hands-on experiences, such as drawing, usually provide a high rate of success for special needs students.

TEACHING STUDENTS WITH SPECIAL NEEDS

The teacher will generally have a wide range of special needs students in his/her classes. The range includes students with learning disabilities, mild retardation, emotional disturbances, speech impairments, hearing impairments, visual impairments, and physical disabilities. The students' success depend, to a large extent, on how the teacher approaches their needs and modifies his/her teaching to meet these needs. The following suggestions can be incorporated into the teaching practice to help the special needs students be successful:

1. Furnish reading material appropriate for the reading level.
2. Provide outlines of subject matter to help the student follow the lecture and instructional material that the special education teacher may use when working with the student.
3. Simplify hand-outs as much as possible by using diagrams, drawings, etc.
4. Provide work that is simple and short in length.
5. Give encouragement frequently.
6. Emphasize the students' success rather than failures.
7. Integrate special needs students with remainder of the class, whenever possible, through group projects and class discussion, etc. Encourage participation.
8. Use several different teaching techniques— group projects, group discussions, individual research projects, etc.
9. Simplify processes into smaller segments.
10. Return assignments and evaluations results quickly with helpful comments and discussion.
11. Design repetitive activities appropriate to the student's ability to help build skill.
12. Utilize oral and written tests using a variety of test questions.
13. Be consistent, reasonable in expectations, and flexible.
14. Pair the special needs student with a student who can help with the assignment.
15. Permit extra time for the special needs student to complete activities and assignments.
16. Work in cooperation with the student and the special education instructor to develop a suitable grading and evaluating system.

When working with hearing-impaired students, face the student when speaking, maintain eye contact, speak clearly, distinctly, and in a normal voice. Be sure that you have the student's attention when making assignments. Allow the vision-impaired student to examine the classroom at the beginning of the course to become familiar with the layout. Use materials with large type when possible. Be specific when referring to parts of a drawing, for instance. The vision- and hearing-impaired students should sit near the front of the classroom.

Students with physical disabilities may require ramps instead of stairs and access to drawing or computer tables. Tables should be at least 31" from the floor to accommodate a wheelchair. Special drawing or computer tables may be necessary for students with physical disabilities. Clearance space of 36" is needed for a wheelchair to pass between objects. As many physical barriers as possible should be eliminated from the classroom.

Teachers can use their influence, creativity, and imagination to ensure the success of the special needs students. They may experiment with a variety of instructional techniques before finding which are successful with the students. The ultimate goal is to challenge these students to work up to their potential and realize their specific goals.

IDENTIFYING GIFTED STUDENTS

It is probable that the majority of gifted students entering the classroom will have been identified. Generally, the school counselor works with the gifted students to guide them into interesting and challenging classes. The school counselor identifies the gifted students to the classroom instructor and works with the classroom instructor to lend any assistance needed to create a positive learning atmosphere.

However, there may be gifted students who have not been identified. Identifying gifted students may be a little more difficult than identifying the special needs students. However, like special needs students, unless gifted students are identified and modifications made to challenge their learning potential, behavior problems may result.

In some cases, gifted students may intentionally conceal their identity and become difficult to distinguish from the remaining students in the classroom. However, several behavior characteristics normally exhibited by gifted students help to make their identification possible. The teacher should be aware of these characteristics in order to help identify any gifted students in the classroom. Some behaviors may include finishing work well before the remaining students in the class, boredom or restlessness, and uniformly high test scores.

Physically, gifted students are often stronger, taller, healthier, and tend to have more energy than their classmates. Mentally, they learn quickly and are skillful thinkers, imaginative, creative, persevering, and curious. Socially, they display leadership, self-confidence, and friendliness. They are usually charitable and critical of themselves as well as others. In addition, there are other characteristics often exhibited by gifted students. The following is not a comprehensive list, but should help the instructor determine whether gifted students are in the classroom.
- Ability to deal with abstraction to a great degree.
- Can generalize at a high level.
- Are self-directed.
- Are capable of considerable independent study.

- Possess an abundant amount of background knowledge from which to make application to new objects quickly and easily.
- Have long attention spans.
- Have well above-average vocabularies.
- Have many and varied interests.
- Ask relevant questions.
- Desire challenges.
- Love learning for its intrinsic rewards.
- Have unusual abilities to build meanings and concepts and to establish relationships.
- Are extremely interested in experimenting with ideas and objects.
- Have tremendous ability to solve problems, invent new objects, and construct technical devices.
- Are very sensitive.
- Have high ideals.
- Have a worthy set of values and objectives.
- Have a great ability to work independently.
- Exhibit high levels of attention, concentration, and interest in intellectual things.
- Interested in knowing how and why things work.
- Become completely preoccupied in their work.
- Great organizational ability.
- Uncomfortable with clutter and may organize the clutter.
- Have an abundance of general and specific information.
- Have high expectations of themselves and those around them.
- Are very critical of the system when it prevents them from expanding their learning experiences.
- Are extremely deep thinkers.
- Become completely absorbed in the problem at hand.

Gifted students perform best in an unrestricted learning environment which provides an atmosphere for their abilities and diverse interests to grow. They have many achievements when they are given the opportunity to learn in surroundings compatible to their interests and abilities.

TEACHING GIFTED STUDENTS

Programs for teaching gifted students differ from those used for special needs students or students with average abilities. The teacher needs to understand gifted students and should be willing to provide the appropriate atmosphere for creative learning activities to take place. The teacher must determine the program modifications which will result in the greatest achievements. The students' capabilities to think critically, establish relationships, and construct meanings and concepts should be refined. Their self-direction, independence, and desire to experiment with ideas and objects should be encouraged. Gifted students need to understand the amount and kind of education required to develop their abilities. The thrill of uncovering ideas, meanings, and relationships, as well as from building a broad base of knowledge provide the challenge of learning for gifted students.

There are a number of features which can be incorporated into a program to address the needs of gifted students. The following list includes several features to be considered:

- Employment of resources outside the classroom.
- Encouragement of individual research and problem solving.
- Provision for a research-oriented classroom.
- Development of a self-motivating and challenging learning atmosphere.
- Surroundings which do not set boundaries to learning.
- Decision-making practices which are problem solving, creative, and current.
- Self-directed exploration, development, and communicating activities.
- A program which is inherently inter- and intra-disciplinary.
- A fast-track program of in-depth technical subjects which is highly individualized.
- Student outcomes should result in delayed success — not failure.
- Teacher-student ratio of 1:10 is considered ideal.
- Use of small groups to conduct research or investigations.
- Development of abstract concepts and models.
- Instructor is a resource person as well as a stimulator.
- Recent technical and research developments in science, math, and technology should be known and understood.
- Research tools, equipment, and communication skills should be employed.
- Involvement of community agencies and businesses to enhance classroom experiences.

Additionally the instructor can provide activities to challenge any gifted students in his/her classroom. They may serve as an aid or assistant to the instructor to help other students having difficulty. They may be paired with slower students to give assistance. They may be encouraged to work ahead on their own or be given more advanced work to challenge their potential. They may work on a project for a local organization or industry under the instructor's guidance. This would not only give them a chance to tap their potential, but also provide experience in the world outside the classroom.

The relationship of the instructor to the gifted students will be somewhat different than with the average-ability student. The instructor is no longer the total authority, but rather the focal point for interaction. The new role as the resource person requires that the instructor be aware of where answers are to be found. This requires that an instructor be willing to experiment and not feel threatened by any perceived loss of authority.

ADDITIONAL STUDENT EXPERIENCES

Student interest and learning can be expanded by providing a variety of activities in addition to those listed in the chapter resources. Students learn inside as well as outside the classroom. There are a number of student experiences and resources the teacher can utilize to expand the students' knowledge. They include architecture and construction resources, field trips, student organizations, and summer work experience. Architecture and construction resources provide reading material to give students a broader understanding of the field, to research a particular topic, or to learn of new innovations in architecture and construction. Field trips enable the students to see first-hand current building practices or techniques. Student organizations help students to develop professionally and summer work experience provides valuable practice in the field of architecture and construction. The teacher can create an atmosphere capable of imparting an abundance of knowledge to the students by providing as many activities and experiences as time allows.

ARCHITECTURE AND CONSTRUCTION RESOURCES

In the Suggested Activities section of the texbook and the Problems/Activities section of the workbook, an abundance of experiences are planned and presented for students to expand their learning experiences. In addition, there are associations and publications whose main purpose is to enlighten the public, provide information, and generally publicize the field, products, or purpose of their association, group, etc. The following list is not meant to be comprehensive, but includes a number of architectural and construction resources that should help the teacher in gathering ideas and materials to enhance the teaching/learning process.

ASSOCIATIONS AND INSTITUTES

Access for the Handicapped
5014 42nd Street, NW
Washington, DC 20016

Acoustical Society of America
500 Sunnyside Blvd.
Woodberry, NY 11797

Adhesive and Sealant Council, Inc.
1500 North Wilson Blvd.
Arlington, VA 22209

Air-Conditioning and Refrigeration
 Institute
1501 Wilson Blvd.
Arlington, VA 22209

Air Conditioning Contractors of America
1513 16th St.
Washington, DC 20036

Allied Construction Employers Association
180 N. Executive Drive
Brookfield, WI 53008

Aluminum Association
900 19th St., NW
Washington, DC 20006

American Association of State Highway and
 Transportation Officials
444 N. Capitol St., NW, Suite 225
Washington, DC 20001

American Building Contractors Association
11100 Valley Blvd., Suite 120
El Monte, CA 91731

American Concrete Institute
22400 W. Seven Mile Rd.
Detroit, MI 48219

American Gas Association, Inc.
1515 Wilson Blvd.
Arlington, VA 22209

American Hardboard Assn.
520 N. Hicks Road
Palatine, IL 60067

American Hardware Mfgrs. Assn.
931 N. Plum Grove Rd.
Schaumburg, IL 60173

American Home Lighting Inst.
435 N. Michigan Ave., Suite 1717
Chicago, IL 60611

American Institute of Architects
1735 New York Ave., NW
Washington, DC 20006

American Institute of Constructors
20 S. Front St.
Columbus, OH 43215

American Institute of Steel Construction
400 N. Michigan Ave.
Chicago, IL 60611

American Institute for Design and Drafting
3119 Price Road
Bartlesville, OK 74003

American Institute of Architects
1735 New York Ave., NW
Washington, DC 20006

American Institute of Constructors
1140 NW 63rd St.
Oklahoma City, OK 73116

American Institute of Steel Construction, Inc.
400 N. Michigan Ave.
Chicago, IL 60611

American Institute of Timber Construction
11818 SE Mill Plain Blvd.
Vancouver, WA 98684

American Iron and Steel Institute
1133 15th St., NW, Suite 300
Washington, DC 20005

American Lumber Standards Committee
PO Box 210
Germantown, MD 20874

American National Standards Institute
1430 Broadway
New York, NY 10018

American Pipe Fitting Assn.
8136 Old Keene Mill Rd. #B-311
Springfield, VA 22152

American Plywood Association
PO Box 11700
Tacoma, WA 98411

American Soc. of Civil Engineers
345 E. 47th St.
New York, NY 10017

American Society of Concrete Construction
426 S. Westgate
Addison, IL 60101

American Society of Heating, Refrigeration, and
 Air-Conditioning Engineers, Inc.
1791 Tullie Circle, NE
Atlanta, GA 30329

American Society of Interior Designers
200 Lexington Ave.
New York, NY 10016

American Society of Mechanical Engineers
United Engineering Center
345 E. 47th St.
New York, NY 10017

American Society of Professional Estimators
3617 Thousand Oaks Blvd.
Suite 210
Westlake, CA 91362

American Society of Sanitary Engineers
PO Box 40362
Bay Village, OH 44140

American Society for Testing and Materials
1916 Race St.
Philadelphia, PA 19103

American Subcontractors Assn.
1004 Duke St.
Alexandria, VA 22314

American Welding Society, Inc.
550 NW LeJeune Rd.
Miami, FL 33126

American Aluminum Mfgrs. Association
2700 River Rd., Suite 118
Des Plaines, IL 60018

Architectural Precast Assn.
825 E. 64th St.
Indianapolis, IN 46220

Architectural Woodwork Institute
2310 S. Walter Reed Dr.
Arlington, VA 22206

Asbestos Information Association/
 North America
1745 Jefferson Davis Hwy.
Suite 509
Arlington, VA 22202

Asphalt Institute
Asphalt Institute Building
College Park, MD 20740

Associated Builders and Contractors, Inc.
729 15th St., NW
Washington, DC 20005

Associated General Contractors of America
1957 East Street, NW
Washington, DC 20006

Associated Sheet Metal Contractors, Inc.
3121 W. Hallandale Beach Blvd.
Suite 114
Hallandale, FL 33009

Associated Specialty Contractors
7315 Wisconsin Ave.
Bethesda, MD 20814

Association of Bituminous Contractors
2020 K St., NW, Suite 800
Washington, DC 20006

Association of the Wall & Ceiling Industries Intl.
25 K St., NE, Suite 300
Washington, DC 20002

Brick Institute of America
11490 Commerce Park Dr.
Suite 300
Reston, VA 22091

Builder's Hardware Mfgrs. Association, Inc.
60 E. 42nd St., Rm. 511
New York, NY 10165

Building Officials and Code Administrators
 International
4051 W. Flossmoor Rd.
Country Club Hills, IL 60477

Building Materials Research Institute, Inc.
501 5th Ave., #1402
New York, NY 10017

Building Research Board
2101 Constitution Ave., NW
Washington, DC 20418

Building Stone Institute
420 Lexington Ave., Suite 2800
New York, NY 10170

Building Systems Council
15th and M St., NW
Washington, DC 20005

California Redwood Association
591 Redwood Highway, Suite 3100
Mill Valley, CA 94941

Carpet and Rug Institute
PO Box 2048
Dalton, GA 30722-2048

Cast Iron Soil Pipe Institute
1499 Chain Bridge Rd., Suite 203
McLean, VA 22101

Ceilings and Interior Systems Construction
  Association
104 Wilmot, Suite 201
Deerfield, IL 60015

Center for Building Technology
National Bureau of Standards
Washington, DC 20234

Ceramic Tile Institute
700 N. Virgil Ave.
Los Angeles, CA 90029

Chain Link Fence Manufacturers Institute
1776 Massachusetts Ave., NW
Suite 500
Washington, DC 20036

Concrete Reinforcing Steel Institute
933 N. Plum Grove Rd.
Schaumburg, IL 60195

Construction Industry Employers Association
625 Ensminger Rd.
Tonawanda, NY 14150

Construction Industry Mfgrs. Assn.
111 E. Wisconsin Ave., Suite 940
Milwaukee, WI 53202-4879

Construction Products Manufacturing Council
PO Box 21008
Washington, DC 20009-0508

Construction Specifications Institute
601 Madison St.
Alexandria, VA 22314

Copper Development Association, Inc.
Greenwich Office Park 2
51 Weaver St.
Grant, CT 06836

Corps of Engineers/U.S. Department of
  the Army
20 Massachusetts Ave., NW
Washington, DC 20314

Council of American Building Officials
5203 Leesburg Pike, Suite 708
Falls Church, VA 22041

Door and Hardware Institute
7711 Old Springhouse Rd.
McLean, VA 22102-0374

Ductile Iron Pipe Research Association
245 Riverchase Parkway E.
Suite 0
Birmingham, AL 35244

Environmental Protection Agency
401 M St., SW
Washington, DC 20460

Expanded Shale, Clay and Slate Institute
6218 Montrose Rd.
Rockville, MD 20852

Facing Tile Institute
PO Box 8880
Canton, OH 44711

Federal Housing Administration
451 7th St., SW, Rm. 3158
Washington, DC 20410

Forest Products Research Society
2801 Marshall Ct.
Madison, WI 53705

General Building Contractors Association
36 S. 18th St.
PO Box 15959
Philadelphia, PA 19103

Gypsum Association
1603 Orrington Ave., Suite 1210
Evanston, IL 60201

Hardwood Plywood Manufacturers Association
PO Box 2789
Reston, VA 22090

Illuminating Engineering Society of
  North America
345 E. 47th St.
New York, NY 10017

Indiana Limestone Institute of America
Stone City Bank Bldg., Suite 400
Bedford, IN 47421

Industrial Heating Equipment Association
1901 N. Moore St.
Arlington, VA 22209

Institute of Electrical and Electronics Engineers
345 E. 47th St.
New York, NY 10017

Insulation Contractors Assn. of America
15819 Crabbs Branch Way
Rockville, MD 20855

International Assn. of Lighting Designers
18 E. 16th St., Suite 208
New York, NY 10003

International Assn. of Plumbing and
 Mechanical Officials
20001 Walnut Dr., S
Walnut, CA 91789

International Brotherhood of Electrical Workers
1125 15th Street, NW
Washington, DC 20005

International Brotherhood of Painters and
 Allied Trades
1750 New York Avenue, NW
Washington, DC 20006

International Council of Bldg. Officials
5360 S. Workman Mill Rd.
Whittier, CA 90601

International Institute for Lath & Plaster
795 Raymond Ave.
St. Paul, MN 55114

International Masonry Institute
823 15th St., NW, Suite 1001
Washington, DC 20005

International Union of Bricklayers & Allied
 Craftsmen
Bowen Building
815 15th St., NW
Washington, DC 20005

International Union of Operating Engineers
1125 17th Street, NW
Washington, DC 20036

Laborers' International Union of
 North America
905 16th Street, NW
Washington, DC 20006-1765

Manufactured Housing Institute
1745 Jefferson Davis Hwy. #511
Arlington, VA 22202

Maple Flooring Manufacturers Association
60 Revere Dr., Suite 500
Northbrook, IL 60062

Marble Institute of America
33505 State St.
Farmington, MI 48024

Mason Contractors Assn. of America
17W 601 14th St.
Oakbrook Terrace, IL 60181

Mechanical Contractors Assn. of America
5410 Grosvenor, Suite 120
Bethesda, MD 20814

Metal Lath/Steel Framing Assn.
600 S. Federal, Suite 400
Chicago, IL 60605

Mineral Insulation Mfgrs. Assn.
1420 King Street
Alexandria, VA 22314

National Asphalt Pavement Assn.
6811 Kenilworth Ave., Suite 620
PO Box 517
Riverdale, MD 20737

National Association of Demolition
 Contractors
4415 W. Harrison St.
Hillside, IL 60162

National Association of Floor Covering
 Distributions
13-126 Merchandise Mart
Chicago, IL 60654

National Association of Home Builders
15th and M Streets, NW
Washington, DC 20005

National Association of Housing Redevelopment
 Officials
1320 18th St., NW
Washington, DC 20036

National Association of Plumbing, Heating,
 & Cooling Contractors
PO Box 6808
Falls Church, VA 22046

National Assn. of Reinforcing Steel Contractors
10382 Main St.
PO Box 225
Fairfax, VA 22030

National Association of Women in Construction
327 S. Adams St.
Fort Worth, TX 76104

National Building Code
American Insurance Association
85 John Street
New York, NY 10038

National Building Manufacturers Association
142 Lexington Ave.
New York, NY 10016

National Building Material Distributors
 Association
1701 Lake Ave., Suite 170
Glenview, IL 60025

National Bureau of Standards
Center for Building Technology
Washington, DC 20234

National Concrete Masonry Association
PO Box 781
Herndon, VA 22070

National Conference of States on Building
 Codes & Standards
481 Carlisle Dr.
Herndon, VA 22070

National Constructors Assn.
1101 15th St., NW, Suite 1000
Washington, DC 20005

National Council on Radiation Protection
 and Measurement
7910 Woodmont Ave., Suite 800
Bethesda, MD 20814

National Electrical Contractors Association
7315 Wisconsin Ave.
13th Floor, West Building
Bethesda, MD 20814

National Electrical Mfgrs. Association
2101 L St., NW, Suite 300
Washington, DC 20037

National Fire Protection Assn.
Batterymarch Park
Quincy, MA 02269

National Forest Products Assn.
1250 Connecticut Ave., NW
Suite 200
Washington, DC 20036

National Glass Association
8200 Greensboro Dr., Suite 302
McLean, VA 22102

National Housing Rehabilitation Assn.
1726 18th St., NW
Washington, DC 20009

National Kitchen Cabinet Assn.
PO Box 6830
Falls Church, VA 22046

National Lime Association
3601 N. Fairfax Dr.
Arlington, VA 22201

National Lumber and Building Material
 Dealers Assn.
40 Ivy St., SE
Washington, DC 20003

National Oak Flooring Mfgrs. Association
PO Box 3009
Memphis, TN 38173-0009

National Paint & Coatings Assn.
1500 Rhode Island Ave., NW
Washington, DC 20005

National Particleboard Assn.
2306 Perkins Pl.
Silver Spring, MD 20919

National Precast Concrete Assn.
825 E. 64th St.
Indianapolis, IN 46220

National Ready Mixed Concrete Assn.
900 Spring St.
Silver Spring, MD 20910

National Roofing Contractors Assn.
1 O'Hare Center
6250 River Rd.
Rosemont, IL 60018

National Society of Professional Engineers
1420 King St.
Alexandria, VA 22314

National Stone Association
1415 Elliot Pl., NW
Washington, DC 20007

National Terrazzo & Mosiac Assn.
3166 Des Plaines Ave., Suite 132
Des Plaines, IL 60018

National Wood Window & Door Assn.
205 Touhy Ave.
Park Ridge, IL 60068

National Woodwork Manufacturers' Association
400 W. Madison St.
Chicago, IL 60606

Operative Plasters' and Cement Masons'
  International Assn. of the United States
  and Canada
1125 177th St., NW, 6th Floor
Washington, DC 20036

Painting & Decorating Contractors of America
7223 Lee Hwy.
Falls Church, VA 22046

Passive Solar Industries Council
2836 Duke St.
Alexandria, VA 22314

Plastics Pipe Institute
355 Lexington Ave.
New York, NY 10017

Plumbing and Drainage Institute
1106 W. 77th St., S. Dr.
Indianapolis, IN 46260

Plumbing-Heating-Cooling Information Bureau
303 E. Wacker Dr., Suite 711
Chicago, IL 60601

Plumbing Manufacturers Institute
800 Roosevelt Rd., Bldg. C.
Suite 20
Glen Ellyn, IL 60137

Portland Cement Association
5420 Old Orchard Rd.
Skokie, IL 60077

Prestressed Concrete Institute
175 W. Jackson Blvd., Suite 1859
Chicago, IL 60604

Red Cedar Shingle & Handsplit Shake Bureau
Suite 275, 515 - 116th Ave., NE
Bellevue, WA 98004

Reinforced Concrete Research Council
5420 Old Orchard Rd.
Skokie, IL 60077

Resilient Floor Covering Institute
966 Hungerford Dr., Suite 12B
Rockville, MD 20850

Resilient Flooring and Carpet Assn., Inc.
14570 E. 14th, Suite 511
San Landro, CA 94578

Scaffolding, Shoring, & Forming Institute, Inc.
1230 Keith Building
Cleveland, OH 44115

Screen Manufacturers Assn.
655 Irving Park, Suite 201
Chicago, IL 60613-3198

Sealant & Waterproofers Institute
3101 Broadway, Suite 300
Kansas City, MO 64111

Sealed Insulating Glass Mfgrs. Association
111 E. Wacker Dr., Suite 600
Chicago, IL 60601

Sheet Metal & Air Conditioning Contractors
  National Assn. Inc.
8224 Old Courthouse Rd.
Vienna, VA 22180

Sheet Metal Workers International Association
1750 New York Ave., NW
Washington, DC 20006

Small Homes Council
Building Research Council
University of Illinois
One East Saint Mary's Road
Champaign, IL 61820

Southern Bldg. Code Congress International, Inc.
900 Montclair Rd.
Birmingham, AL 35213

Southern Forest Products Assn.
P.O. Box 52468
New Orleans, LA 70152

Steel Door Institute
712 Lakewood Center N.
14600 Detroit Ave.
Cleveland, OH 44107

Steel Joist Institute
1205 48th Ave., N, Suite A
Myrtle Beach, SC 29577

Steel Structures Painting Council
4400 5th Ave.
Pittsburgh, PA 15213

Steel Window Institute
1230 Keith Building
Cleveland, OH 44115

Stucco Manufacturers Assn.
14006 Ventura Blvd.
Sherman Oaks, CA 91423

Systems Builders Assn.
P.O. Box 117
West Milton, OH 45383

Thermal Insulation Mfgrs. Association
29 Bank St.
Stanford, CT 06901

Tile Contractors Assn. of America, Inc.
112 N. Alfred Street
Alexandria, VA 22314

Tile Council of America
P.O. Box 2222
Princeton, NJ 08540

Tilt-up Concrete Association
5420 Old Orchard Rd.
Skokie, IL 60077

Truss Plate Institute
583 D'Onofrio Drive, Suite 200
Madison, WI 53719

Underwriters' Laboratories, Inc.
333 Pfingsten Rd.
Northbrook, IL 60062

United Assn. of Journeymen & Apprentices of
the Plumbing & Pipe Fitting Industry of the
United States & Canada
901 Massachusetts Ave., NW
Washington, DC 20001

United Brotherhood of Carpenters and
Joiners of America
101 Constitution Ave., NW
Washington, DC 20001

U.S. Department of Labor/Occupational
Safety & Health Adm.
200 Constitution Ave., NW
Washington, DC 20210

U.S. Forest Products Laboratory
One Gifford Pinchot Dr.
Madison, WI 53705-2398

United Union of Roofers, Waterproofers &
Allied Workers
1125 17th Street, NW, 5th Floor
Washington, DC 20036

Valve Manufacturers Association of America
1050 17th St., NW, Suite 701
Washington, DC 20036

Vermiculite Association
52 Executive Park South
Atlanta, GA 30329

Vinyl Siding Institute
355 Lexington Avenue
New York, NY 10017

Wallcovering Manufacturers Assn.
355 Lexington Ave.
New York, NY 10017

Western Wood Products Assn.
1500 Yeon Building
Portland, OR 97204

Wire Reinforcement Institute
8361-A Greensboro Dr.
McLean, VA 22102

Wood Truss Council of America
111 Wacker Drive
Chicago, IL 60601

In addition to these resources, a number of other references should be made available to the students in the classroom or the school library. These references include ANSI manuals, Architectural Graphic Standards, Timesaver Standards, Sweets Architectural File, and texts on architecture, design and drafting, construction, manufacturing, materials, and processes. The following publications indicate the variety of information available to enhance learning.

PUBLICATIONS

Academic Computing
Academic Computing Publications, Inc.
200 West Virginia
McKinney, TX 75069-4425

Architectural Digest
Architectural Digest Publishing Corp.
5900 Wilshire Blvd.
Los Angeles, CA 90036

Architectural Record
McGraw-Hill, Inc.
1221 Avenue of the Americas
New York, NY 10020

Builder
A Hanley-Wood, Inc. Publication
P.O. Box 2029
Marion, OH 43305

Builder & Contractor
Associated Builders & Contractors, Inc.
729 15th Street, NW
Washington, DC 20005

Building Design & Construction
Cahners Publishing Company
275 Washington St.
Newton, MA 02158-1630

Computer-Aided Design Report
CAD/CAM Publishing
841 Turquoise St.
San Diego, CA 92109

Computer-Aided Engineering
Penton Publishing
1100 Superior Avenue
Cleveland, OH 44114

Computer Graphics Review Technology &
  Business Communications, Inc.
730 Boston Park Rd.
Sudbury, MA 01776

Computer Graphics Today
Media Horizons, Inc.
50 West 23rd St.
New York, NY 10010

Computer Graphics World
Pennwell Publishing Co.
119 Russell St., P.O. Box 1112
Littleton, MA 01460

Computers for Design & Construction
310 E. 44th St.
New York, NY 10017

Concrete Construction
Aberdeen Group
426 South Westgate
Addison, IL 60101

Concrete Technology Today
Portland Cement Association
5420 Old Orchard Road
Skokie, IL 60077-1083

Construction Digest
Construction Digest, Inc.
7355 Woodland Dr.
Indianapolis, IN 46278

Construction Equipment
Cahners Plaza
1350 E. Touhy Avenue
P.O. Box 5080
Des Plaines, IL 60017-5080

Design Graphics World
Communication Channels, Inc.
6255 Barfield Rd.
Atlanta, GA 30328

Design News
Cahners Publishing Co.
275 Washington St.
Newton, MA 02158

Exteriors
Edgell Communications, Inc.
7500 Old Oak Blvd.
Cleveland, OH 44130

Fine Woodworking
The Taunton Press
63 South Main Street
Box 355
Newton, CT 06470-9989

Heating/Piping/Air Conditioning
Penton Publishing, Inc.
1100 Superior Avenue
Cleveland, OH 44114

High Technology
High Technology Publishing Corp.
38 Commercial Wharf
Boston, MA 02110

Historic Preservation
1785 Massachusetts Ave., NW
Washington, DC 20036

Interior Construction
104 Wilmot Road, Suite 201
Deerfield, IL 60015-5195

Interior Design
A Cahners Publication
P.O. Box 1970
Marion, OH 43305

The Journal of Light Construction
P.O. Box 686
Holmes, PA 19043

Journal of Research of the National
  Bureau of Standards
U.S. Government Printing Office
Washington, DC 20402

Laboratory Planning & Design
859 Willamette Street
P.O. Box 10460
Eugene, OR 97440-2460

Lighting
859 Willamette Street
P.O. Box 10460
Eugene, OR 97440-2460

Masonry Construction
Aberdeen Group
426 South Westgate
Addison, IL 60101

Metal Construction News
7450 N. Skokie Blvd.
Skokie, IL 60077

MicroCAD News
Ariel Communications, Inc.
12710 Research Blvd.
Austin, TX 78759

Modern Steel Construction
The Wrigley Building
400 N. Michigan Ave.
Chicago, IL 60611

Multi-Housing News
Gralla Publications
1515 Broadway
New York, NY 10036

Nation's Building News
The National Association of Home Builders
15th and M Streets, NW
Washington, DC 20005

PC Magazine
Ziff-Davis Publishing Co.
P.O. Box 54093
Boulder, CO 80322

Plan & Print
International Reprographic Association
611 E. Butterfield Rd.
Lombard, IL 60148

Practical Homeowner
Practical Homeowner Publishing Co.
825 Seventh Ave.
New York, NY 10019

Progressive Architecture
Rheinhold Publishing
1100 Superior Ave.
Cleveland, OH 44106

Professional Builder
Reed Publishing USA
275 Washington St.
Newton, MA 02158-1630

Qualified Remodeler
20 E. Jackson Blvd.
Chicago, IL 60604

Woodshop News
Pratt Street
Essex, CT 06426

Woodsmith
2200 Grand Avenue
Des Moines, IA 50312

FIELD TRIPS

Field trips are a valuable source of information for students. The local community generally has a number of sites which can provide first-hand knowledge in the field of architecture and construction. A prearranged field trip can be utilized to show the students how the activities they are involved in the classroom relate to industry.

Most companies are willing to cooperate with instructors and welcome student groups if arrangements are made ahead of time. An instructor should make contact with a representative from the company well in advance of the trip. The instructor should maintain a working relationship with the representative so that all parties involved have a complete understanding of areas to be covered, date, time, and other related information. Some companies may provide materials to be used in the classroom to help prepare the students for the trip.

Prior to the trip, the students should be briefed on the day's activities. Any background information should be presented that will help the students understand what they will see on the trip. After the field trip is completed, the instructor should discuss the trip with the students and evaluate the field trip with them.

Field trips provide students with information which they cannot learn in the classroom. They have an opportunity to learn about careers in the field. They can actually see the duties that must be performed by employees of architecture and construction firms. Materials, as well as techniques and construction practices, can also be viewed.

Some possible field trip experiences include home construction sites, architectural firms, building material centers, and companies manufacturing industrialized homes. Other possibilities are in the area of recent innovations in architecture — residential construction utilizing solar applications, dome structures, and earth sheltered dwellings. Restoration of older homes is yet another source.

STUDENT ORGANIZATIONS

Participating in recognized student organizations provides many rewards. Opportunities for developing leadership skills, interacting with professionals in the field, and helping students grow as individuals are some of the many positive aspects of student organizations. The variety of activities which organizations offer expand student interest and participation as well as help to develop technical skills. Organizations which offer activities for students in architecture and construction include the following:

American Institute of Design and Drafting (AIDD)
966 Hungerford Dr., Suite 10B
Rockville, MD 20850

American Vocational Association (AVA)
1410 King St.
Alexandria, VA 22314

International Technology Education Association (ITEA)
1914 Association Dr.
Reston, VA 22091

National Computer Graphics Association
2722 Merrilee Dr., Suite 200
Fairfax, VA 22031

Vocational Industrial Clubs of America (VICA)
Box 3000
Leesburg, VA 22075

Student competitions are often sponsored by industry, organizations, training centers, or state education associations. Contact these various organizations in your community and state for information.

SUMMER WORK EXPERIENCE

Summer work experience provides short-term opportunities to work in the fields they have chosen for responsible students who have completed advanced courses. The instructor may help students locate the work experience or the students may find it on their own. To be most beneficial, the summer work experience should coincide with the student's career goals.

There are several advantages of summer work experience. For example, it is an excellent way for students to gain actual work experience. It gives them an opportunity to use and refine the skills they have learned in the classroom as well as learn new skills. Students gain a better understanding of all the aspects involved in the career of their choice by actually performing the day-to-day activities. They also have an opportunity to learn about other careers. The students can earn money while the employer benefits by getting a good worker at little cost.

EVALUATION

Purposeful evaluation is an important factor in the teaching/learning process. Appropriate evaluation should also be an important part of the teacher's method of teaching. There should be a conscious effort on the part of the teacher to evaluate each and every learning activity. Evaluation involves the influence of the class on the students in addition to their performance in the class. It includes deciding how students are performing as well as their feelings about the class. The conscientious teacher will constantly be aware of the students' thoughts and how they are growing intellectually. The instructor should care about the students' comprehension as well as their outlook. He/she should also be concerned about the students' capabilities in addition to what they accomplish.

Evaluation indicates not only the quality of teaching, but also how well students learn. Evaluation reveals to the instructor whether his/her teaching methods and strategies are effective. The evaluation methods that the teacher uses should help the students to better comprehend and utilize the theory to be mastered in the class.

The overall goal of effective teaching is to assist the students in meeting the required objectives. A combination of the teacher's efforts and student learning can accomplish this goal. The students' ability to learn, plus the effectiveness of the teaching, is evident by an evaluation of the technical skills obtained, the concepts learned, and the mental processes of identifying and solving problems.

Evaluation should be an ongoing process — a process that the instructor as well as the student can use. Some typical methods used for evaluation purposes include observations, self-evaluations, tests and examinations, progress charts, and individual as well as group project evaluations. By using a wide variety of methods to evaluate student progress, an ongoing process of measurement by the teacher and the students should result.

The evaluation process is started by the instructor presenting the overall objectives to the students and letting them know exactly what is expected from them. The instructor should relate to them what they are expected to know, how they should perform, what class behavior is acceptable, as well as the various class procedures. The students should have a clear understanding of what will be taught, what they are expected to learn, and how they will be evaluated.

A vital part of the evaluation process is immediate feedback. The observation technique does just that. The student knows immediately if he/she is correctly applying the knowledge learned. The instructor should always emphasize what the student is doing correctly and show the student areas that require improvement. The instructor should always return drawings, tests, etc., as quickly as possible and make suggestions for improvement as well as commend good work.

A variety of evaluation techniques should be used to evaluate student progress. These techniques should be integrated into the teaching/learning process wherever possible. For instance, the instructor can use several evaluation techniques during a single class period. As material is presented, the instructor should observe the expressions on the students' faces. Do they understand the presentation or are there puzzled looks on their faces? If the teacher notices that the students do not understand the material being presented, it should be reviewed again or presented to them in a different way to ensure understanding. An instructor should encourage students to enter into the discussion so that he/she is sure that the students understand the concepts being presented. As the students begin to draw, observe them at their workstations. Is their work correct or should suggestions be made for improvement? Let the students know immediately if their performance is correct or if they need to make changes.

Using a variety of evaluation methods permits students to express themselves in different ways. Students with good eye/hand coordination frequently can perform successfully using drawing equipment. Those who can visualize a completed project before even starting the drawing process can be successful using the computer or traditional techniques. Other students can perform well on written work. The teacher should provide opportunities for each student to find success.

The evaluation method used should be appropriate to achieve the desired results. Some methods are more suitable for one type of evaluation than others. If necessary, the instructor should make note of the various methods used for each situation and make reference to it periodically.

The evaluation should always be based on guidelines and models. For example, several guidelines are given in the textbook for good window design. When evaluating designs for windows, base the evaluation on whether the design follows these guidelines. The drawings in the textbook should be used as models for the student to follow. In other words, they should serve as models for the students to pattern their work after. When evaluating the students' drawings, use the models for comparison. How does the students' work compare to the work shown in the models?

The instructor should use evaluation methods that differentiate. The methods used should indicate how the students behave, how they comprehend, or how they carry out their work. The methods used should not only measure small differences, but meaningful differences as well. The instructor can determine which methods differentiate to the fullest extent for any given situation by experimenting with various methods.

The weight (emphasis) given to evaluations should vary among the different projects. All of the projects should not be worth the same amount. Values should be assigned to the projects so that the students will know the worth of each one. For example, a set of plans for a structure should have greater value than a quiz. The students should be told at the beginning of the course the values placed on the various projects.

The instructor should use evaluation methods that are dependable, effective, and complete. Dependable evaluation methods produce similar results time after time. Effective evaluation methods produce results that they are expected to produce. In other words, a test item designed to measure a certain concept should measure that concept. If it does not, then the test item is not effective. Evaluation methods that are complete should cover the concepts presented. The methods should be inclusive to the point that they cover the objectives to be learned. The instructor should keep these points in mind when selecting evaluation methods.

The instructor can use demonstration as an evaluation technique. He/she can set up a drawing table and actually draw a project along with the students. The students can see a professional at work. They gain confidence in their instructor's ability and this, in turn, helps to build confidence in themselves. The students can observe habits, drawing procedures, techniques, as well as sequence of methods demonstrated. They can see what the drawing actually looks like. The students will then set higher expectations for themselves when they see the instructor's performance.

Meaningful evaluation includes commending students when they succeed. It also includes constant feedback. It entails providing constant motivation and encouragement for students to reach their goals. Meaningful evaluation also involves teaching students to be responsible for their own development.

Flexibility in teaching methods may be required to use evaluation effectively. An instructor may need to modify teaching methods to meet the various needs of the students. Extra attention and time may be required for some students to complete their projects. The laboratory should be available for student use in addition to class time to enable students who need extra time to complete their projects and provide time for advanced students who wish to work on extra projects.

CHAPTER RESOURCES

The Teacher's Resource Guide (TRG) includes chapter resources for each chapter in the textbook and workbook. Each chapter resource section contains objectives for each chapter, displays for bulletin boards, and teaching strategies. Also included are answers to the review questions in the textbook and answers to the review questions and problems/activities in the workbook. A chapter exam is also provided in the chapter resources.

OBJECTIVES

The objectives are the same as those found at the beginning of each chapter in the textbook. They are included in each chapter resource section in the TRG to aid the instructor in developing the lesson plan.

DISPLAYS

Display suggestions for bulletin boards, etc., are provided for each chapter. These displays are designed to create interest, provide information, or display student work. This is an excellent medium for displaying informational leaflets such as those showing the latest building components available or current building techniques. Encourage student participation in collecting the items to be displayed and in arranging the display itself.

INSTRUCTIONAL MATERIALS

The resources necessary to teach the content of each chapter are listed in the instructional materials section. Instructors should answer the review questions in the textbook and workbook, complete the problems/activities in the workbook, and answer the exam questions in the TRG before assignments are made to the students. This enables an instructor to thoroughly understand the material and be prepared to explain every detail. It also gives an instructor an idea of the length of time required by the students to complete a given project or where they may encounter difficulties in comprehending concepts or mastering techniques.

TEACHING STRATEGY

Suggestions and strategies for teaching the content of the chapter are presented in this section. Instructors are given information on using the textbook including the review questions and suggested activities and the workbook review questions and problems/activities. The instructor can utilize as many of the suggestions and activities he/she desires in the time allotted. Some modifications will most likely be necessary to meet the needs of the students and curriculum. The instructor should keep a record of the teaching strategies and suggestions he/she finds effective and continue to add ideas to keep his/her teaching current and relevant.

TRANSPARENCY/DUPLICATING MASTERS

Transparency and duplicating masters may be utilized to reinforce concepts presented in the teaching strategies. They may be created from the solutions to the problems/activities presented in the workbook or from illustrations presented in the textbook. Transparency masters can reduce the time required to construct drawing examples on the chalkboard. They can be used as precise models for the students to observe. Duplicating masters are designed to be used in class or for out-of-class assignments. In some instances, concepts may be presented best by using a combination of transparency and duplicating masters.

CHAPTER EXAM

Different kinds of questions are included in the chapter exam. The chapter exam is the last thing the student should complete for a given chapter. The chapter exam is designed to sample the students' understanding of materials and procedures and serve as a good measure of their understanding of the chapter content.

The World of Architecture

■ OBJECTIVES

After studying this chapter, the student will be able to:
☐ Identify the historical influences that helped shape today's home designs.
☐ Recognize and describe the elements of contemporary dwellings.
☐ Discuss current trends in architecture.

■ DISPLAYS

1. House Styles. Select several photos of homes, each representing a different basic style. Identify the styles represented. Form an attractive arrangement on your bulletin board.
2. Famous House. Make a large "blueprint" from a slide of a famous house like the Fallingwater House at Bear Run, Pennsylvania designed by Frank Lloyd Wright. Display the print on your bulletin board. Use the following procedure to make the "blueprint." Set up a slide projector in a dark room. Select the slide you wish to make a print from and focus the image on a wall so that it is about the size of a sheet of blueprint (blue line or black line) paper. Tape a sheet of print paper to the wall and make a test copy by covering most of the unexposed sheet with cardboard. Expose the uncovered portion for 5 minutes. Move the cardboard over to expose another portion and expose that section for another 5 minutes. Continue the process until the first step has had an exposure of about 30 minutes. Develop the sheet and select the exposure time best suited for your slide. Expose a new sheet for the appropriate amount of time to produce a blueprint of the slide. The exposure time will depend on the speed of the print paper and density of the slide.

■ INSTRUCTIONAL MATERIALS

Text: Pages 7-24
  Review Questions, Suggested Activities
Workbook: Pages 7-8
  Review Questions, Problems/Activities
Teacher's Resource Guide:
  Chapter 1—Teaching Strategy
  Chapter 1—Exam

■ TEACHING STRATEGY

- Prepare Display #1 to set the stage for this chapter.
- Review chapter objectives.
- Introduce the world of architecture by showing photos or slides of a variety of architectural styles. Point out similarities and differences.
- Discuss several historical influences that helped shape home designs. Study characteristics of the Cape Colonials (Cape Cod and Cape Ann), Garrison, Salt Box, and Southern Colonial.
- Prepare Display #2 to coincide with discussion of influences of home styles.
- Discuss and illustrate a variety of contemporary home designs. Emphasize the structure as related to the local environment—south, west, north, etc.
- Share information concerning trends in residential architecture. For example, cover post-modern architecture, revival of previous styles, and experimentation with unique materials and building techniques.
- Assign one or more of the Suggested Activities in the text.
- Chapter Review
  —Assign Review Questions in the text. Discuss the correct answers.
  —Assign Review Questions in the workbook. Have students check their own answers.

- Evaluation
  - Administer the Chapter 1—Exam. Correct the exam and return.

■ ANSWERS TO REVIEW QUESTIONS, TEXT
Page 23

1. climate conditions
2. a. Sensitivity to design.
   b. Skill in drawing techniques.
   c. Knowledge of the latest construction materials.
3. b. Containers in village stores.
4. a. Separate corner posts on each floor can be shorter and stronger.
   b. Straight lines provide economy of framing materials.
   c. The overhang provides extra second floor space.
5. a. The front colonnade.
   b. The giant portico.
6. The roof pitch is abruptly changed between the ridge and eaves.
7. a. Some distinctive features are borrowed from the past.
   b. Individuals often want their own tastes reflected in their homes.
   c. Architects have a wider range of materials to design with.
8. low-pitched
9. a. New design concepts.
   b. Additions to the basic ranch styles.
10. a. Dramatic yet comfortable living styles.
    b. Homes designed to fit particular sites.
    c. Provide a feeling of openness.
    d. Retain necessary privacy.
11. post-modern.
12. fiberglass.

■ ANSWERS TO REVIEW QUESTIONS, WORKBOOK

PART I: MATCHING

1. g. Salt Box.
2. a. Cape Ann.
3. d. Garrison.
4. h. Southern Colonial.
5. b. Cape Cod.
6. f. Ranch.
7. c. Contemporary.
8. e. New England Gambrel.

PART II: COMPLETION

1. hillside
2. provide openness
3. Post-modern
4. energy-efficient
5. restored
6. Zanadome

PART III: SHORT ANSWER/LISTING

1. A. The separate corner posts on each floor make it possible to user shorter, stronger posts.
   B. The short, straight lines provide economy in framing materials.
   C. Extra space is added at the second level by the overhang at very little extra cost.
2. A. Post-modern architecture.
   B. Restoration of older homes.
   C. Experimentation of new materials and new designs such as the Zanadome.

■ ANSWERS TO CHAPTER 1—EXAM

TRUE—FALSE

1. T	4. F
2. T	5. T
3. F	

MULTIPLE CHOICE

1. D	5. D
2. B	6. C
3. C	7. A
4. A	

Chapter 1—Exam
THE WORLD OF ARCHITECTURE

Name _____

Period _____ **Date** _____ **Score** _____

TRUE—FALSE
Circle T if the statement is true or F if the statement is false.

T　　F　　1. Many traditional residential styles were designed to meet climatic conditions.

T　　F　　2. The name of some house styles is related to their shape.

T　　F　　3. The Cape Cod originated as a large house with a steep roof and no overhang.

T　　F　　4. An advantage of the gambrel roof is the ease of building it.

T　　F　　5. One of the most gracious of all the Colonials is the traditional Southern Colonial.

MULTIPLE CHOICE
Choose the answer that correctly completes the statement. Write the corresponding letter in the space provided.

_____ 1. Two popular home styles developed over _____ years ago are the Cape Cod and Cape Ann.
  A. 1000
  B. 600
  C. 400
  D. 200

_____ 2. The Cape Cod is one of the earliest and best known of the traditional _____ styles.
  A. Southern
  B. Colonial
  C. Eastern
  D. European

_____ 3. A primary feature of the Cape Cod home style was its _____.
  A. large windows
  B. double entry doors
  C. central chimney
  D. metal roofing

_____ 4. The basic roof style of the Cape Ann style is a _____ roof.
  A. gambrel
  B. gable
  C. mansard
  D. hip

_____ 5. The _____ style house gets its name from the shape of coffee, tea, cracker, and salt boxes found in colonial stores.
  A. Cape Ann
  B. Gambrel
  C. Garrison
  D. Salt Box

_____ 6. The _____ home style is basically a long, low, one-story house that originated in the southwest part of the United States.
A. contemporary
B. split-level
C. ranch
D. Cape Cod

_____ 7. A current trend in architecture that combines traditional and contemporary influences is called _____.
A. post-modern
B. revival
C. modern
D. art deco

2
CHAPTER

Basic House Design

■ OBJECTIVES

After studying this chapter, the student will be able to:
- ☐ Recognize the four basic house designs.
- ☐ List the chief advantages of each design.
- ☐ Map the traffic circulation for maximum efficiency.
- ☐ Compare the relative cost of heating and cooling for each design.

■ DISPLAYS

1. Basic House Designs. Form a bulletin board display from the best basic house designs submitted by your students for Suggested Activities #1 in the text.
2. House Styles. Contact real estate firms to secure photos of ranch, two-story, and split-level homes they are marketing. Group the photos according to house style to form a bulletin board display.

■ INSTRUCTIONAL MATERIALS

Text: Pages 25-36
   Review Questions, Suggested Activities
Workbook: Pages 9-13
   Review Questions, Problems/Activities
Teacher's Resource Guide:
   Chapter 2—Teaching Strategy
   Chapter 2—Exam

■ TEACHING STRATEGY

- Prepare Display #1 to show basic house designs.
- Review chapter objectives.

- Introduce the four basic designs—one-story or ranch, one-and-one-half-story, two-story, and split-level.
- Assign one or more of the Suggested Activities in the text.
- Discuss one-story ranch designs with respect to advantages, disadvantages, characteristics, and variations within the design.
- Discuss one-and-one-half-story designs. Again cover advantages, disadvantages, characteristics, and variations within the design.
- Discuss two-story designs. Cover advantages, disadvantages, characteristics, and variations within the design.
- Prepare Display #2.
- Discuss split-level designs in the same way as previous designs.
- Discuss traffic circulation in terms of functional analysis.
- Assign Problem 2-1 in workbook.
- Assign one or more of the Suggested Activities in the text.
- Chapter Review
   —Assign Review Questions in the text. Discuss the correct answers.
   —Assign Review Questions in the workbook. Have students check their own answers.
- Evaluation
   —Administer the Chapter 2—Exam. Correct the exam and return.
   —Return Problem 2-1 with grade and comments.

■ ANSWERS TO REVIEW QUESTIONS, TEXT
Page 34

1. a. Ranch or one-story.
   b. One-and-one-half-story.
   c. Two-story.
   d. Split-level.

2. a. Absence of stairs.
    b. Easy to maintain.
    c. Simplified construction.
    d. Lends itself to indoor-outdoor living.
    e. Good seller.
    Also: Lends itself to expansion and modification.
3. a. Usually costs more to build.
    b. Requires a larger lot.
    c. Heating may be a problem.
    d. Maintenance is costly.
    e. Too much hall space.
4. steep roof, dormers.
5. economy, expansibility.
6. two-story
7. a. Not very popular.
    b. Exterior maintenance costly.
    c. Does not lend itself to variations in style.
    d. May appear out-of-place unless located among other similar styles.
8. split-level
9. a. Basement.
    b. Intermediate.
    c. Living.
    d. Sleeping.
10. a. Side-by-side.
    b. Front-to-back.
    c. Back-to-front.
11. It lends itself to indoor-outdoor living.
12. To provide additional light and ventilation.
13. c. 40 to 60 percent.
14. The back-to-front split-level.

■ ANSWERS TO REVIEW QUESTIONS WORKBOOK

PART I: MULTIPLE CHOICE

1. c. Easily adapted to indoor-outdoor living.
2. a. One-story ranch design.
3. b. Low-pitched roof.
4. b. One-and-one-half-story design.
5. d. All of the above.
6. c. It is economical to build, requires a smaller lot, and has a small roof and foundation area compared to interior space of most other designs.
7. a. Heating is relatively simple and economical because heat naturally rises from the first to the second floor.
8. c. Two-story design.
9. d. Split-level design.
10. b. Intermediate level.
11. d. All of the above.

PART II: SHORT ANSWER/LISTING

1. Zoned heating (separate thermostats for various areas of the house) should solve the problem.
2. A. Side-by-side.
    B. Front-to-back.
    C. Back-to-front.
3. The front-to-back split-level.
4. It is a split entry (the foyer is half way between levels).
5. The foyer should be centrally located and convenient to all areas of the house, since some family members and all guests will be using this entrance. The distance from the garage to the kitchen should be direct for transporting food and household items.
6. A. One-story ranch design.
    B. One-and-one-half-story design.
    C. Two-story design.
    D. Split-level design.

■ ANSWERS TO PROBLEMS/ACTIVITIES WORKBOOK

PART III: PROBLEMS/ACTIVITIES

1. Solution on page 33.

■ ANSWERS TO CHAPTER 2 EXAM

TRUE—FALSE

1. T
2. T
3. T

4. T
5. T

MULTIPLE CHOICE

1. A
2. D
3. C

4. B
5. D

SHORT ANSWER

1. A. One-story or ranch.
    B. One-and-one-half-story.
    C. Two-story.
    D. Split-level.
2. (Choose five)
    A. Space available for the house.
    B. Site contour.
    C. Climate.
    D. Convenience.
    E. Cost.
    F. Surroundings.
    G. Personal preference.
3. A. Side-by-side.
    B. Front-to-back.
    C. Back-to-front.

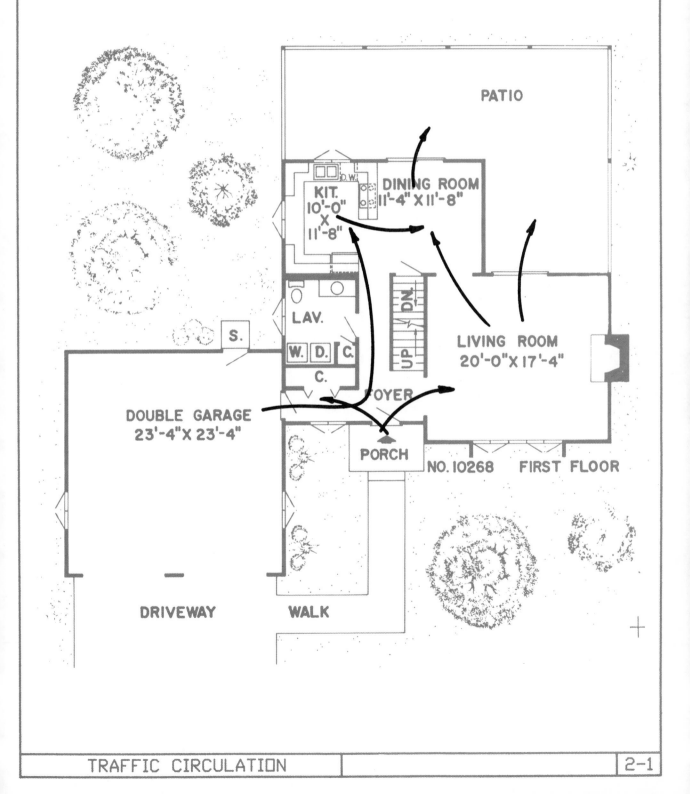

PATIO

DINING ROOM
11'-4" X 11'-8"

KIT.
10'-0"
X
11'-8"

D.W.

LAV.

W. D. C.

C.

DN.

UP

LIVING ROOM
20'-0"X 17'-4"

FOYER

S.

DOUBLE GARAGE
23'-4"X 23'-4"

PORCH

NO. 10268   FIRST FLOOR

DRIVEWAY   WALK

TRAFFIC CIRCULATION   2-1

Chapter 2—Exam
BASIC HOUSE DESIGN

Name _____

Period _____ **Date** _____ **Score** _____

TRUE—FALSE
Circle T if the statement is true or F if the statement is false.

T   F   1. One chief advantage of the ranch design is that it lends itself to indoor-outdoor living.

T   F   2. The ranch design may have a basement or crawl space.

T   F   3. Ranch homes generally require a considerable amount of hall space.

T   F   4. Compared to ranch and one-and-one-half-story houses, the two-story house is more economical to build.

T   F   5. The split-level house was conceived for the hilly or sloping site.

MULTIPLE CHOICE
Choose the answer that correctly completes the statement. Write the corresponding letter in the space provided.

_____ 1. The reason that a ranch design is generally more expensive to build than a two-story home of the same size is that _____.
A. it requires more roof area and more foundation length
B. it requires more windows and doors
C. builders don't like to build ranch homes
D. permits cost more to build a ranch home

_____ 2. One-and-one-half story homes generally have _____ to provide additional light and ventilation.
A. skylights
B. glass sliding doors
C. picture windows
D. dormers

_____ 3. One disadvantage of a two-story house is that _____.
A. it is more costly to heat because of the heights
B. it has little resale value
C. general exterior maintenance is usually more difficult and costly
D. the second floor is too far from the furnace

_____ 4. In the _____ split-level home design, the house looks like a ranch in the front and a two-story house from the back.
A. back-to-front
B. front-to-back
C. side-by-side
D. reversed split-level

_____ 5. An analysis should be made of _____ to determine if the house plan is as functional as possible.
A. walking paths
B. air circulation
C. traffic movement
D. traffic circulation

Name _____

SHORT ANSWER

Answer the following questions using short answers.

1. List the four basic designs that a residential home designer has to choose from.

   A. _____

   B. _____

   C. _____

   D. _____

2. List five of the factors that should play a role in the final decision of a house design.

   A. _____

   B. _____

   C. _____

   D. _____

   E. _____

   F. _____

   G. _____

3. List the three basic variations of the split-level home design.

   A. _____

   B. _____

   C. _____

Primary Considerations

■ OBJECTIVES

After studying this chapter, the student will be able to:
- ☐ Evaluate a given site with respect to important considerations.
- ☐ Discuss key site consideration, restrictions, zoning, and codes.
- ☐ Record topographical features of a site.
- ☐ List family needs that should be considered when planning a dwelling.
- ☐ Describe the basic construction drawings used to build a structure.

■ DISPLAYS

1. Our Community. Secure a large map of your school district and mount it on the bulletin board. Have each student locate his/her residence on the map by placing a map tack at the location. Shade in shopping areas, churches, recreation areas, and other services offered by the community. Locate the school with a distinct symbol.
2. Permits Required to Build a Home. Display sample permits required in your area to build a new residence. Attach an estimation of cost for each permit for an "average" new home in your community.
3. Site Considerations. Use materials generated by Suggested Activity #6 to develop a bulletin board that illustrates the advantages of proper site considerations when planning a house.

■ INSTRUCTIONAL MATERIALS

Text: Pages 37-48
Review Questions, Suggested Activities

Workbook: Pages 15-20
Review Questions, Problems/Activities

Teacher's Resource Guide:
Chapter 3 — Teaching Strategy
Chapter 3 — Exam

■ TEACHING STRATEGY

- Prepare Display #1 which shows the local community.
- Review chapter objectives.
- Discuss site considerations as a part of the total planning process.
- Discuss the community influence in terms of planning a particular residence.
- Prepare Display #2. Discuss cost and restrictions.
- Discuss zoning and codes that affect building practices in your area.
- Introduce topographical features.
- Prepare Display #3.
- Emphasize family needs as a primary consideration. Review the list of activities in the text.
- Review modular aspects and quality of living as two additional factors to be considered.
- Describe in detail the various drawings included in a set of construction plans. Refer to drawings in the text.
- Assign one or more of the Suggested Activities in the text.
- Chapter Review
  — Assign Review Questions in the text. Discuss the correct answers.
  — Assign Review Questions in the workbook. Have students check their own answers.

- Evaluation
  - Administer the Chapter 3—Exam. Correct the exam and return.
  - Return graded problems with comments.

■ ANSWERS TO REVIEW QUESTIONS, TEXT
Pages 47-48

1. a. Site considerations.
   b. Community.
   c. Cost.
   d. Zoning restrictions.
   e. Style.
   f. Location.
   g. Schools.
   h. Neighbors.
   i. Climate.
   j. Shopping.
   k. Transportation.
   l. Room for expansion.
2. title.
3. deed.
4. a. Slope.
   b. Contour.
   c. Size.
   d. Shape.
   e. Elevation.
   f. Trees.
   g. Rocks.
   h. Soil conditions.
5. one acre
6. The lifestyle of those who occupy it.
7. a. Preparing food.
   b. Dining.
   c. Entertaining.
   d. Hobbies.
   e. Laundering.
   f. Studying.
   g. Dressing.
   h. Sleeping.
   i. Relaxing.
   j. Working.
   Also: Storage, bathing, housekeeping, accommodating guests, and planning.
8. To reduce waste and lower costs.
9. four
10. a. Plot plan.
    b. Foundation plan.
    c. Floor plan.
    d. Elevations.
    e. Electrical plan.
    f. Construction details.
    g. Pictorial presentation.
11. To determine if there are any legal claims against the property.
12. The quality of living provided for the owner.
13. local conditions.

■ ANSWERS TO REVIEW QUESTIONS, WORKBOOK

PART I: COMPLETION

1. site
2. split-level
3. site.
4. title
5. Zoning
6. building
7. building
8. shape
9. size
10. materials
11. standard
12. 4' x 8'
13. 4
14. 15
15. quality

PART II: MATCHING

1. h. Title search.
2. b. Deed.
3. e. Restrictions.
4. c. Easements.
5. a. Building codes.
6. g. Surveyor.
7. i. Topographical drawings.
8. d. Modular construction.
9. f. Specifications.

PART III: MULTIPLE CHOICE

1. d. Electrical plan.
2. a. Construction details.
3. c. Location of the house on the site, utilities, topographical features, site dimensions, and other buildings on the property.
4. b. Shows size and material of the support structure. May serve as the basement plan. Gives information pertaining to excavation, waterproofing, and supporting structures.
5. b. Plumbing plan.
6. c. Floor plan.

PART IV: SHORT ANSWER/LISTING

1. A. Is the community a "planned" community or one with no central theme?
   B. Are the homes within the price range of the proposed home?
   C. Are the neighbors in about the same socioeconomic category as the prospective homeowner?
   D. Is the community alive and growing or run-down and dying?
   E. Does it have room for growth or is it restricted?
   F. Are the residents people who take pride in their homes or seem indifferent toward them?
   G. Does the community have modern churches, quality schools, and shopping areas?
   H. Are such facilities as fire protection, water, sewer, natural gas, and garbage collection available in the community?
   I. Is the site near the prospective owner's place of work?
   J. Is public transportation available in the community?
   K. Does the community have a high rate of turnover due to the resale of homes?

2. A. Needed improvements such as grading, fill, tree removal, and drainage.
   B. Amount of frontage.
   C. Whether or not it is a corner lot.
3. A. The owner must provide his/her own sewer and water. If the water is very hard, has iron, or there is a lack of water, special equipment is needed to handle these problems which create greater expense for the homeowner.
   B. A site smaller than one acre may not meet the code requirements.
4. A. Preparing food.
   B. Dining.
   C. Entertaining.
   D. Family Recreation.
   E. Hobbies.
   F. Laundering.
   G. Studying.
   H. Dressing.
   I. Sleeping.
   J. Relaxing.
   K. Working.
   L. Storage.
   M. Bathing.
   N. Housekeeping.
   O. Accommodating guests.
   P. Planning.
5. A. Plot plan.
   B. Foundation plan.
   C. Floor plan.
   D. Elevations.
   E. Electrical plan.
   F. Construction details.
   G. Pictorial presentations.

■ ANSWERS TO CHAPTER 3—EXAM

TRUE—FALSE
1. T
2. F
3. T
4. T
5. T

MULTIPLE CHOICE
1. C
2. A
3. D
4. D
5. A
6. C

SHORT ANSWER
1. (Choose five.)
   A. Slope.
   B. Contour.
   C. Size.
   D. Shape.
   E. Elevation.
   F. Trees.
   G. Rocks.
   H. Soil conditions.
2. (Choose twelve.)
   A. Preparing food.
   B. Dining.
   C. Entertaining.
   D. Family recreation.
   E. Hobbies.
   F. Working.
   G. Laundering.
   H. Studying.
   I. Dressing.
   J. Sleeping.
   K. Relaxing.
   L. Storage.
   M. Bathing.
   N. Housekeeping.
   O. Accommodating guests.
   P. Planning.
3. A. Plot Plan.
   B. Foundation Plan.
   C. Floor Plan.
   D. Elevations.
   E. Electrical Plan.
   F. Construction Details.
   G. Pictorial Presentation.

Chapter 3—Exam
PRIMARY CONSIDERATIONS

Name _____

Period _____ **Date** _____ **Score** _____

TRUE—FALSE
Circle T if the statement is true or F if the statement is false.

T   F   1. Site considerations are just as important as the size and room arrangement of a house.

T   F   2. The house should appear to stand apart from its surroundings.

T   F   3. A planned community is preferred over one that has no central theme.

T   F   4. Building codes ensure a prescribed level of quality.

T   F   5. A truly functional house represents the life-styles of those who occupy it.

MULTIPLE CHOICE
Choose the answer that correctly completes the statement. Write the corresponding letter in the space provided.

_____ 1. Corner lots generally have higher _____ because the length of frontage is longer than a typical lot.
   A. resale potential
   B. risk factors
   C. assessments
   D. insurance costs

_____ 2. A _____ search should be instituted before purchasing a lot to determine if there are any legal claims against the property.
   A. title
   B. library
   C. quit claim deed
   D. property

_____ 3. A house measuring _____ would be more economical to build than one that did not apply modular principles.
   A. 28' x 59'
   B. 50' x 51'
   C. 39' x 59'
   D. 40' x 60'

_____ 4. Exterior walls of residential structures should be multiples of _____ feet.
   A. 16
   B. 10
   C. 8
   D. 4 or 2

_____ 5. Plywood and paneling are produced in sheets that are generally _____ in size.
   A. 4' x 8'
   B. 3' x 6'
   C. 4' x 12'
   D. 6' x 12'

_____ 6. The construction drawing that shows the front or rear side of the house is called a(n) _____.

    A. Floor Plan
    B. Pictorial Presentation
    C. Elevation
    D. Foundation Plan

SHORT ANSWER

Answer the following questions using short answers.

1. List five topographical features that may limit the type of structure that may be built on a site.

    A. _____

    B. _____

    C. _____

    D. _____

    E. _____

2. Identify twelve individual and family activities that should be provided for in a functional house.

    A. _____

    B. _____

    C. _____

    D. _____

    E. _____

    F. _____

    G. _____

    H. _____

    I. _____

    J. _____

    K. _____

    L. _____

3. List the seven drawings which are frequently included in a set of typical residential construction drawings.

    A. _____

    B. _____

    C. _____

    D. _____

    E. _____

    F. _____

    G. _____

Drawing Instruments and Techniques

■ OBJECTIVES

After studying this chapter, the student will be able to:
☐ Define the three principal views in orthographic projection.
☐ List and explain the use of architectural drafting equipment.
☐ Discern the difference between size and scale.
☐ Reproduce the standard alphabet of lines.
☐ Demonstrate an acceptable architectural lettering style.
☐ Explain the use of several architectural drawing time-savers.

■ DISPLAYS

1. Typical Manual Drafting Equipment. Using photos from drafting equipment supply company catalogs, prepare a bulletin board display which shows the type of drafting equipment commonly used by manual drafters.
2. Modern CADD System. Secure photos of the components of a modern CADD system. Attach the photos to the bulletin board using a residential CADD drawing as a background. Identify each of the CADD system components.
3. Architectural Lettering Styles. Display several samples of architectural lettering styles produced by your students. Encourage the class members to examine these examples in an effort to improve their individual lettering styles.

■ INSTRUCTIONAL MATERIALS

Text: Pages 49-72
    Review Questions, Suggested Activities
Workbook: Pages 21-29
    Review Questions, Problems/Activities

Teacher's Resource Guide:
    Chapter 4—Teaching Strategy
    Chapter 4—Exam

■ TEACHING STRATEGY

- Prepare Display #1.
- Review chapter objectives.
- Review basic orthographic projection.
- Assign Problems 4-1 and 4-2 in the workbook.
- Discuss the principal views in architecture. Use Transparency #1.
- Cover traditional architectural drafting equipment.
- Discuss CADD drafting. Prepare Display #2 for reference.
- Explain how to use the scale and describe how to draw to scale. Assign Problem 4-3.
- Discuss the alphabet of lines. Draw them on the chalkboard.
- Assign Problem 4-4 in workbook.
- Discuss architectural lettering. Show students how to make each letter on the chalkboard.
- Assign Problem 4-5 in workbook.
- Prepare Display #3.
- Discuss architectural drawing time-savers. Illustrate the use of each method.
- Assign one or more of the Suggested Activities in the text.
- Chapter Review
    —Assign Review Questions in the text. Discuss the correct answers.
    —Assign Review Questions in the workbook. Have students check their own answers.
    —Use answers to Problems 4-4 and 4-5 in workbook to make transparencies for review with the class.
- Evaluation
    —Administer the Chapter 4—Exam. Correct

the exam and return.

—Return graded problems with comments.

■ ANSWERS TO REVIEW QUESTIONS, TEXT
Pages 69-70

1. right side
2. floor plan.
3. erasing shield.
4. 11 x 17 in., 12 x 18 in.
5. straightedge.
6. 30°-60°, 45°
7. 1/2°.
8. engineer's
9. 1/2" = 1".
10. 1/4" = 1'-0".
11. dividers.
12. compass.
13. lettering guide.
14. communicate ideas.
15. border
16. object
17. hidden
18. dimension
19. lettering
20. artistic.
21. variable.
22. 1/8", 3/32"
23. a. Templates.   c. Stencils.
    b. Burnishing plates. d. Underlays.
24. a. Overlays.   d. Photo drawings.
    b. Drafting tapes.   e. Stamps.
    c. Transfer symbols.
25. To handle the entire process; from conceptual design to the production of the construction drawings.
26. a. Data processing section or logic section.
    b. Memory or control section.
    c. Data transfer mechanism or data bus.
27. It details the operations that are to be performed on the data by the computer.
28. AEC package.
29. Pen plotter.

■ ANSWERS TO REVIEW QUESTIONS, WORKBOOK

PART I: MATCHING

1. f. Dimension lines.
2. g. Drafting tapes.
3. h. Grids.
4. b. Burnish plates.
5. d. Computer symbols library.
6. j. Orthographic projection.
7. i. Illustration boards.
8. l. Technical fountain pens.
9. e. Data processing unit.
10. c. CADD software.
11. k. Photoplotters.
12. a. Alphabet of lines.

PART II: MULTIPLE CHOICE

1. A. A.
2. B. 18 x 24 in.
3. C. Hold the blade with the left hand and draw from left to right.
4. C. The drawing is only half as large as the object in real life.
5. D. All of the above.
6. D. All of the above.
7. C. "C."
8. C. Hidden lines.
9. A. Center lines.
10. C. H.
11. A. 6H.

PART III: COMPLETION

1. top
2. front
3. side, lead
4. vellum
5. plastics
6. drafting
7. vernier
8. twelve
9. 1/2 in.
10. F
11. Lettering
12. engineering
13. memory
14. pen
15. long
16. Section
17. construction
18. lower

PART IV: SHORT ANSWER/LISTING

1. A. Front elevation.
   B. Right side elevation.
   C. Left side elevation.
   D. Rear elevation.
2. A. Choose one that will erase all traces of the lead without destroying the surface.
   B. Choose one that will not leave eraser color which detracts from the appearance of the drawing.
3. A. 45°.
   B. 30°-60°.
4. A. Semicircular.
   B. Circular.
5. A. To divide a line into proportional parts.
   B. To provide a quick method of measuring a length which must be used a number of times.

6. Hold the compass between the thumb and forefinger and rotate in a clockwise manner while leaning it slightly forward.
7. Line up at least four points and draw the line through three of the points.
8. A. Drum plotter.
   B. Flatbed plotter.
9. To communicate ideas accurately and clearly.
10. Cutting plane lines.
11. Allow about the same distance between words as the letters are high.

PART V: PROBLEMS/ACTIVITIES

1. Solution on page 46.
2. Solution on page 47.
3. Solution on page 48.
4. Solution on page 49.
5. Solution on page 50.

■ ANSWERS TO CHAPTER 4—EXAM

TRUE—FALSE

1. T	4. F
2. T	5. T
3. F	

MULTIPLE CHOICE

1. B	5. A
2. C	6. A
3. B	7. C
4. C	

SHORT ANSWER

1. A. Top.
   B. Front.
   C. Right side.
2. A. Architect's scale.
   B. Engineer's scale.
   C. Combination scale.
3. A. A data processing or logic section.
   B. A memory or control section.
   C. A data transfer mechanism or data bus.
4. A. Pen plotters.
   B. Electrostatic plotters.
   C. Photoplotters.
   D. Printers.
5. A. Templates.
   B. Underlays.
   C. Overlays.
   D. Drafting tapes.
   E. Transfer letters and symbols.
   F. Stencil letter guides.
   G. Grids.
   H. Rubber stamps.
   I. Burnish plates.

MATCHING

1. D	6. E
2. F	7. I
3. H	8. G
4. C	9. B
5. A	

1.

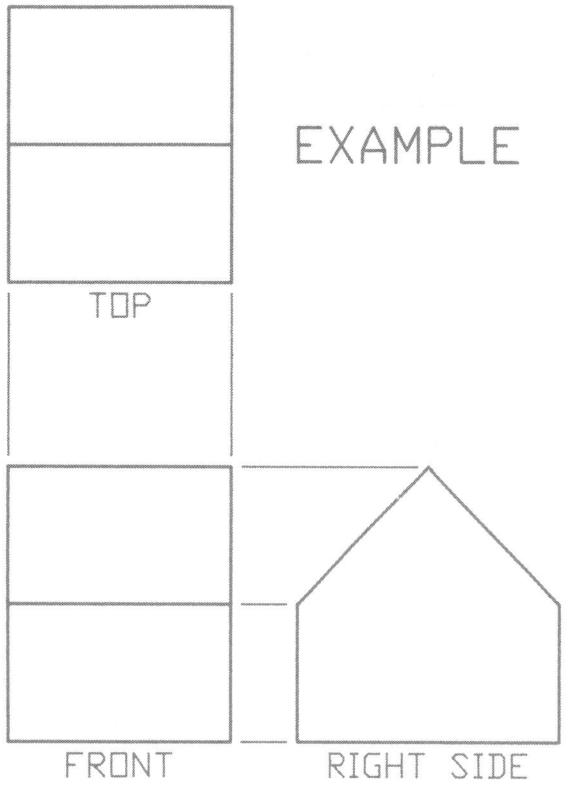

EXAMPLE

TOP

FRONT   RIGHT SIDE

A

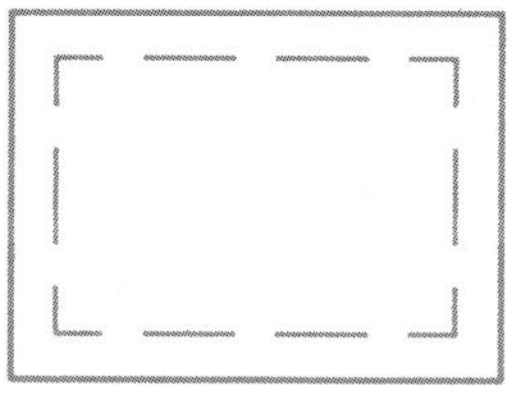

DIRECTIONS:
Draw the
Front View
in the space
provided.

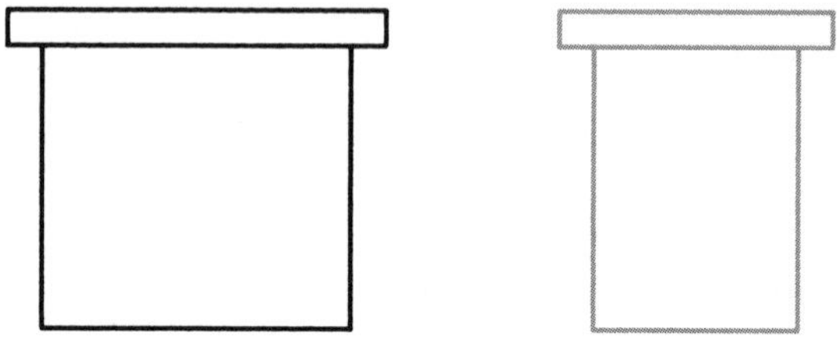

B

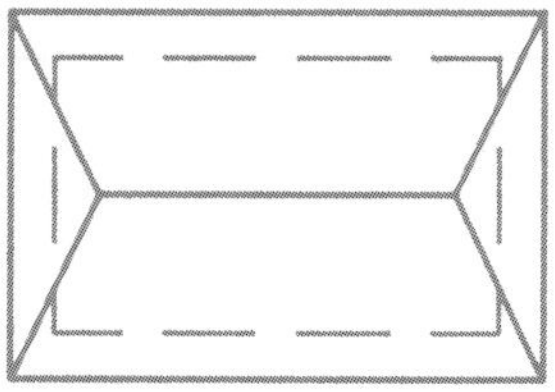

DIRECTIONS:
Draw the
Front View
in the space
provided.

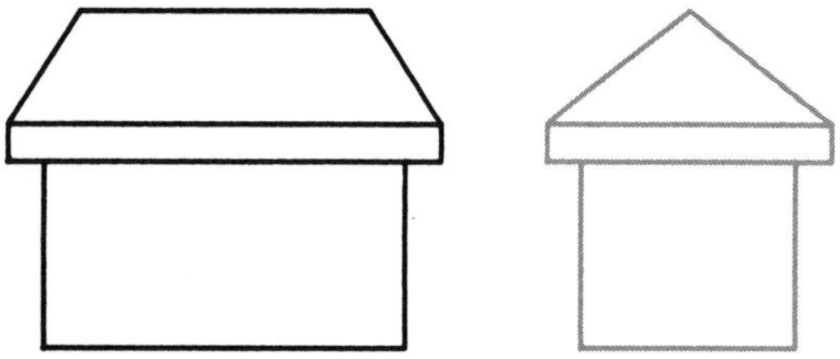

C

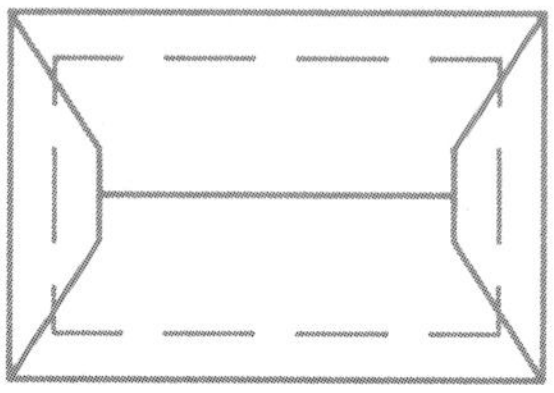

DIRECTIONS:
Draw the
Front View
in the space
provided.

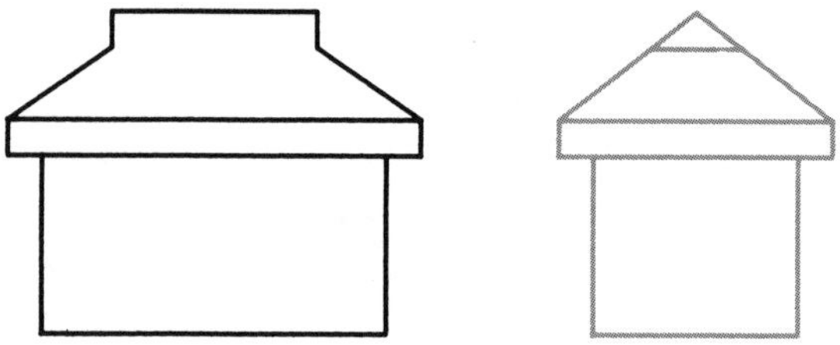

ORTHOGRAPHIC PROJECTION   4-1

2.

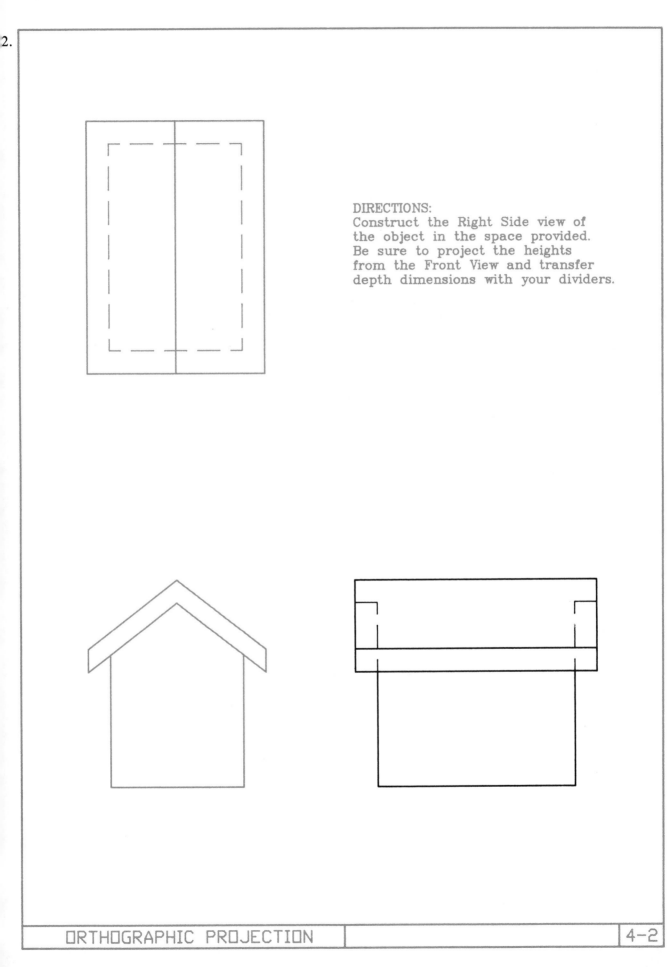

DIRECTIONS:
Construct the Right Side view of
the object in the space provided.
Be sure to project the heights
from the Front View and transfer
depth dimensions with your dividers.

3.

DIRECTIONS:
Measure each of the lines below using the scale indicated and letter the
length of the line 1/8" high just above the dimension line.   Use guidelines.

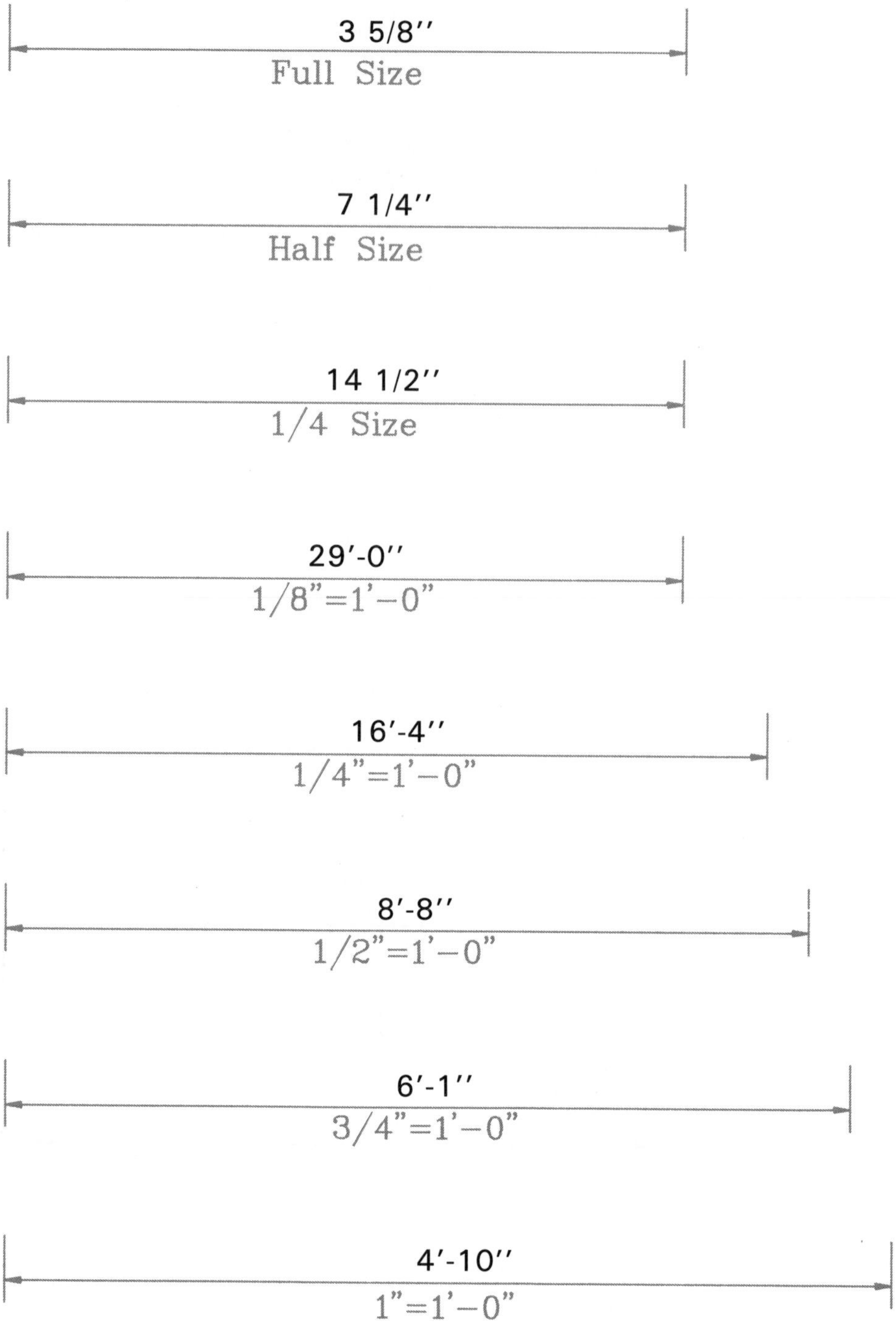

3 5/8''
Full Size

7 1/4''
Half Size

14 1/2''
1/4 Size

29'-0''
1/8"=1'-0"

16'-4''
1/4"=1'-0"

8'-8''
1/2"=1'-0"

6'-1''
3/4"=1'-0"

4'-10''
1"=1'-0"

MEASURING TO SCALE | | 4-3

DIRECTIONS:
Draw each of the lines illustrated below in the space provided to the
right of each line. Be sure to pay close attention to the thickness of
each line and the size of each element.

BORDER
LINE

OBJECT
LINE

CUTTING
PLANE LINE

SHORT BREAK
LINE

HIDDEN
LINE

CENTER
LINE

LONG BREAK
LINE

LEADER

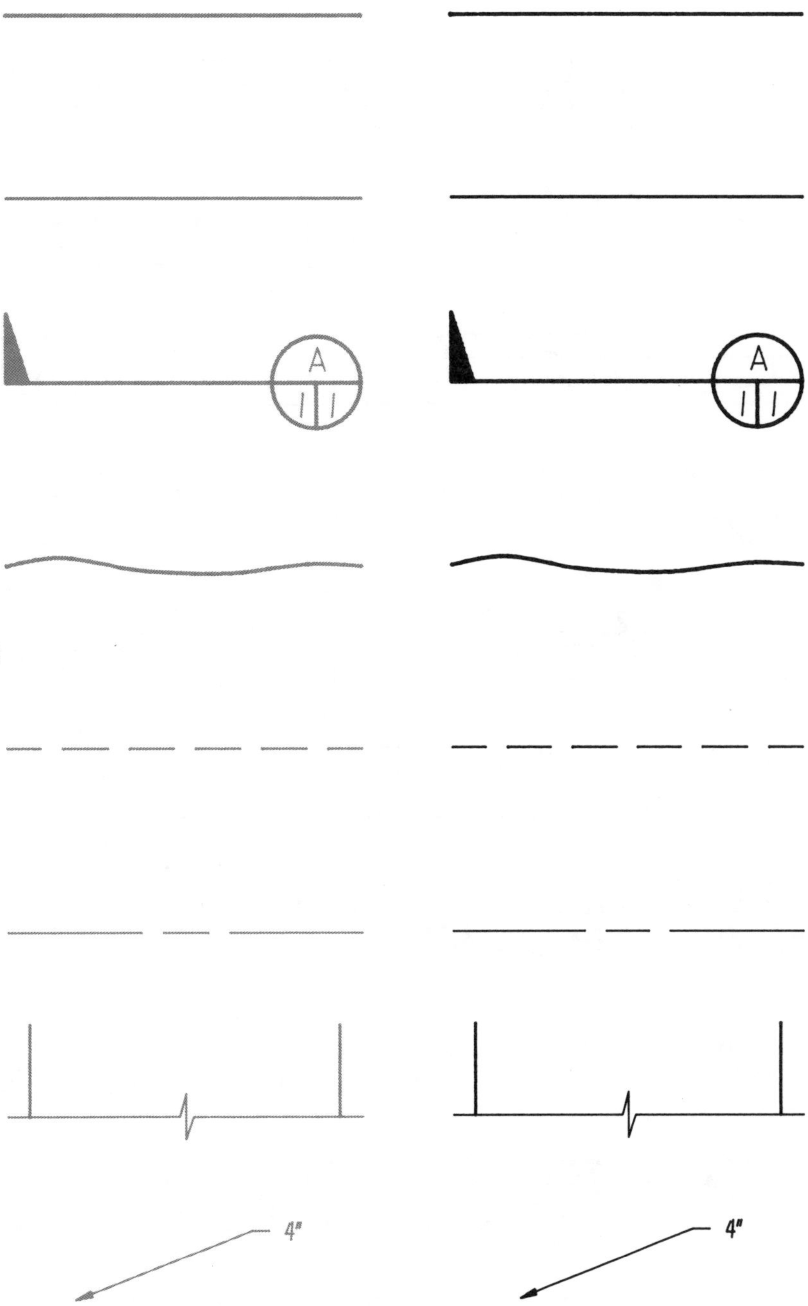

ALPHABET OF LINES | 4-4

5.

DIRECTIONS:
Practice lettering the alphabet and numbers using a style similar to one illustrated in the text. Practice "your" style until it becomes a part of you and flows easily.

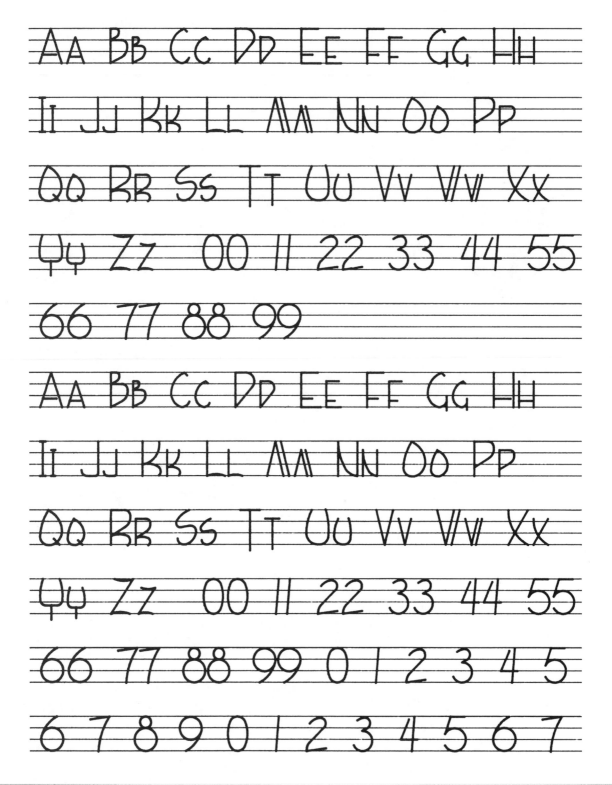

Chapter 4—Exam
DRAWING INSTRUMENTS AND TECHNIQUES

Name _____

Period _____ **Date** _____ **Score** _____

TRUE—FALSE
Circle T if the statement is true or F if the statement is false.

T   F   1. In orthographic projection, projection lines are parallel to each other.

T   F   2. The plan view is used as the basis for most other views in a house plan.

T   F   3. Architectural drawing sheets are based on multiples of 8 1/2" x 11".

T   F   4. An engineer's scale is based on 10 units to the foot.

T   F   5. A drawing of an object made at 1/8 size will be larger than the same drawing made at 1/2 scale.

MULTIPLE CHOICE
Choose the answer that correctly completes the statement. Write the corresponding letter in the space provided.

_____ 1. The top view of an object in mechanical drawing is comparable to the _____ plan of a house.
    A. floor
    B. roof
    C. plot
    D. perspective

_____ 2. The size of a standard architectural drawing "C" size sheet is _____.
    A. 24" x 36"
    B. 22" x 34"
    C. 18" x 24"
    D. 17" x 22"

_____ 3. A traditional drafting device that allows the drafter to draw a line at any angle is a(n) _____.
    A. straightedge
    B. adjustable triangle
    C. scale
    D. protractor

_____ 4. The _____ is used to draw circles and arcs.
    A. dividers
    B. protractor
    C. compass
    D. irregular curve

_____ 5. The acronym CADD stands for _____.
    A. Computer-Aided Drafting and Design
    B. Coded Architectural Drafting and Design
    C. Cost Analysis Design Differences
    D. Computer-Assisted Detail Drawing

_____ 6. CADD _____ details the operations to be performed on the data by the computer.
    A. software
    B. RAM
    C. monitor chip
    D. main memory

_____ 7. Most experienced drafters choose a _____ to produce a final hardcopy of their drawings.
    A. blueprint
    B. dot matrix printer
    C. pen plotter
    D. photocopier

SHORT ANSWER
Answer the following questions using short answers.

1. List the three principal views in orthographic projection.

    A. _____

    B. _____

    C. _____

2. Identify the three principal types of scales used in architectural drawing.

    A. _____

    B. _____

    C. _____

3. List the three components included in a computer or processor.

    A. _____

    B. _____

    C. _____

4. List four typical CADD hardcopy output devices.

    A. _____

    B. _____

    C. _____

    D. _____

5. List five architectural drawing time-savers.

    A. _____

    B. _____

    C. _____

    D. _____

    E. _____

MATCHING

Select the answer that correctly matches each term. Place your answer in the space provided.

_____ 1. Border lines

_____ 2. Object lines

_____ 3. Cutting plane lines

_____ 4. Short break lines

_____ 5. Hidden lines

_____ 6. Center lines

_____ 7. Guidelines

_____ 8. Construction lines

_____ 9. Dimension lines

A. Objects that are not visible.
B. Used to show location and size.
C. Freehand line.
D. Forms a boundary.
E. Indicates the center of symmetrical objects.
F. Interior walls, steps, and doors.
G. For the drafter's use.
H. Shows where the object is to be sectioned.
I. Used in lettering.

Room Planning, Sleeping Area

■ OBJECTIVES

After studying this chapter, the student will be able to:
☐ Discuss factors that are important in the design of bedrooms.
☐ Plan the size and location of closets for a typical residence.
☐ Apply the furniture cut-out method in planning a room arrangement.
☐ Implement important design considerations for bathrooms.
☐ Plan a bathroom that follows solid design principles.

■ DISPLAYS

1. Bedrooms. Select several examples (floor plans) of well- designed bedrooms which represent a broad range in size, complexity, and furniture arrangement. Display them in an attractive arrangement for the class to study.
2. Bedroom Furniture Arrangement. Secure several 8 x 10 black-and-white glossy photos of bedroom arrangements from furniture manufacturers to illustrate the importance of planning for furniture arrangement in the bedroom.
3. Bathrooms. Secure several 8 x 10 black-and-white glossy photos of bathroom arrangements from fixture manufacturers to illustrate the importance of planning for fixture arrangement in the bathroom.

■ INSTRUCTIONAL MATERIALS

Text: Pages 73-88
  Review Questions, Suggested Activities
Workbook: Pages 31-40
  Review Questions, Problems/Activities

Teacher's Resource Guide:
  Chapter 5 — Teaching Strategy
  Chapter 5 — Exam

■ TEACHING STRATEGY

- Prepare Display #1 for class members to study.
- Review chapter objectives.
- Discuss bedrooms — size, groupings, furnishings, arrangement.
- Assign Problem 5-1 in workbook.
- Prepare Display #2.
- Assign Problem 5-2 in the workbook.
- Discuss bathrooms — size, fixtures, arrangement.
- Assign Problems 5-3 and 5-4 in the workbook.
- Assign Problem 5-5 in the workbook.
- Assign one or more of the Suggested Activities in the text.
- Chapter Review
  — Assign Review Questions in the text. Discuss the correct answer.
  — Assign Review Questions in the workbook. Have students check their own answers.
- Evaluation
  — Administer the Chapter 5 — Exam. Correct the exam and return.
  — Return graded problems with comments.

■ ANSWERS TO REVIEW QUESTIONS, TEXT
Page 87

1. a. No electrical switches should be reachable from the tub.
   b. Use ground fault circuit interrupters.
2. a. Sleeping area.
   b. Living area.
   c. Service area.
3. pocket doors

4. a. Ceramic tile.
   b. Terrazzo.
   c. Marble.
5. corner
6. six, four
7. a. 100 square feet.
8. 5' x 8'.
9. 30" x 60".
10. a. Sliding.
    b. Bi-fold.
    c. Accordion.
    d. Flush.
11. functional.
12. 30".
13. a. Ease of cleaning.
    b. Accessible to a disabled person.

■ ANSWERS TO REVIEW QUESTIONS, WORKBOOK

PART I: MULTIPLE CHOICE

1. C. 1/3.
2. A. Size of the family.
3. C. Three-bedroom.
4. D. Master bedroom.
5. B. 100.
6. C. Master bedroom.
7. B. 2.
8. C. Near the bedroom entrance.
9. D. All of the above.
10. A. On two walls.
11. D. 3'-0".
12. B. Near a corner.

PART II: COMPLETION

1. 1 1/2
2. sleeping
3. half
4. three-quarter
5. 5
6. bidet.
7. mirror
8. 30 in.
9. 30 x 60 in.
10. fiberglass
11. terrazzo
12. vanities.
13. Jacuzzis™
14. exhaust
15. Electrical switches
16. GFCI
17. 2'-6"

PART III: SHORT ANSWER/LISTING:

1. A. Determine the size of furniture to be used.
   B. Draw the plan view of each item to the same scale as the floor plan.
   C. Cut out each furniture representation.
   D. Place the cut-outs on the floor plan in the desired arrangement.
   E. Trace around each one to "fix" the location.
   F. Remove the cut-outs and darken in the lines.
2. A. Ease of cleaning.
   B. Resistance to moisture.
   C. Pleasing atmosphere.
3. A. Flooring materials should not become slick when wet.
   B. Horizontal grab bars may be installed around shower stalls and tubs.
   C. Devices in faucets to control water temperature thermostatically to prevent burns.
   D. Devices to automatically decrease hot water pressure when cold water pressure is decreased.
   E. Use non-shatter glass in tub and shower enclosures.
4. A. Dressing.
   B. Exercising.
5. A. Sleeping.
   B. Living.
   C. Service.

PART IV: PROBLEMS/ACTIVITIES

1. Solution on page 57.
2. Solution on page 58.
3. Solution on page 59.
4. Instructor will evaluate the plan according to design principles suggested in the text.

■ ANSWERS TO CHAPTER 5—EXAM

TRUE—FALSE

1. T		5. T	
2. T		6. T	
3. F		7. F	
4. T			

MULTIPLE CHOICE

1. C		7. B	
2. C		8. A	
3. A		9. B	
4. B		10. C	
5. C		11. A	
6. D		12. D	

DIRECTIONS:
Using colored pencils, crayons, felt tip markers, or adhesive—backed (semi—transparent) overlays, shade each of the three basic areas of the house using three colors. Include a legend for clarity.

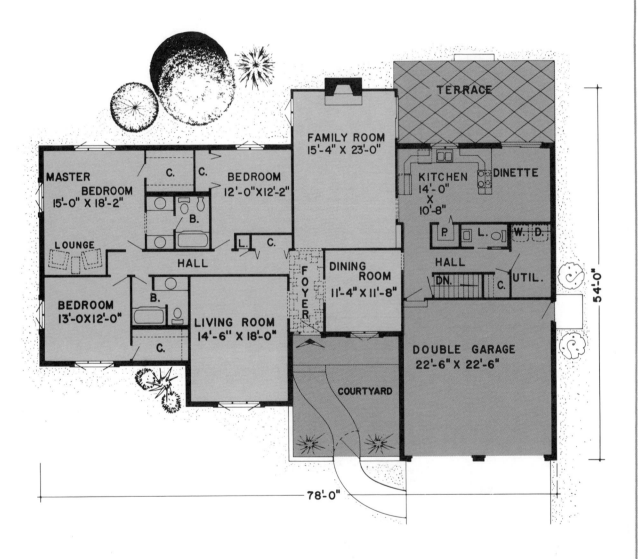

- SLEEPING
- LIVING
- SERVICE

BASIC AREAS | 5-1

2.

DIRECTIONS:
Remove the "Furniture Cut-Outs" page from your workbook and carefully cut out each furniture piece for use in this assignment or use a furniture template. Plan a functional arrangement for each of the bedrooms below using the cut-outs or template. Observe the spacing shown in Fig. 5-12 in the text. Trace the location of each item and label.

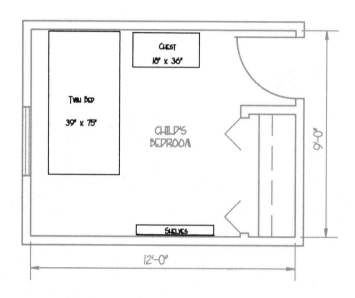

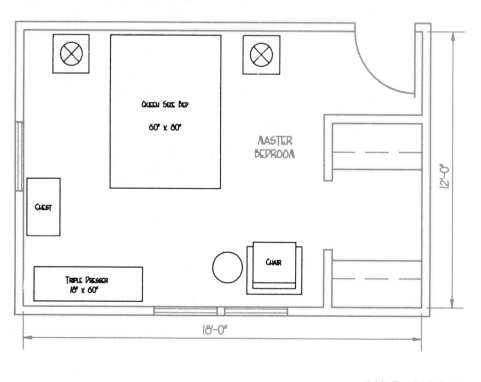

SCALE: 1/4"=1'-0"

BEDROOM PLANNING

5-2

3.

DIRECTIONS:
Plan a functional arrangement of fixtures for each of the baths shown below. Study Figs. 5-30 through 5-34 in your text for arrangement ideas and clearances. Use a template to draw the fixtures.

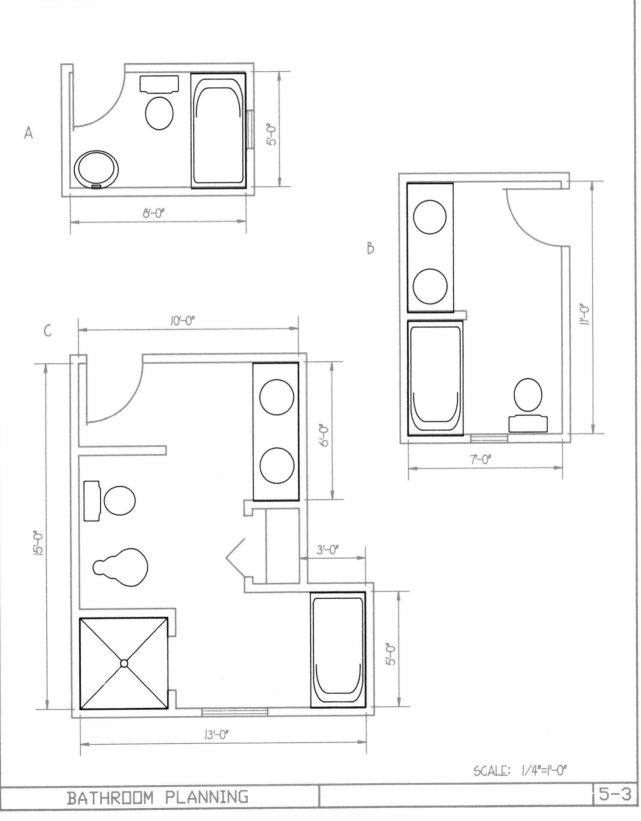

SCALE: 1/4"=1'-0"

BATHROOM PLANNING | 5-3

Chapter 5—Exam
ROOM PLANNING, SLEEPING AREA

Name _____

Period _____ **Date** _____ **Score** _____

TRUE—FALSE
Circle T if the statement is true or F if the statement is false.

T   F   1. A residential structure may be divided into three basic areas.

T   F   2. The purpose of each room must be understood if a functional plan is to be developed.

T   F   3. If possible, the sleeping area should have a north or northeast orientation.

T   F   4. The largest bedroom is usually considered to be the master bedroom.

T   F   5. The FHA recommends more closet rod space for a woman than for a man.

T   F   6. An interior door should swing into the room.

T   F   7. Bathroom doors are usually the same width as bedroom doors.

MULTIPLE CHOICE
Choose the answer that correctly completes the statement. Write the corresponding letter in the space provided.

_____ 1. The _____ is where the family relaxes, entertains guests, dines, and meets together.
A. sleeping area
B. entertaining area
C. living area
D. service area

_____ 2. Usually about _____ of the house is dedicated to the sleeping area.
A. 1/8
B. 1/4
C. 1/3
D. 1/2

_____ 3. The Federal Housing Administration recommends _____ square feet as the minimum size for a bedroom.
A. 100
B. 150
C. 200
D. 250

_____ 4. It is necessary for each bedroom to have a _____.
A. bathroom
B. closet
C. double window
D. ceiling fan

_____ 5. The minimum depth of a clothes closet is _____.
A. 12"
B. 18"
C. 24"
D. 30"

_____ 6. The usual height of an interior door is _____.
   A. 6'-0"
   B. 6'-2"
   C. 6'-4"
   D. 6'-8"

_____ 7. A half bath is one that usually has only a _____.
   A. water closet and bidet
   B. water closet and lavatory
   C. water closet and shower
   D. water closet and tub

_____ 8. A 5' x 8' bath would be considered a(n) _____ bath.
   A. small
   B. average
   C. large
   D. very large

_____ 9. Most water closets require a space at least _____ inches wide for installation.
   A. 24"
   B. 30"
   C. 36"
   D. 40"

_____ 10. The most common size bathtub is _____.
   A. 26" x 48"
   B. 30" x 50"
   C. 30" x 60"
   D. 32" x 72"

_____ 11. Standard bathroom vanity sizes are 21" deep by _____ " high.
   A. 30
   B. 32
   C. 34
   D. 36

_____ 12. A _____ receptacle should be used in the bathroom.
   A. shielded
   B. grounded
   C. waterproof
   D. ground fault circuit interrupter

Room Planning, Living Area

■ OBJECTIVES

After studying this chapter, the student will be able to:

☐ Identify the rooms and areas that comprise the living area.
☐ Apply design principles to planning a living room.
☐ Integrate the furniture in a living room plan.
☐ Analyze a dining room using good design principles.
☐ Design a functional entryway and foyer.
☐ Communicate the primary design considerations for a family recreation room.
☐ Synthesize patios, porches, and courts into the total floor plan of a dwelling.

■ DISPLAYS

1. Living Area. Select a floor plan of a residence that has a well-designed living area. Shade the living area on the plan using colored pencils, magic markers, or transparent, adhesive-backed overlay material. Display the floor plan while the class is studying living areas of the home.
2. Living Rooms. Display several of the living room presentation plans prepared by students for Suggested Activities #1 in the text. Change the display to feature presentation plans of dining rooms, foyers, recreation rooms, and outdoor living areas as the class completes each of these areas.

■ INSTRUCTIONAL MATERIALS

Text: Pages 89-126
Review Questions, Suggested Activities

Workbook: Pages 41-51
Review Questions, Problems/Activities
Teacher's Resource Guide:
Chapter 6 — Teaching Strategy
Chapter 6 — Exam

■ TEACHING STRATEGY

- Prepare Display #1.
- Review chapter objectives.
- Discuss Living Rooms — shapes, sizes, furniture, arrangement, location.
- Prepare Display #2.
- Assign Problem 6-1 in the workbook.
- Discuss Dining Rooms — shapes, sizes, furniture, arrangement, location.
- Assign Problem 6-2 in the workbook.
- Discuss Entryways and Foyers — types, features, placement, provisions. Study the examples in the text with the students.
- Assign Problem 6-3 in the workbook.
- Discuss Family Recreation Rooms and Special-Purpose Rooms.
- Assign Problem 6-4 in the workbook.
- Discuss Patios, Porches, and Courts.
- Assign Problems 6-5 and 6-6 in the workbook.
- Assign one or more of the Suggested Activities in the text.
- Chapter Review
  — Assign Review Questions in the text. Discuss the correct answers.
  — Assign Review Questions in the workbook. Have students check their own answers.
- Evaluation
  — Administer the Chapter 6 — Exam. Correct the exam and return.
  — Return graded problems with comments.

ANSWERS TO REVIEW QUESTIONS, TEXT
Pages 123-124

1. 3'-0".
2. A place to greet guests and remove overcoats and overshoes.
3. large
4. a. Using a flower planter.
   b. Furniture arrangement.
   c. A screen.
   d. Variation in floor level.
5. a. What furniture is planned for the room?
   b. How often will it be used?
   c. Is it to be a multi-purpose room?
   d. Is the size proportional to the remainder of the house?
6. one-third
7. a. A more open plan with fewer rooms or cubicles.
   b. The living area is not restricted to the interior of the structure.
   c. The living area has become the showplace.
   d. Is the place for recreation, entertaining, and relaxing?
8. a. Main entry.
   b. Service entry.
   c. Special-purpose entry.
9. 6'-8".
10. a. Living room.
    b. Dining room.
    c. Foyer.
    d. Patios, decks, and terraces.
11. a. Atrium or greenhouse.
    b. Ham radio room.
    c. Home office.

ANSWERS TO REVIEW QUESTIONS, WORKBOOK

PART I: COMPLETION

1. 250
2. furniture
3. lower
4. patios
5. foyer
6. north
7. sliding
8. dining
9. divider
10. texture

PART II: MULTIPLE CHOICE

1. B. 120.
2. A. 6 to 8.
3. B. 2'-0".
4. C. Living room.
5. D. Open plan.
6. A. Living room.
7. D. All of the above.
8. B. Main.
9. D. All of the above.
10. C. Provide natural light to an interior part of the house which has no exterior wall space.

PART III: MATCHING

1. D. Entry.
2. C. Double doors.
3. K. Mud room.
4. O. Sliding doors.
5. F. Foyer.
6. I. Foyer floor.
7. G. Foyer coat closet.
8. J. Mirror wall.
9. H. Foyer decor.
10. E. Family recreation room.
11. L. Patios.
12. M. Play patio.
13. N. Porches.
14. B. Deck.
15. A. Courts.

PART IV: SHORT ANSWER/LISTING

1. A. Living room.
   B. Dining room.
   C. Foyer.
   D. Recreation or family room.
   E. Special-purpose rooms, such as sunroom or home office.
   F. Outside patios.
2. A. What furniture is planned for this particular room?
   B. How often will the room be used?
   C. How many people will be expected to use the room at any one time?
   D. How many functions are combined in this one room?
   E. Is the living room size in proportion to the remainder of the house?
3. A. The number of people who use the facilities at any one time.
   B. The furniture to be included in the room.
   C. Clearance allowed for traffic through the room.
4. A. Table.
   B. Chairs.
   C. Buffet.
   D. China closet.
   E. Server or cart.
5. A. Large overhang.
   B. Recessed entry.
6. A. The size of the house.
   B. Cost of the house.
   C. Location.
   D. Personal preference.

7. A. Near the dining or living room.
   B. Between the kitchen and the garage.
   C. Adjacent to a patio.
   D. In the basement.
8. When a person in a wheelchair will be using the room.
9. A. Home office.
   B. Sunroom or atrium.
   C. Greenhouse.
   D. Ham radio room.
10. A. Privacy.
    B. Special lighting.
    C. Plumbing.
    D. Unique storage requirements.
11. A. Relaxing.
    B. Playing.
    C. Entertaining or living.
12. A. Concrete.
    B. Brick.
    C. Stone.
    D. Redwood or pressure-treated lumber.
13. On the quiet side of the home near bedrooms.
14. The back of the house.
15. A. Flowers.
    B. Pools.
    C. Screens.
16. Near or adjacent to a family recreation room or service entrance.
17. Screens or glass.

PART V: PROBLEMS/ACTIVITIES

1. Solution on page 66.
2. Solution on page 67.
3. Solution on page 68.
4. Solution on page 69.
5. Solution on page 70.

■ ANSWERS TO CHAPTER 6—EXAM

TRUE—FALSE

1. T	4. T
2. F	5. T
3. T	6. F

MULTIPLE CHOICE

1. D	5. A
2. A	6. D
3. C	7. A
4. B	

MATCHING

1. B	9. C
2. A	10. B
3. B	11. C
4. C	12. B
5. C	13. A
6. B	14. B
7. A	15. B
8. B	

SHORT ANSWER

1. A. What furniture is planned for the room?
   B. How often will the room be used?
   C. How many people are expected to use the room at any one time?
   D. How many functions are combined in the room?
   E. Is the room size in proportion to the remainder of the house?
2. A. Main entry
   B. Service entry
   C. Special-purpose entry
3. A. Patios
   B. Porches
   C. Courts

1.

DIRECTIONS:
Plan the furniture arrangement in Living Room "A" around a music center. The room should provide seating for five people. Living Room "B" may be planned around a theme of your choice. Use standard size furniture from Fig. 6-7 in your text for both rooms.

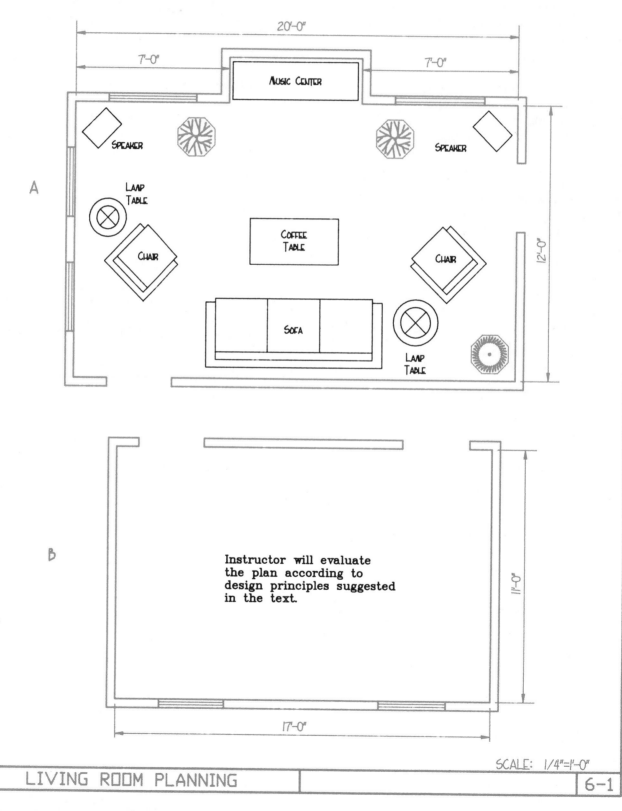

LIVING ROOM PLANNING

SCALE: 1/4"=1'-0"

6-1

2.

DIRECTIONS:
Plan an arrangement of the following furniture pieces (table with 6 chairs, buffet, or china cabinet) in the dining room below. In the remaining space, design a medium size dining room (180–200 square feet) which provides seating for 8 and storage for dishes, table linens, silverware, and accessories.

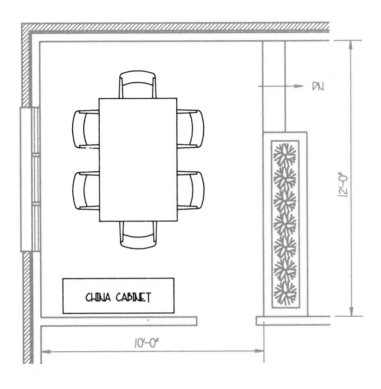

Instructor will evaluate the plan according to design principles suggested in the text.

SCALE: 1/4"=1'-0"

DINING ROOM PLANNING

6-2

3.

DIRECTIONS:
Complete the entry/foyer below by adding the following: slate
floor, brick veneer exterior, entry arrow, plant in foyer, and
closet shelf and rod.

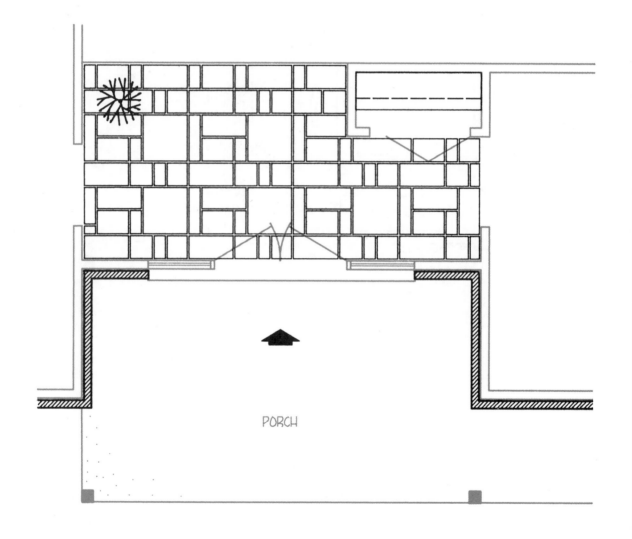

PORCH

SCALE: 1/4"=1'-0"

ENTRY/FOYER PLANNING

6-3

4.

DIRECTIONS:
Plan a functional arrangement of furniture in the Family Recreation Room below which includes a sofa, upholstered chair, coffee table, lamp table and lamp, and built-in cabinets along the wall opposite the fireplace. Draw an elevation view of the storage units in the space provided.

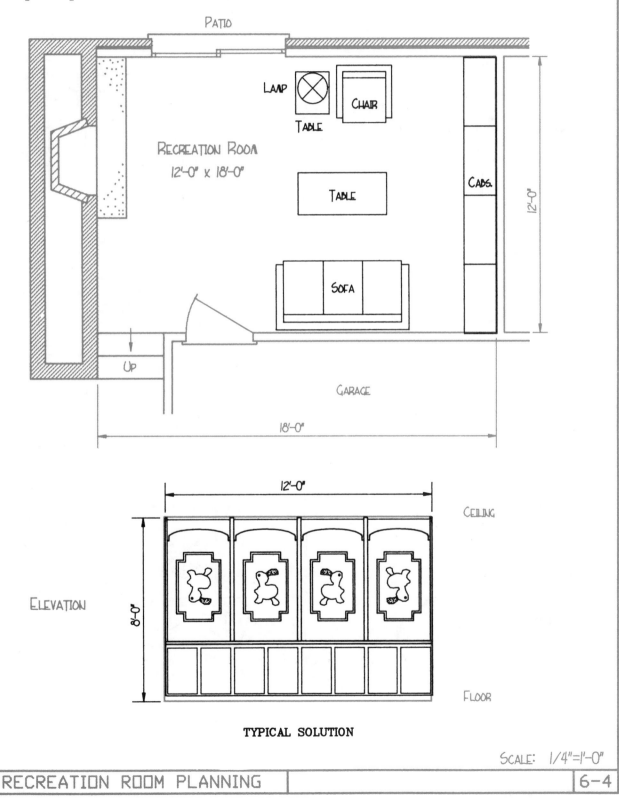

TYPICAL SOLUTION

SCALE: 1/4"=1'-0"

RECREATION ROOM PLANNING | 6-4

5.

DIRECTIONS:
Complete the plan below (covered porch on the right and patio on the left). Include clay tile pavers on the porch, concrete patio divided into 4'-0" square grid, seating along long porch wall, two lounge chairs and round table on patio, plants along front privacy wall, hedge between living room and patio, and several plants in pots on the patio and porch.

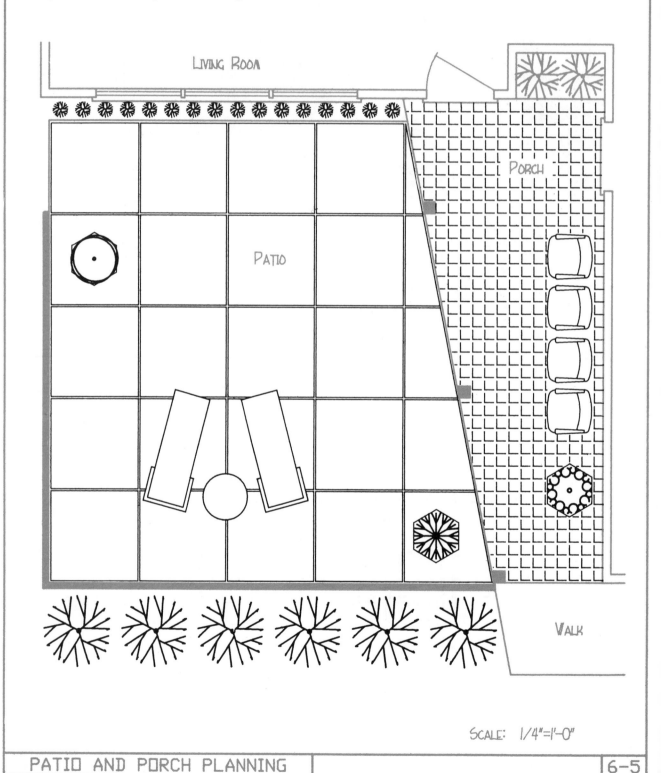

SCALE: 1/4"=1'-0"

PATIO AND PORCH PLANNING | | 6-5

Chapter 6—Exam
ROOM PLANNING, LIVING AREA

Name _____

Period _____ **Date** _____ **Score** _____

TRUE—FALSE
Circle T if the statement is true or F if the statement is false.

T   F   1. The living area of the home is designed for all activities not included in the sleeping and service areas.

T   F   2. Traffic should be planned through the living room because it is the center of activity.

T   F   3. The main outside entrance should not open directly into the living room.

T   F   4. For efficient use, the dining room should be adjacent to the kitchen and living room.

T   F   5. The function and efficiency of the rooms in the living area will be enhanced by using the open plan.

T   F   6. A closet is optional in the foyer.

MULTIPLE CHOICE
Choose the answer that correctly completes the statement. Write the corresponding letter in the space provided.

_____ 1. An average size living room is about _____ square feet.
  A. 100
  B. 152
  C. 200
  D. 250

_____ 2. A small dining room capable of seating four people around a table and providing space for a buffet would require about _____ square feet of space.
  A. 120
  B. 200
  C. 250
  D. 300

_____ 3. The _____ entry should be centrally located to provide easy access to various parts of the house.
  A. service
  B. special purpose
  C. main
  D. side

_____ 4. A major consideration in the design of an entryway is _____.
  A. the appearance of neighboring homes
  B. protection from the weather
  C. visibility of the play area
  D. wind direction

_____ 5. The _____ functions as a place to greet guests and remove coats and boots.
  A. foyer
  B. mudroom
  C. entryway
  D. living room

_____ 6. The basic purpose of a _____ room is to provide a place where the family can play or pursue hobbies.
  A. music room
  B. living room
  C. TV room
  D. family recreation room

_____ 7. The following are examples of special-purpose rooms.
    A. Atrium, greenhouse, ham radio room
    B. Darkroom, family recreation room, greenhouse
    C. Shop, darkroom, living room
    D. Kitchen, atrium, ham radio room

MATCHING
Select the answer that correctly matches each term. Place your answer in the space provided.

_____ 1. Patios, decks, and terraces   A. Sleeping area of the home

_____ 2. Master bath   B. Living area of the home

_____ 3. Foyer   C. Service area of the home

_____ 4. Garage

_____ 5. Shop

_____ 6. Dining room

_____ 7. Bedroom

_____ 8. Living room

_____ 9. Kitchen

_____ 10. Family room

_____ 11. Clothes care center

_____ 12. Home office

_____ 13. Dressing room

_____ 14. Sunroom

_____ 15. Library

SHORT ANSWER
Answer the following questions using short answers.

1. List five important questions to ask regarding the size and design of a living room.

    A. _____

    B. _____

    C. _____

    D. _____

    E. _____

2. List the three basic types of entryways.

    A. _____

    B. _____

    C. _____

3. List three separate, but similar, living areas of the home that extend living to the outside.

    A. _____

    B. _____

    C. _____

Room Planning, Service Area

■ OBJECTIVES

After studying this chapter, the student will be able to:

☐ Apply good design principles to planning the service area of a home.
☐ Design a functional kitchen to meet a family's needs.
☐ Select appliances for a modern kitchen.
☐ Plan a modern, efficient clothes care center.
☐ Describe appropriate dimensions for garage space.

■ DISPLAYS

1. Service Area. Select pictures from magazines or actual photos of various service areas of the home and display them in an attractive arrangement on your bulletin board.
2. Student Work. Display outstanding student work to encourage better work from all students in the class. Workbook Problem/Activity 7-3, Kitchen Design, is a possible choice for the bulletin board display.

■ INSTRUCTIONAL MATERIALS

Text: Pages 127-150
   Review Questions, Suggested Activities
Workbook: Pages 53-62
   Review Questions, Problems/Activities
Teacher's Resource Guide:
   Chapter 7—Teaching Strategy
   Chapter 7—Exam

■ TEACHING STRATEGY

- Prepare Display #1.
- Review chapter objectives.
- Discuss the Service Area of the home.
- Discuss the kitchen in terms of styles, sizes, work triangle, appliances, cabinets, and location.
- Hand out "Appliance Symbols with Dimensions."
- Assign Problems 7-1, 7-2, and 7-3 in the workbook.
- Prepare Display #2.
- Assign one or more of the Suggested Activities in the text.
- Discuss the Clothes Care Center—appliances, sizes, operations.
- Assign Problem 7-4 in the workbook.
- Discuss garages and carports in terms of size, arrangement, doors, turnarounds.
- Assign Problems 7-5, 7-6, and 7-7 in the workbook.
- Chapter Review
   —Assign Review Questions in the text. Discuss the correct answers.
   —Assign Review Questions in the workbook. Have students check their own answers.
   —Make a transparency of workbook Problem 7-6 to use for review with the class.
- Evaluation
   —Administer the Chapter 7—Exam. Correct the exam and return.
   —Return graded problems with comments.

■ ANSWERS TO REVIEW QUESTIONS, TEXT Page 150

1. 3
2. 11' x 19'.
3. 10'.
4. a. Washing.   d. Ironing.
   b. Drying.   e. Mending.
   c. Folding.   f. Storing.

5. a. Straight line.   d. U-shaped.
   b. Corridor.   e. Peninsula.
   c. L-shaped.   f. Island.
6. 21
7. a. Kitchen.   d. Utility.
   b. Laundry.   e. Garage.
   c. Work center.   f. Storage.
8. 34 1/2
9. attic.
10. a. Wood.
    b. Fiberglass.
    c. Plastic.
    d. Aluminum or steel.
11. 25
12. 26

■ ANSWERS TO REVIEW QUESTIONS, WORKBOOK

PART I: MATCHING

1. F. Service area.
2. G. Straight line kitchen.
3. D. L-shaped kitchen.
4. A. Corridor kitchen.
5. H. U-shaped kitchen.
6. E. Peninsula kitchen.
7. C. Island kitchen.
8. B. Garage or carport.

PART II: MULTIPLE CHOICE

1. D. 34 1/2" high, 24" deep, in width increments in 3" multiples.
2. C. Near the service entrance and the dining room.
3. B. A hood with a fan.
4. D. All of the above.
5. B. 20 x 20 to 25 x 25.
6. A. Garage.
7. D. All of the above.
8. A. 16 ft. wide and 7 ft. high.

PART III: COMPLETION

1. most
2. 22
3. cooking
4. 6 in.
5. cabinets.
6. hidden
7. food preparation
8. 26
9. Carports
10. service
11. 7
12. 10
13. turnaround

PART IV: SHORT ANSWER/LISTING

1. A. Kitchen.
   B. Clothes care center.
   C. Garage or carport.
   D. Utility.
   E. Storage.
2. A. Food preparation center.
   B. Cleanup center.
   C. Cooking center.
3. Measure from the center front of the sink to the center front of the range to the center front of the refrigerator and back to the center front of the sink.
4. A main ceiling fixture or fixtures plus lighting over the sink, cooking center, and food preparation areas.
5. To provide the location and facilities for washing, drying, pressing, folding, storing, and mending clothes.
6. A. The number of automobiles to be housed.
   B. The size and layout of the house.
   C. The space available.
7. A. The floor should be at least 4 in. thick concrete reinforced with steel or wire mesh.
   B. The floor should have good drainage.
   C. Ample windows and artificial lighting are needed.
   D. Check local building codes for fire protection requirements for attached garages.

PART V: PROBLEMS/ACTIVITIES

1. Solution on page 76.
2. Solution on page 77.
3. Solution on pages 78-84.
4. Solution on page 85.
5. Solution on page 86.
6. Solution on page 87.

■ ANSWERS TO CHAPTER 7—EXAM

TRUE—FALSE

1. T   4. F
2. T   5. T
3. T

MULTIPLE CHOICE

1. C   5. A
2. D   6. C
3. D   7. B
4. C

SHORT ANSWER

1. (Choose four.)
   A. Kitchen.
   B. Clothes care center or laundry.

C. Garage or carport.
D. Utility and storage.
E. Mudroom.
2. A. Straight line.
   B. L-shaped.
   C. Corridor.
   D. U-shaped.
   E. Peninsula.
   F. Island.
3. A. It provides plenty of work space.
   B. It is attractive.
   C. It is easily joined to the dining room using the peninsula as a divider.

4. A. Washing.
   B. Drying.
   C. Pressing.
   D. Folding.
   E. Storing.
   F. Mending.

MATCHING

1. E		6. D
2. C		7. B
3. A		8. A
4. D		9. C
5. B		

1.

DIRECTIONS:
Draw the base and wall cabinets, appliances, and work triangle for each of the kitchens below. Use standard size units.

U–SHAPED KITCHEN: The available space is 12' by 12'. Include a 36" wide range on the right side wall, a 36" wide refrigerator on the left side wall, and a sink under the window. Label appliances.

PENINSULA KITCHEN: The available space is 12' by 16'. The peninsula is designed to accommodate four stools. The range is to be located on the right, the refrigerator on the left, and sink below the window.

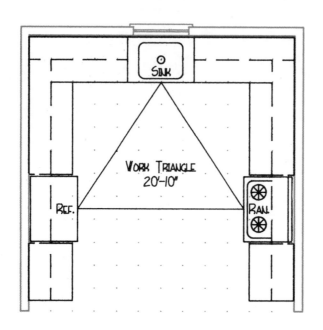

U–SHAPED
KITCHEN

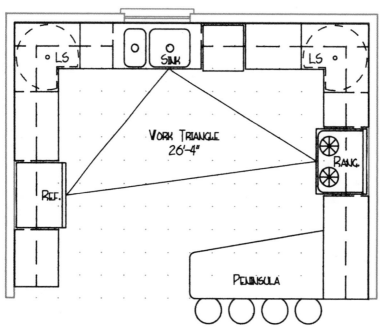

PENINSULA
KITCHEN

SCALE: 1/4"=1'-0"

KITCHEN PLANNING | 7-1

DIRECTIONS:
Study the configuration of this large, complex kitchen to determine the most functional layout. Include the following: refrigerator, range, dishwasher, planning desk, sink, breakfast bar with cabinets above and stools below. Show ceramic tile floor as 12" square grid. Label appliances.

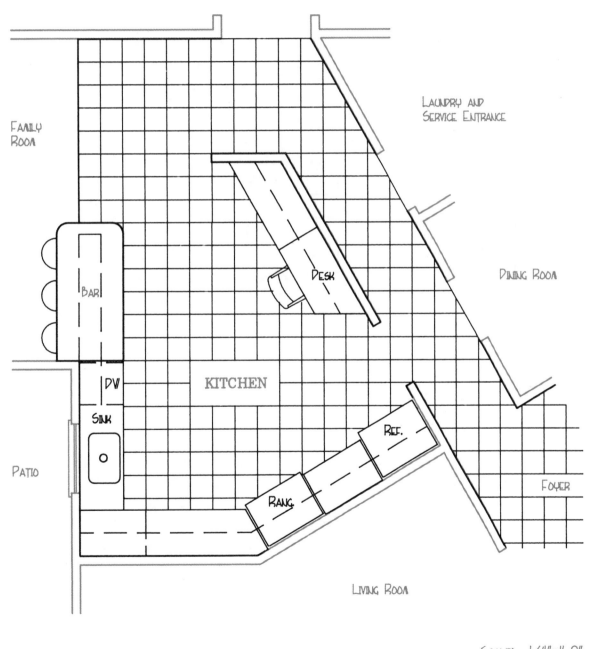

SCALE: 1/4"=1'-0"

KITCHEN PLANNING   7-2

3.

TYPICAL SOLUTION

KITCHEN
DESIGN

BY JOHN Q. STUDENT

ASSIGNMENT 7-3

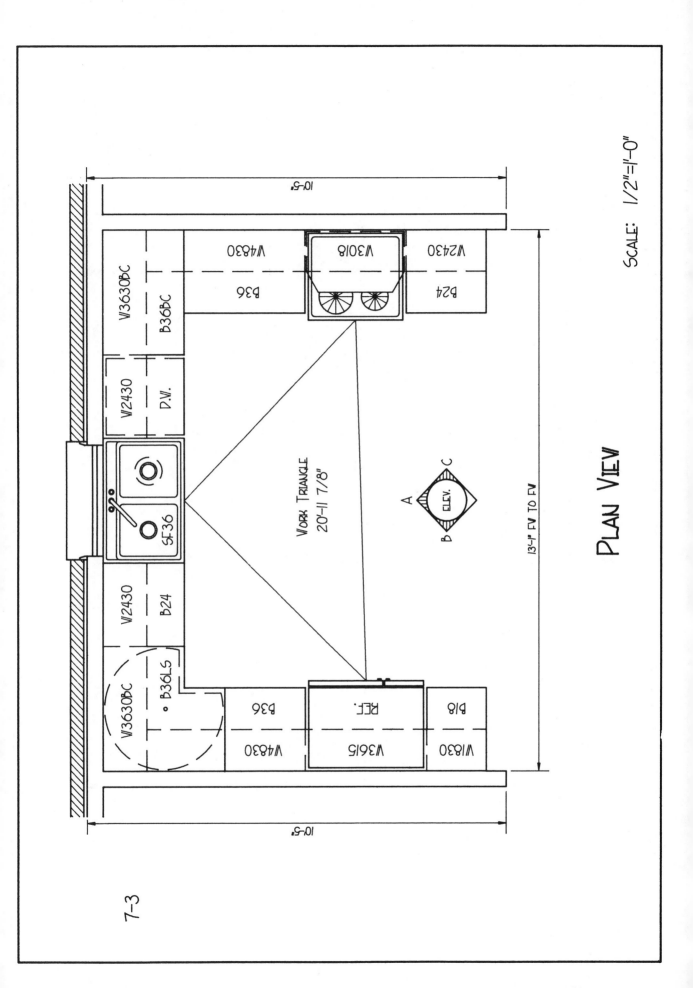

PLAN VIEW

SCALE: 1/2"=1'-0"

7-3

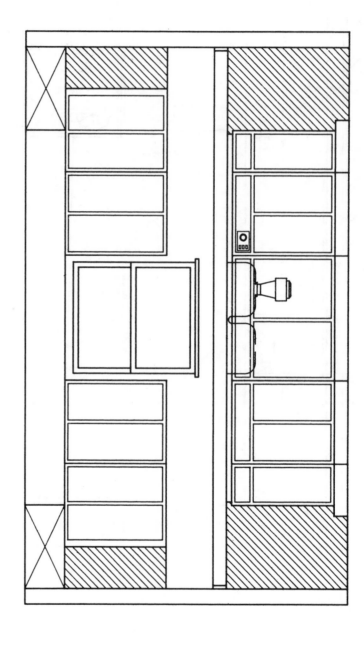

7-3

V3630BC

V2430
B24

SF-36

V2430
D.V.

V3630BC
B36BC

B36LS

ELEVATION A

SCALE: 1/2"=1'-0"

7-3

V1830
B18

V3615
REF.

V4830
B36

B36LS

V3630PC

ELEVATION B

SCALE: 1/2"=1'-0"

7-3

W3630BC

B36BC

W4830
B36

W3018

W2430
B24

ELEVATION C

SCALE: 1/2"=1'-0"

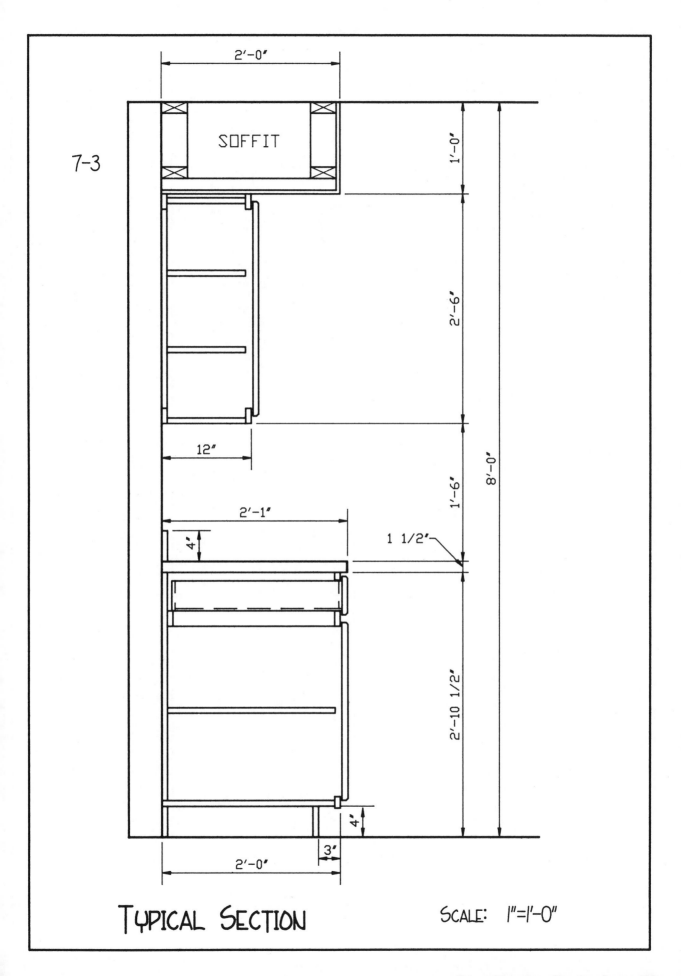

7-3

2'-0"

SOFFIT

1'-0"

2'-6"

12"

8'-0"

2'-1"

1'-6"

4"

1 1/2"

2'-10 1/2"

4"

3'

2'-0"

TYPICAL SECTION

SCALE: 1"=1'-0"

Cabinet & Appliance Schedule

Appliances

# Reqd.	Mfg. #	Manufacturer	Model	Remarks
1	46G5769IN	Sears Kenmore	Side by Side Ref./Freezer	58 7/8" H x 35 3/4" W x 30 5/8" D
1	22G16965N	Sears Kenmore	Dishwasher	34 1/2" H x 23 5/16" W x 25 1/2" D
1	22G45588N	Sears Kenmore	Cooktop Range/Oven	30 3/4" H x 30" W x 26 3/4" D
1	AH 133 791	Gaggenau	Hood	3 5/16" H x 35 1/16" W x 19 11/16" D
1	GC 430	Jenn-Air	Garbage Disposal	7 1/2" Dia. x 14" H
1	K 5924	Kohler	Double Sink	9 5/8" H x 33" W x 22" D

Cabinets

# Reqd.	Mfg. #	Manufacturer	Model	Remarks
1	B 18	Scheirich/Gardencourt	Base Cabinet	34 1/2" H x 18" W x 24" D
2	B 24	Scheirich/Gardencourt	Base Cabinet	34 1/2" H x 24" W x 24" D
2	B 36	Scheirich/Gardencourt	Base Cabinet	34 1/2" H x 36" W x 24" D
1	CB 36	Scheirich/Gardencourt	Base Cabinet	34 1/2" H x 36" W x 24" D
1	LSB 36	Scheirich/Gardencourt	Base Cabinet	34 1/2" H x 36" W x 36" D
1	SB 36	Scheirich/Gardencourt	Base Cabinet	34 1/2" H x 36" W x 24" D
1	W 30 18	Scheirich/Gardencourt	Wall Cabinet	30" H x 18" W x 12" D
1	W 36 15	Scheirich/Gardencourt	Wall Cabinet	15" H x 36" W x 12" D
2	W 48 30	Scheirich/Gardencourt	Wall Cabinet	30" H x 48" W x 12" D
2	CW 30 30	Scheirich/Gardencourt	Wall Cabinet	30" H x 30" W x 12" D
3	W 30 24	Scheirich/Gardencourt	Wall Cabinet	30" H x 24" W x 12" D
1	W 18 30	Scheirich/Gardencourt	Wall Cabinet	18" H x 30" W x 12" D

7-3

DIRECTIONS:
Plan a functional arrangement for the Clothes Care Center below which includes the following items: fold—down ironing board, washer, dryer, laundry tub, countertop space for folding and sewing with base cabinets below, wall cabinets for storage, and planning area. Draw an elevation of the wall (which includes the window) in the space provided. Label each component in the Plan View.

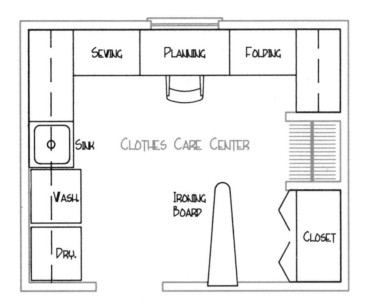

PLAN VIEW

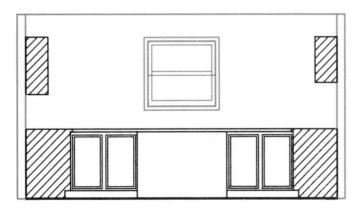

ELEVATION

SCALE: 1/4"=1'-0"

CLOTHES CARE CENTER PLANNING

7—4

5.

DIRECTIONS:
The pictorial below shows a detached garage of frame construction. Draw a Plan View of this garage which assumes the following: garage is 22'-0" long by 20'-0" wide, door is 16'-0" wide, a 3'-0" side door leads to the house, garage has two windows on the left side, and shelves at the rear of the garage. Garage walls are 5 1/4" thick. Scale is 1/4"=1'-0".

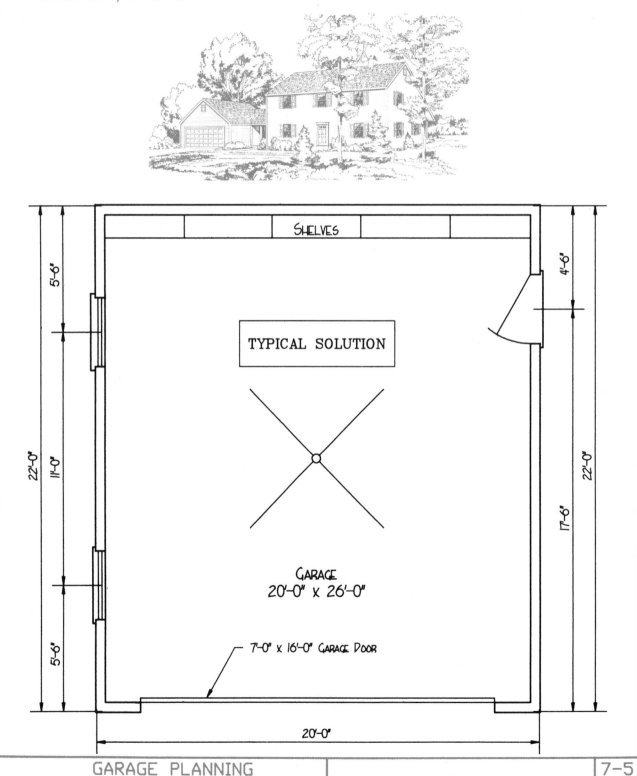

SHELVES

TYPICAL SOLUTION

GARAGE
20'-0" x 26'-0"

7'-0" x 16'-0" GARAGE DOOR

5'-6" 11'-0" 5'-6"   22'-0"

4'-6"   17'-6"   22'-0"

20'-0"

GARAGE PLANNING

7-5

6.

DIRECTIONS:
Plan a driveway with turnaround which meets the following criteria:
Drive is 18'–0" wide at garage with turning radius beginning 6'–0"
in front of garage on the right side. Turnaround is 20'–0" wide and
proceeds 6'–0" beyond the turning radius tangent point. Width of the
drive between turnaround and street is 10'–0". Show all tangent
points, centers, and dimensions.

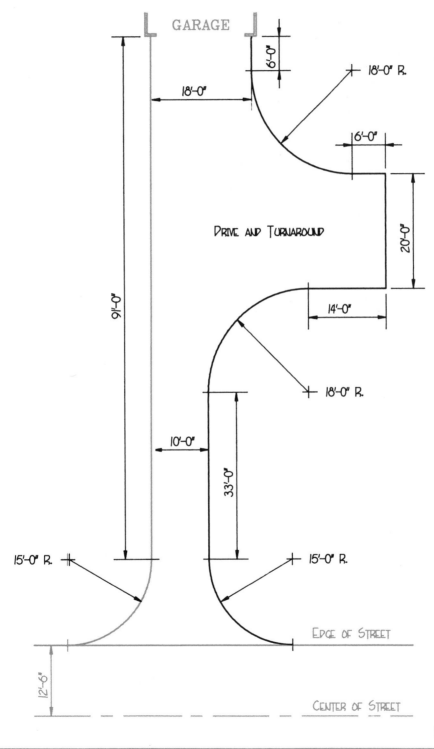

GARAGE

18'–0" R.

6'–0"

18'–0"

6'–0"

DRIVE AND TURNAROUND

20'–0"

14'–0"

91'–0"

18'–0" R.

10'–0"

33'–0"

15'–0" R.

15'–0" R.

EDGE OF STREET

12'–6"

CENTER OF STREET

SCALE: 1/16"=1'–0"

| DRIVEWAY TURNAROUND PLANNING | | 7–6 |

Chapter 7—Exam
ROOM PLANNING, SERVICE AREA

Name _____

Period _____ **Date** _____ **Score** _____

TRUE—FALSE
Circle T if the statement is true or F if the statement is false.

T   F   1. The kitchen triangle is one measure of kitchen efficiency.

T   F   2. The straight line kitchen is generally used in cottages and apartments.

T   F   3. Corridor kitchens are usually small to medium in size.

T   F   4. Exhaust from the kitchen may be expelled into the attic.

T   F   5. A lowered ceiling makes a room appear larger.

MULTIPLE CHOICE
Choose the answer that correctly completes the statement. Write the corresponding letter in the space provided.

_____ 1. For practical kitchen design, the length of the work triangle should not exceed _____ feet.
A. 10
B. 20
C. 22
D. 30

_____ 2. The L-shaped kitchen is located along two _____ walls.
A. opposite
B. outside
C. interior
D. adjacent

_____ 3. The most popular kitchen design is the _____ kitchen.
A. L-shaped
B. corridor
C. straight line
D. U-shaped

_____ 4. At least _____ feet of clearance should be provided on all sides of the island in an island kitchen.
A. 2
B. 3
C. 4
D. 5

_____ 5. The preferred material for the floor of a clothes care center is _____.
A. ceramic tile
B. carpet
C. hardwood flooring
D. asbestos floor tile

_____ 6. A garage designed for two cars may be as small as _____.
A. 11' x 19'
B. 16' x 20'
C. 20' x 20'
D. 24' x 24'

_____ 7. The floor of a garage or carport should be at least _____-in. thick concrete reinforced with steel or wire mesh.
   A. 2
   B. 4
   C. 6
   D. 8

SHORT ANSWER
Answer the following questions using short answers.

1. The service area of the home supplies equipment and space for maintenance, storage, and services. List four "rooms" of the home that are included in the service area.

   A. _____

   B. _____

   C. _____

   D. _____

2. List the six basic styles of kitchens.

   A. _____

   B. _____

   C. _____

   D. _____

   E. _____

   F. _____

3. List three reasons why the peninsula kitchen is popular.

   A. _____

   B. _____

   C. _____

4. List six functions performed in the clothes care center.

   A. _____

   B. _____

   C. _____

   D. _____

   E. _____

   F. _____

MATCHING
Select the answer that correctly matches each term. Place your answers in the spaces provided.

_____ 1. Countertop height

_____ 2. Base cabinet widths

_____ 3. Base cabinet height

_____ 4. Wall cabinet heights

_____ 5. Countertop width (front to back)

A. 34 1/2"
B. 25"
C. 12" to 48" in increments of 3"
D. 12" to 30" in increments of 3"
E. 36"

_____ 6. Minimum driveway width

_____ 7. Turnaround radius

_____ 8. Garage door height

_____ 9. Garage apron thickness

A. 7'
B. 18'
C. 6"
D. 10'

8
CHAPTER

Plot Plans

■ OBJECTIVES

After studying this chapter, the student will be able to:
☐ Identify the various features shown on a typical plot plan.
☐ Visualize land elevations from contour lines.
☐ Recognize typical topographical symbols and apply them to site considerations.
☐ Properly locate a building on a site.
☐ Draw a plot plan using correct symbols and conventions.

■ DISPLAYS

1. Plot Plan Elements. Select examples of each of the elements typically included on a residential plot plan. Cut out the elements and display them with identification. Include all the items covered in this chapter.
2. Site Topography. Display a site plan which illustrates an interesting topography along with a model made from cardboard to the same scale represented on the drawing. Cut cardboard pieces to represent the various contours. (See Fig. 31-10.)

■ INSTRUCTIONAL MATERIALS

Text: Pages 151-160
   Review Questions, Suggested Activities
Workbook: Pages 63-73
   Review Questions, Problems/Activities
Teacher's Resource Guide:
   Chapter 8—Teaching Strategy
   Chapter 8—Exam

■ TEACHING STRATEGY

• Prepare Display #1.
• Review chapter objectives.
• Discuss the definition and purpose of plot plans.
• Cover the elements of property lines.
• Discuss bearing angles.
• Discuss contour lines.
• Prepare Display #2.
• Assign one or more of the Suggested Activities in the text.
• Discuss topographical features.
• Assign Problem/Activity 8-1 in the workbook.
• Assign Problems/Activities 8-2, 8-3, and 8-4 in the workbook.
• Discuss location of a structure on the site.
• Present the procedure for drawing a plot plan.
• Assign Problems/Activities 8-5 and 8-6 in the workbook.
• Discuss landscape plot plans.
• Chapter Review
   —Assign Review Questions in the text. Discuss the correct answers.
   —Assign Review Questions in the workbook. Have students check their own answers.
   —Make a transparency of the answers for Problems/Activities 8-1, 8-2, and 8-3 of the workbook to review principles taught in Chapter 8.
• Evaluation
   —Administer the Chapter 8—Exam. Correct the exam and return.
   —Return graded problems with comments.

■ ANSWERS TO REVIEW QUESTIONS, TEXT Page 160

1. c. A contour line.
2. surveyor
3. a. Natural contour.
   b. Trees.
   c. View.
   d. Surrounding houses.
   e. Style of house to be built.
   f. Solar orientation.
   g. Winds.
   h. Placement of well or septic tank.

4. scale
5. It indicates magnetic north on the plot plan.
6. short dashed
7. Features   Color
    a. Lakes and streams. a. Blue.
    b. Roads and houses. b. Black.
    c. Vegetation.   c. Green.
    d. Contour lines.   d. Brown.
8. adjacent
9. bearing
10. landscape.

■ ANSWERS TO REVIEW QUESTIONS, WORKBOOK

PART I: MATCHING

1. K. Plot plan.
2. L. Property lines.
3. A. Bearing angles.
4. B. Bench mark.
5. F. Contour line.
6. E. Contour interval.
7. D. Closed contour lines.
8. G. Estimated contours.
9. M. Topographical features.
10. C. Blue.
11. H. Green.
12. J. Meridian arrow.
13. I. Landscape plan.

PART II: SHORT ANSWER/LISTING

1. A. Length and bearing of each property line.
    B. Location, outline, and size of buildings on the site.
    C. Contour of the land.
    D. Elevation of property corners and contour lines.
    E. Meridian arrow (north symbol).
    F. Trees, shrubs, streams, and gardens.
    G. Streets, driveways, sidewalks, and patios.
    H. Location of utilities.
    I. Easements for utilities and drainage, if any.
    J. Well, septic tank, and field.
    K. Fences and retaining walls.
    L. Lot number or address of the site.
    M. Scale of the drawing.
2. Begin at a given corner. Use the bench mark if one is given. Then proceed in a clockwise manner until the beginning point is reached.
3. A series of long (1 to 2 in.), thin freehand lines.
4. Black is used in lettering and features roads, houses, and other structures.
5. Brown indicates land forms such as contour lines.
6. A. Natural contour.
    B. Trees.
    C. View.
    D. Surrounding houses.
    E. Code restrictions.
    F. Style of house to be built.
    G. Solar orientation.
    H. Winds.
    I. Placement of well.
    J. Septic system.
    K. Size and shape of the site.
7. A. Draw the outside of exterior walls. Shade or cross hatch the area covered by the house.
    B. Draw the exterior walls as hidden lines with the roof shown as solid lines.
    C. Draw the exterior walls thickened.
8. Letter the elevation of each contour line and property corner.
9. After all topographical features have been drawn.
10. A. Boundary lines.
    B. Meridian arrow.
    C. Outline of the house.
    D. Driveway.
    E. Walks.
    F. Patios.
    G. Contour lines.

PART III: COMPLETION

1. surveyor
2. engineer's
3. Contour
4. Relative
5. steep
6. even.
7. Irregular
8. different
9. right
10. overhang
11. outside
12. 1" = 30'-0".

PART IV: PROBLEMS/ACTIVITIES

1. Solution on page 96.
2. Solution on page 97.
3. Solution on page 98.
4. Solution on page 99.
5. Solution on page 100.
6. Solution on page 101.

■ ANSWERS TO CHAPTER 8—EXAM

TRUE—FALSE

1. F		4. T	
2. T		5. T	
3. T		6. F	

MULTIPLE CHOICE

1. C		5. B	
2. C		6. D	
3. A		7. C	
4. D			

IDENTIFICATION

1. X	11.
2. X	12. X
3.	13. X
4. X	14.
5. X	15. X
6.	16. X
7.	17. X
8. X	18. X
9.	19.
10. X	20. X

SHORT ANSWER

1. A. Show only exterior walls of the house and shade the space covered by the house.
   B. Show the exterior walls as hidden lines and the roof as object lines (typical roof plan).
   C. Show exterior wall thickness with all interior walls. Do not include windows and doors.

1.

DIRECTIONS:
Draw the proper topographical symbol in the space provided.

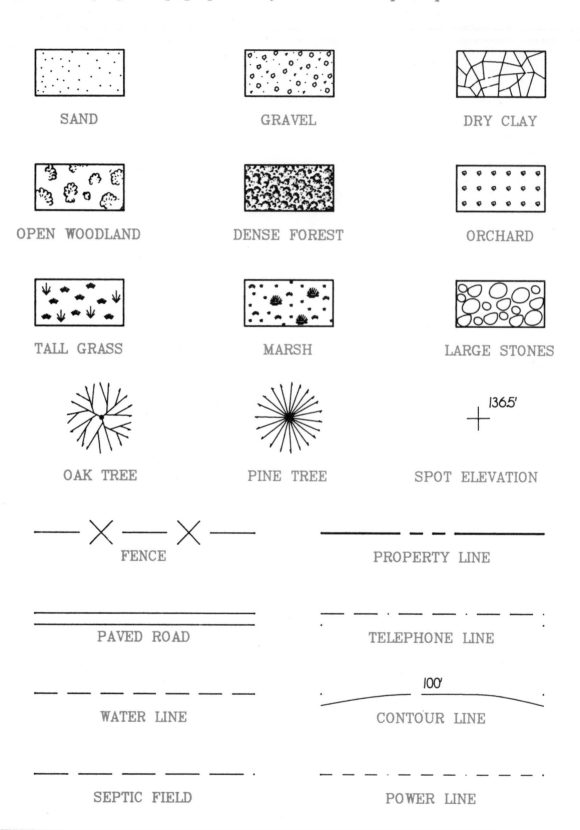

SAND

GRAVEL

DRY CLAY

OPEN WOODLAND

DENSE FOREST

ORCHARD

TALL GRASS

MARSH

LARGE STONES

OAK TREE

PINE TREE

SPOT ELEVATION

FENCE

PROPERTY LINE

PAVED ROAD

TELEPHONE LINE

WATER LINE

CONTOUR LINE

SEPTIC FIELD

POWER LINE

TOPOGRAPHICAL SYMBOLS   8-1

2.

DIRECTIONS:
Plot the following property line directions (bearings) in the circle as shown.
Note the direction of North is generally toward the top of the plate, but
may be any direction desired. Label each line showing its bearing.

N 15° E   S 32°-30' W
N 90°-0'-0" E   S 78°-15' W
S 75° E   N 90° W
Due South   N 45° W

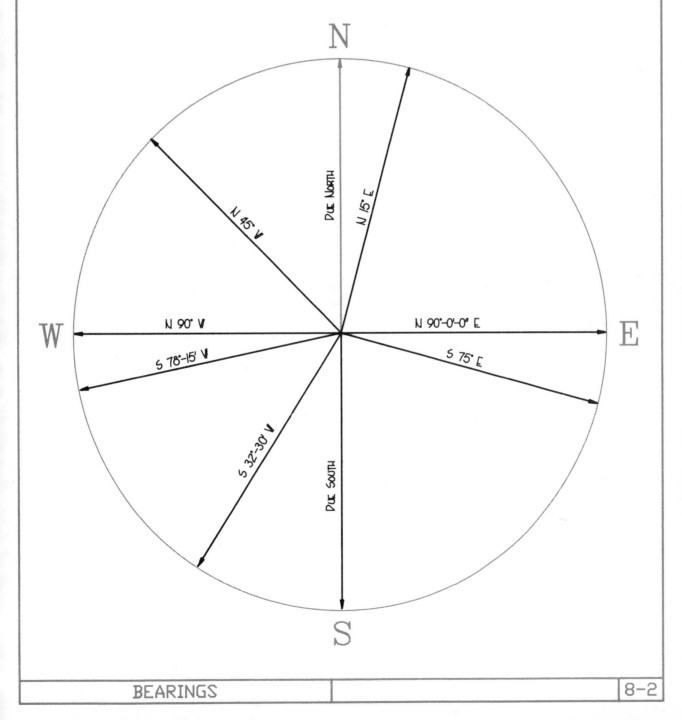

| BEARINGS | | 8-2 |

3.

DIRECTIONS:
Using the property line symbol and format shown in the example below, locate the property boundaries described in the chart. Note the scale and direction of North.

> Begin at point "A".
> Line AB bears Due North for a distance of 150.0'.
> Line BC bears N 75° E for a distance of 112.5'.
> Line CD bears S 56° E for a distance of 45.0'.
> Line DE bears S 15° W for a distance of 142.5'.
> Determine the bearing and length of line EA.
> Label property lines and corners.

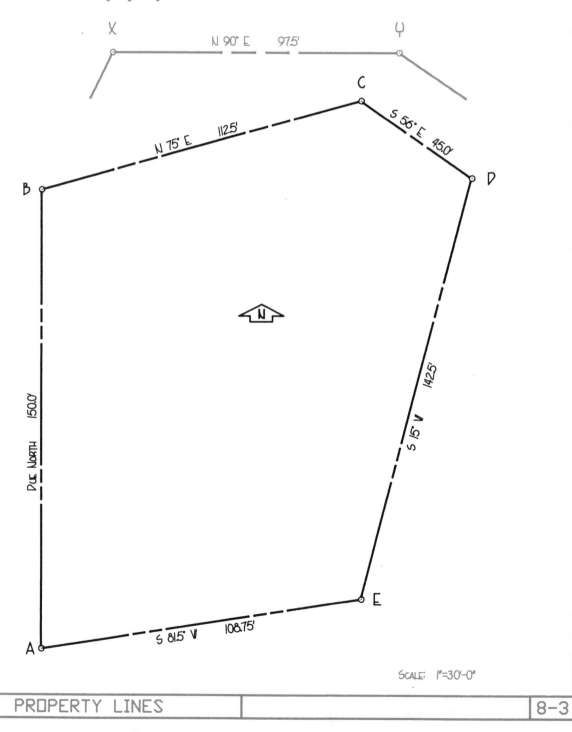

SCALE: 1"=30'-0"

PROPERTY LINES | 8-3

4.

DIRECTIONS:
This assignment consists of two parts——plotting contour lines from an
elevation grid and showing a profile section defined by a cutting plane.
Using the elevation grid at the top of the page, plot the contour lines at
elevations 5, 10, and 15 feet. Use the proper contour line symbol and label.
Draw a profile section of the property defined by Section A,1,1 in the space
provided. Be sure to project the points from the grid above. Hatch the
sectioned area in the profile.

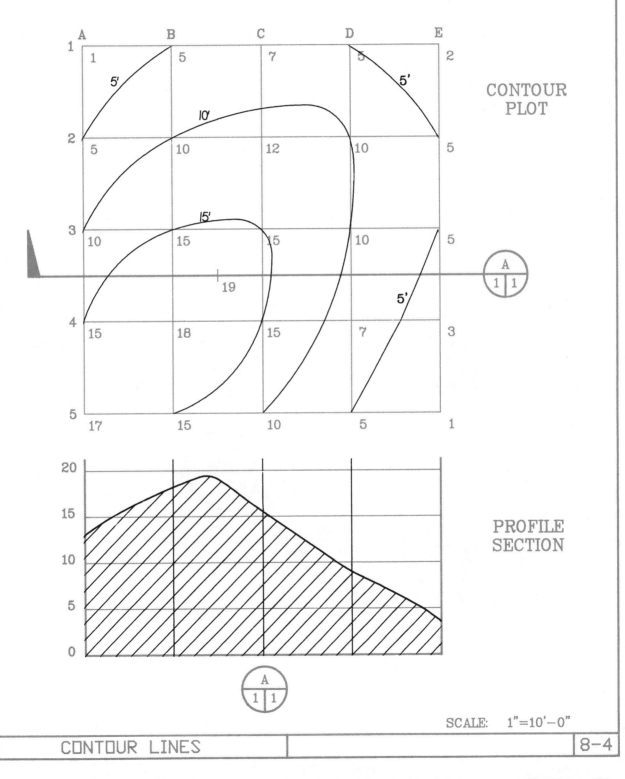

CONTOUR
PLOT

PROFILE
SECTION

SCALE: 1"=10'-0"

CONTOUR LINES

8-4

5.

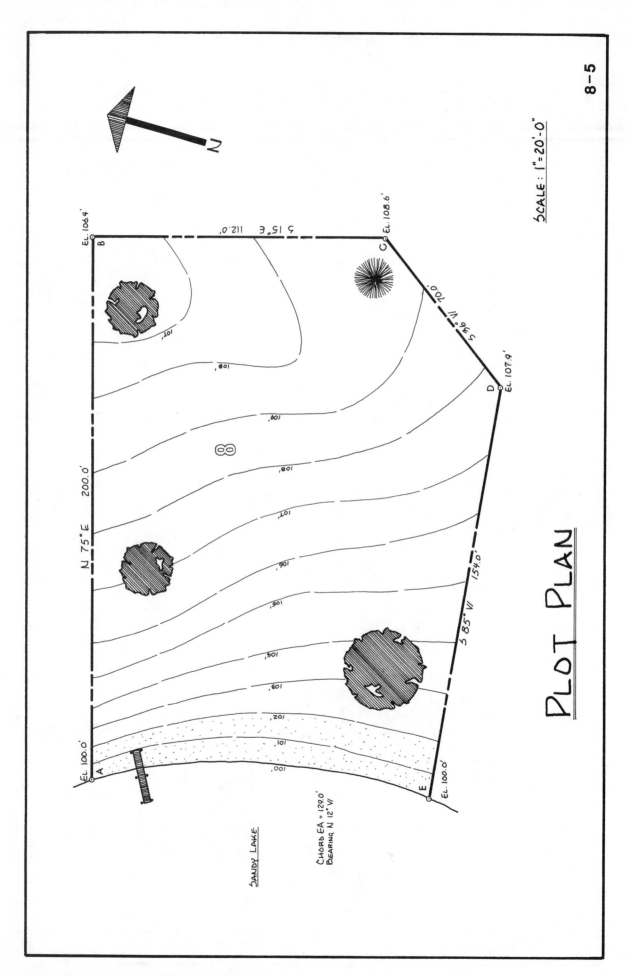

N

PLOT PLAN

SCALE: 1" = 20'-0"

8-5

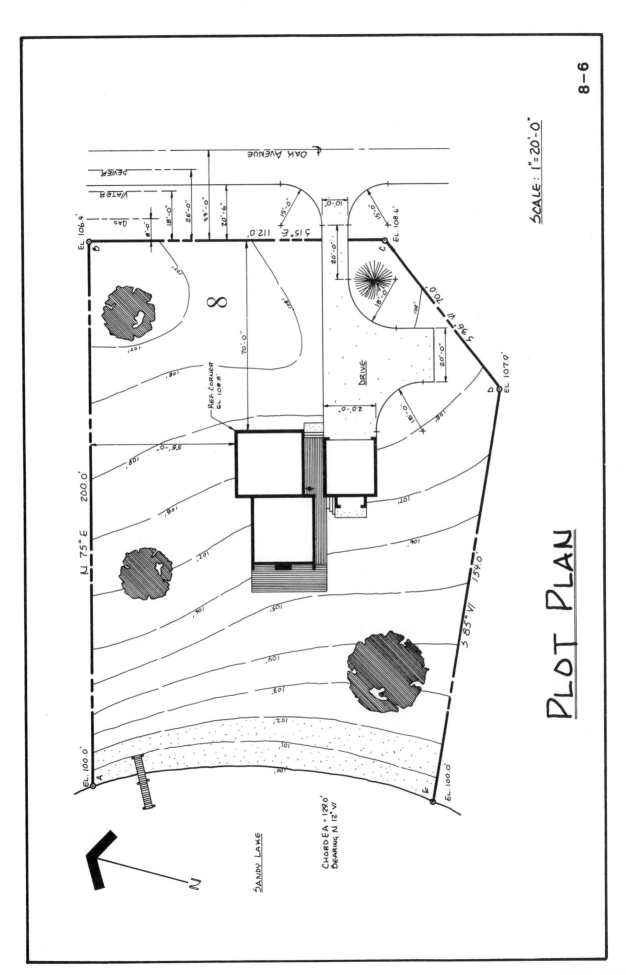

PLOT PLAN

SCALE: 1" = 20'-0"

8-6

Chapter 8—Exam
PLOT PLANS

Name _____

Period _____ **Date** _____ **Score** _____

TRUE—FALSE
Circle T if the statement is true or F if the statement is false.

T   F   1. A plot plan is an elevation view drawing which shows the site and location of the buildings on the property.

T   F   2. Property lines define the site boundaries.

T   F   3. A contour is a line connecting points which have the same elevation.

T   F   4. Contour interval is the vertical distance between two adjacent contours.

T   F   5. Topographical features are represented by symbols.

T   F   6. A plot plan, landscape plan, and site plan are essentially the same.

MULTIPLE CHOICE
Choose the answer that correctly completes the statement. Write the corresponding letter in the space provided.

_____ 1. Property lines are measured with a(n) _____ scale to the nearest 1/100 foot.
    A. architect's
    B. combination
    C. engineer's
    D. metric

_____ 2. The proper format for describing the bearing of a property line is _____.
    A. S 45° N
    B. N 45° 60' 15" E
    C. N 90° E
    D. S 75° 30' 62" W

_____ 3. If a property corner begins or ends on a _____, it is usually identified with a special symbol.
    A. bench mark
    B. contour line
    C. bearing line
    D. meridian arrow

_____ 4. Contour lines help describe the _____ of a site by depicting shape and elevation of the land.
    A. view
    B. entourage
    C. value
    D. topography

_____ 5. When color is used on a topographical drawing, black is used to represent _____.
    A. all land forms
    B. the works of humanity
    C. streams, lakes, marsh, and ponds
    D. vegetation

_____ 6. The standard procedure for dimensioning the location of a house on a site is to dimension _____ of the house from adjacent lot lines.
  A. one side
  B. two sides
  C. two corners
  D. one corner

_____ 7. A typical scale used for a plot plan is _____.
  A. 1" = 1'-0"
  B. 1/4" = 1'-0"
  C. 1" = 30'-0"
  D. 10' = 1'-0"

IDENTIFICATION
Identify the features that are generally shown on a plot plan by placing a check in the space provided.

_____ 1. Scale of the drawing.

_____ 2. Location of utilities.

_____ 3. Window wells and areaways.

_____ 4. Elevation of property corners and contour lines.

_____ 5. Length and bearing of each property line.

_____ 6. Room layout.

_____ 7. Cut and fill calculations.

_____ 8. Location, outline, and size of buildings on the site.

_____ 9. Ornamental plant list.

_____ 10. Meridian arrow (north symbol).

_____ 11. Height of windows and doors.

_____ 12. Streets, driveways, sidewalks, and patios.

_____ 13. Contour of the land.

_____ 14. Footings for buildings on the site.

_____ 15. Trees, shrubs, streams, and gardens.

_____ 16. Well, septic tank, and field.

_____ 17. Fences and retaining walls.

_____ 18. Easements for utilities and drainage, if any.

_____ 19. Electrical distribution panel.

_____ 20. Lot number or address of the site.

SHORT ANSWER
Answer the following question using short answers.

1. Briefly describe the three commonly accepted methods of representing the house on the site.

  A. _____
  _____

  B. _____
  _____

  C. _____
  _____

Footings, Foundations, and Concrete

■ OBJECTIVES

After studying this chapter, the student will be able to:

☐ Describe the procedure for staking out a house location.
☐ List the major considerations when designing a footing for a residential foundation.
☐ Analyze a typical floor plan to determine the appropriate foundation.
☐ Discuss the design considerations for wood, concrete, and masonry foundation walls.
☐ Calculate the load to be supported by a beam.
☐ Explain the purpose of a lintel.

■ DISPLAYS

1. Residential Foundations. Select a floor plan which includes several types of footings and foundations. Display the plan with appropriate details to communicate the construction techniques. Connect each detail with the proper location on the plan view using a string and tack.
2. Wood Foundations. Display an assortment of design materials and ideas related to all-weather wood foundations. Literature which includes specifications, building techniques, and code requirements can be secured from the American Plywood Association as well as companies that produce pressure-treated wood products.

■ INSTRUCTIONAL MATERIALS

Text: Pages 161-182
  Review Questions, Suggested Activities
Workbook: Pages 75-86
  Review Questions, Problems/Activities
Teacher's Resource Guide:
  Chapter 9—Teaching Strategy
  Chapter 9—Exam

■ TEACHING STRATEGY

- Prepare Display #1.
- Review chapter objectives.
- Discuss staking out the house location.
- Present excavation. Discuss the average maximum frost penetration in various areas of the United States.
- Discuss footing shapes and specifications and foundation walls.
- Cover slab foundations.
- Assign Problem 9-1 in the workbook.
- Present pier and post foundations.
- Prepare Display #2.
- Present wood foundations.
- Discuss concrete masonry basement walls.
- Assign workbook Problems 9-2 and 9-3.
- Discuss beams and girders.
- Assign workbook Problem 9-4.
- Discuss lintels, concrete, and masonry.
- Assign one or more of the Suggested Activities in the text.
- Chapter Review
  —Assign Review Questions in the text. Discuss the correct answers.
  —Assign Review Questions in the workbook. Have students check their own answers.
- Evaluation
  —Administer the Chapter 9—Exam. Correct the exam and return.
  —Return graded problems with comments.

■ ANSWERS TO REVIEW QUESTIONS, TEXT Pages 180-181

1. plot
2. Diagonal measurement method.
3. retain the location of the house during excavation.
4. undisturbed earth.

5. soil bearing capacity.
6. foundation wall.
7. building on a hilly terrain.
8. 1/2
9. T-
10. a. Less expensive.
    b. Faster to build.
11. length.
12. All-weather wood foundation.
13. Chemical preservatives.
14. So that the top of the foundation wall will be level.
15. a. Silicon bronze.
    b. Copper.
    c. Hot-dipped zinc-coated steel.
16. 7
17. pilaster
18. tar, cement-based paint.
19. beam
20. a. S-beam.
    b. W-beam.
21. live
22. kips.
23. lintel.
24. a. Cement.
    b. Sand.
    c. Aggregate.
    d. Water.
25. slows
26. screed
27. expansion joints.
28. 7 5/8" x 7 5/8" x 15 5/8".

■ ANSWERS TO REVIEW QUESTIONS, WORKBOOK

PART I: COMPLETION

1. 90
2. plot
3. 15
4. Diagonal
5. batter
6. 4
7. bob
8. control
9. 8
10. 6
11. codes
12. 6
13. footings
14. sandy
15. clay
16. wood.
17. bottom
18. 4
19. three
20. tamping
21. 12 x 10.

PART II: SHORT ANSWER/LISTING

1. Footings increase the supporting capacity of the foundation wall by spreading the load over a larger area.
2. Concrete.
3. The thickness should be the same as the foundation wall and the width should be two times the foundation wall thickness.
4. A variation in settlement may occur because of the compressibility of the different subsoils.
5. The footings should be large enough to minimize any of these differences.
6. When footings are located over soft or poorly drained soils, soils which are not uniform, or over backfilled utility trenches.
7. 12 in. thick.
8. The use of two 1/2 in. steel rods in the horizontal and vertical footings where the steps are located.
9. The foundation walls extend from the first floor to the footing.
10. A. Cast concrete.
    B. Concrete block.
    C. Pressure-treated wood.
    D. Brick.
    E. Stone.
11. A. T-foundation.
    B. Slab foundation.
    C. Pier or post foundation.
    D. Permanent wood foundation.
12. A. The weight to be supported.
    B. The load bearing capacity of the soil.
    C. The location of the foundation in the building.
    D. The climate.
    E. Local building codes.
    F. Preferred building practice.
13. Form boards are made from construction lumber and are used to provide a form for the cast footing used with the T-foundation.
14. Yes.
15. A. Requires less time, expense, and labor to construct.
    B. Excavation is simpler than for the foundation since a separate footing is not required.
    C. Casting the foundation and floor in one operation uses less time.
16. A. They are easier to handle.
    B. They are more readily available.
    C. They do not check as much as solid beams.
17. A. Strength.
    B. Fire resistant.
18. The W-beam has greater strength.
19. Moving or fixed weights which are not structural elements of the house such as furniture, occupants, snow on the roof, wind, etc.
20. They are fixed or static weights of the building

itself such as the weights of roofing, foundation walls, siding, joists, etc.

21. A. Precast concrete.
    B. Cast concrete.
    C. Lintel blocks.
    D. Angle steel.
22. A. In line with interior columns.
    B. Where the slab changes in width.
    C. At a maximum spacing of about 20 ft.
23. A. T-foundation.   D. Post.
    B. Slab foundation.   E. Wood foundation.
    C. Pier.
24.

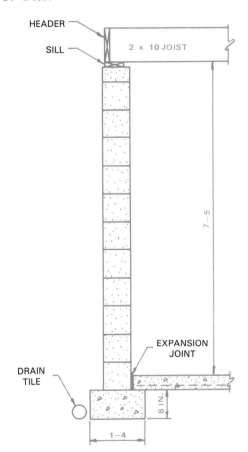

HEADER
SILL
2 x 10 JOIST
7—5
EXPANSION JOINT
DRAIN TILE
8 IN.
1—4

PART III: MULTIPLE CHOICE

1. D. All of the above.
2. C. Climates where traditional concrete foundation work stops in freezing or rainy weather.
3. B. At least 12 in.
4. B. A basement sump is installed in poorly drained soils.
5. D. All of the above.
6. A. Double top plate of the foundation wall.
7. C. After the basement floor has cured and the first floor is installed.
8. A. Support from crosswalls.
9. A. A little shorter than first or second floor walls.
10. A. Metal tiebars.
11. B. Capping may be omitted.

12. C. Applying two 1/4 in. thick coats of cement-mortar or plaster then applying a coat of bituminous waterproofing.
13. D. All of the above.
14. C. 4 x 4 x 3/8 in.
15. C. Condense mortar to the surface ready for final steel-troweling.
16. B. 25.
17. A. 4 to 6.
18. A. 7 5/8 x 7 5/8 x 15 5/8.

PART IV: MATCHING

1. N. Plot plan.
2. P. Saw kerf.
3. S. T-foundation.
4. R. Slab foundation.
5. M. Pier foundation.
6. L. PWF.
7. B. AWWF.
8. A. ACA or CCA.
9. C. Bearing wall.
10. O. S-beam.
11. J. Kip.
12. K. Lintel.
13. E. Concrete.
14. D. Cement.
15. G. Coarse aggregate.
16. Q. Screed.
17. H. Float.
18. T. Trowel.
19. F. Contraction joints.
20. I. Jointing tool.

PART V: PROBLEMS/ACTIVITIES

1. Solution on page 109.
2. Solution on page 110.
3. Solution on page 111.
3. Solution on page 112.

■ ANSWERS TO CHAPTER 9—EXAM

TRUE—FALSE

1. T	4. T
2. T	5. T
3. F	6. T

MULTIPLE CHOICE

1. D	7. C
2. B	8. B
3. D	9. A
4. C	10. C
5. B	11. B
6. D	12. A

MATCHING

1. D
2. A
3. E

4. C
5. B

SHORT ANSWER

1. A. Use pilasters.
   B. Use wall stiffeners.
   C. Use continuous horizontal steel joint rein-forcement.
2. A. A heavy coat of hot tar.
   B. Two coats of cement-based paint designed for this purpose.
3. A. S-beams.
   B. W-beams.
4. A. Live loads.
   B. Dead loads.
5. A. Precast lintels.
   B. Cast concrete lintels.
   C. Lintel blocks.
   D. Angle steel lintels.
6. A. Cement.
   B. Sand.
   C. Coarse aggregate.
   D. Water.
7. 7 5/8" x 7 5/8" x 15 5/8"

DIRECTIONS:
Draw a typical foundation wall section for a thickened-edge slab which includes the following elements:
> Scale: 3/4"=1'-0"
> Foundation 10" thick and 48" from top of slab to bottom of foundation (no footing).   Thickness and depth should conform to code.
> Welded wire fabric in foundation and slab.
> Slab 4" thick on 1" RF insulation and 4" compacted sand.
> Wall on foundation of 8" concrete block with 3/4" RF insulation outside extending 24" below the grade.   Use wood siding over insulation to 2" above the grade.   Flash exposed insulation with aluminum.
> Label and dimension.   Add scale.

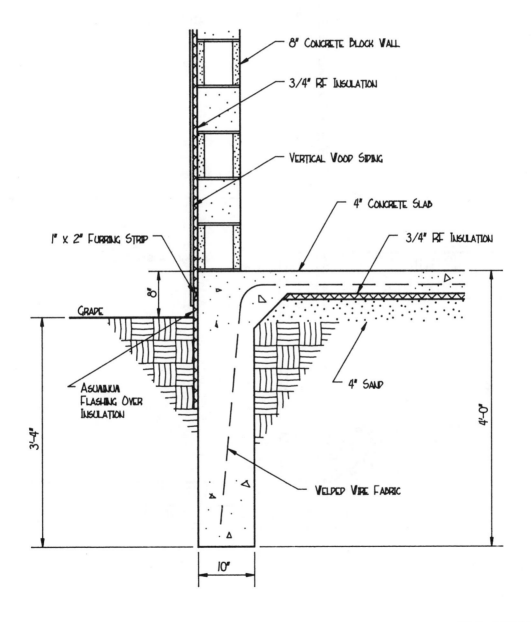

8" CONCRETE BLOCK WALL

3/4" RF INSULATION

VERTICAL WOOD SIDING

4" CONCRETE SLAB

3/4" RF INSULATION

1" x 2" FURRING STRIP

8"

GRADE

ASUMINUM FLASHING OVER INSULATION

3'-4"

4" SAND

4'-0"

WELDED WIRE FABRIC

10"

SCALE: 3/4"=1'-0"

SLAB FOUNDATION SECTION   9-1

Footings, Foundations, and Concrete   109

2.

DIRECTIONS:
Draw a typical foundation wall section for a frame structure with siding which has a crawl space. Include the following elements in your drawing:
> Scale: 3/4"=1'-0"
> Continuous footing 8"x 16" with 2-1/2" re-rods and 4" perforated drain tile in pea gravel.
> 8" concrete block foundation wall (6 courses high or code) with 1/2" parge coat for moisture protection. Grade 8" below top of foundation and crawl space from top of footing to bottom of joists.
> 2"x 8" treated sill plate with 1/2"x 16" anchor bolts and sill sealer.
> 2"x 10" floor joist with 3/4" T&G P.W. glued and nailed.
> Frame wall with 3/4" RF insulation to top of foundation with horizontal siding, 3 1/2" batt insulation, and 1/2" drywall.
> Label and dimension.   Add scale.

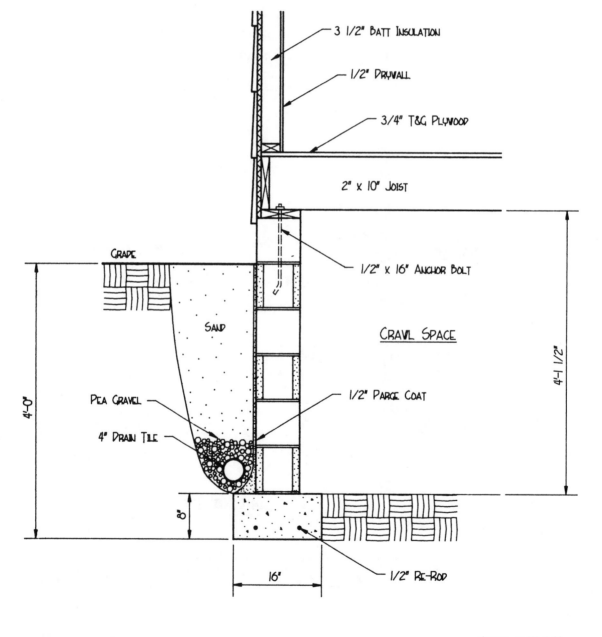

3 1/2" BATT INSULATION

1/2" DRYWALL

3/4" T&G PLYWOOD

2" x 10" JOIST

1/2" x 16" ANCHOR BOLT

CRAWL SPACE

GRADE

SAND

4'-1 1/2"

PEA GRAVEL

1/2" PARGE COAT

4" DRAIN TILE

4'-0"

8"

16"

1/2" RE-ROD

SCALE: 3/4"=1'-0"

FOUNDATION WITH CRAWL SPACE

9-2

DIRECTIONS:
Draw a typical foundation/basement wall section for a brick veneer on frame
residential structure. Include the following elements in your drawing:
> Scale: 3/4"=1'-0"
> Continuous footing 12"x 24" with 2-1/2" re-rods and 4" perforated
  drain tile in pea gravel.
> 12" thick basement wall with 4" brick ledge and dampproofing. Basement
  floor to ceiling should be 7'-10" to 8'-0".
> 4" basement floor slab with welded wire fabric and 4" compacted sand
  with vapor barrier.
> 2"x 8" treated sill plate with sill sealer and 1/2"x 8" anchor bolts.
> Floor system is 14" wood floor trusses to span 24'-0" with 3/4" T&G
  P.W. panels glued and nailed. See Reference Section in text.
> First floor frame wall has 3/4" RF insulation, 3 1/2" batt insulation,
  and 1/2" drywall inside. Veneer is common brick with 1" air space,
  wall ties, and flashing.
> Label and dimension. Add scale.

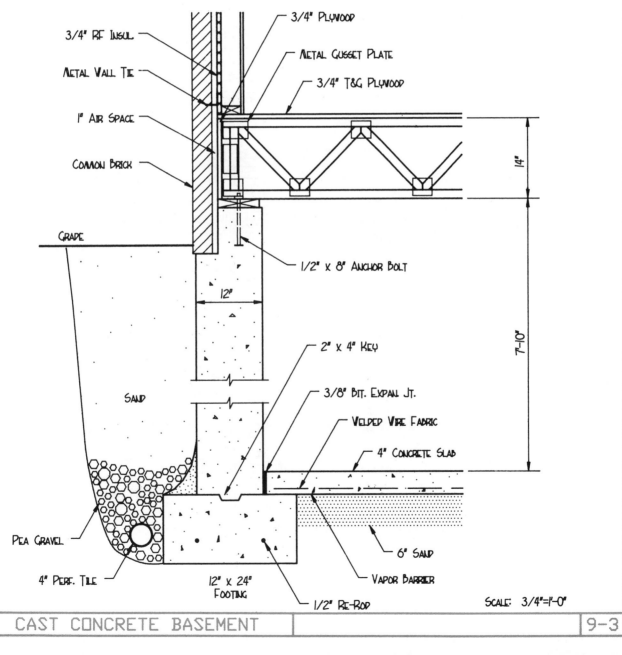

CAST CONCRETE BASEMENT

9-3

4.

DIRECTIONS:
Draw a typical foundation/basement wall section for a residential structure which requires a wood foundation. Include the following elements:
> Scale: 3/4"=1'-0"
> Base for foundation is 8" of crushed stone or gravel.
> Foundation/basement wall is 2"x 6" frame with 2"x 10" footing plate and 3/4" P.W. sheathing covered with polyethylene film. All wood materials are specially treated for this application.
> Include protection strip at grade, double top plate, and 1"x 4" screed.
> Basement floor is 4" thick with welded wire fabric and moisture barrier. Include drain tiles where ground water is a problem.
> First floor system is 2"x 10" joists with 3/4" T&G P.W. glued and nailed.
> Exterior wall is 2"x 4" stud, 3/4" RF insulation, siding, and 1/2" drywall.
> Label and dimension. Add scale.

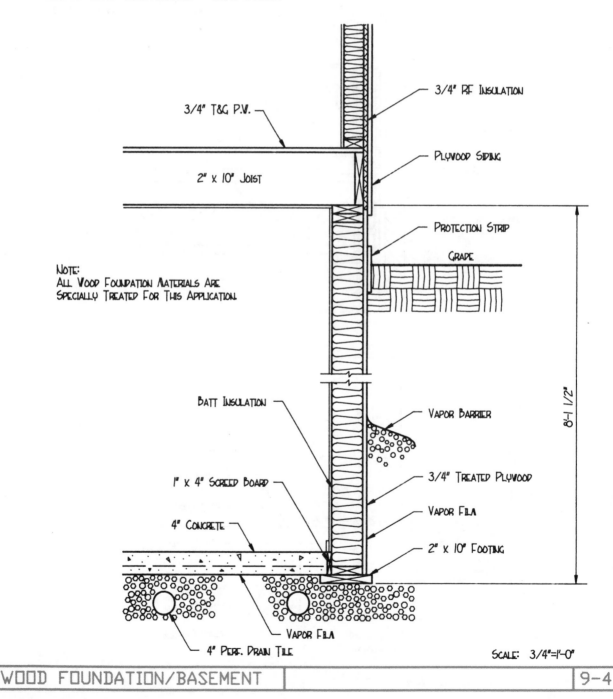

3/4" T&G P.V.

2" x 10" Joist

3/4" RF Insulation

Plywood Siding

Protection Strip

Grade

NOTE:
All Wood Foundation Materials Are Specially Treated For This Application

Batt Insulation

Vapor Barrier

1" x 4" Screed Board

3/4" Treated Plywood

Vapor Film

4" Concrete

2" x 10" Footing

8'-1 1/2"

Vapor Film

4" Perf. Drain Tile

SCALE: 3/4"=1'-0"

WOOD FOUNDATION/BASEMENT   9-4

Chapter 9—Exam
FOOTINGS, FOUNDATIONS, AND CONCRETE

Name _____

Period _____ Date _____ Score _____

TRUE—FALSE
Circle T if the statement is true or F if the statement is false.

T   F   1. Square corners of a rectangle may be laid out using the 9-12-15 unit method.

T   F   2. The finished floor of a house should be at least 8" above the grade.

T   F   3. Residential footings should be at least 12" below the average maximum frost penetration.

T   F   4. Excavations in clay may be nearly vertical.

T   F   5. Footings for most residential structures are made from cast concrete.

T   F   6. The footing for a chimney is generally 12 inches thick.

MULTIPLE CHOICE
Choose the answer that correctly completes the statement. Write the corresponding letter in the space provided.

_____ 1. The plot plan provides the necessary dimensions required for _____.
   A. locating all windows and doors on the plan
   B. building the house foundation
   C. securing a building permit
   D. staking out the location of the house on the site

_____ 2. The exact location of a proposed house foundation is maintained through the use of _____.
   A. angle boards
   B. batter boards
   C. construction boards
   D. building boards

_____ 3. A _____ point is needed to determine the depth of excavation and foundation wall height.
   A. rod
   B. stake
   C. clearance
   D. control

_____ 4. Excavation for residential footings should extend down to a minimum of _____ inches into undisturbed earth.
   A. 2
   B. 4
   C. 6
   D. 12

_____ 5. The _____ spreads the weight of a building over a broad area.
   A. floating slab
   B. footing
   C. site foundation
   D. reinforcing rod

_____ 6. The footing for a residential structure is generally _____ inches wide when the foundation wall is 8" thick.
   A. 8
   B. 10
   C. 14
   D. 16

_____ 7. Reinforcing bars are required in footings _____.
   A. for all residential structures
   B. when the house is built in a 100 year floodplain
   C. when uneven settlement of the structure is anticipated
   D. to prevent frost heave

_____ 8. Stepped footings are frequently necessary when _____.
   A. the house has more than one floor level
   B. when building on hilly terrain
   C. brick veneer is used
   D. two different materials are used

_____ 9. Foundation walls are normally that part of a house which extends _____.
   A. from the first floor to the footing
   B. from the first floor to the soffit
   C. from the frost line to the grade
   D. from the footing to the eaves line

_____ 10. Nails and other fasteners used in an all-weather wood foundation should be made from _____.
   A. aluminum, silicon bronze, or copper
   B. brass, copper, or aluminum
   C. silicon bronze, copper, or hot-dipped zinc-coated steel
   D. copper, brass, or hot-dipped zinc-coated steel

_____ 11. In an AWWF foundation, all lumber and plywood that comes in contact with the ground should be pressure treated with _____.
   A. tar or other decay-resistant material
   B. waterborne preservative salts
   C. special caulking compounds
   D. kerosene

_____ 12. Concrete and masonry basement wall thickness depends on lateral earth pressure and _____.
   A. vertical load to be supported
   B. wishes of the builder
   C. weight of the foundation material
   D. None of the above

MATCHING
Select the answer that correctly matches each term. Place your answer in the space provided.

_____ 1. Permanent wood foundation

_____ 2. Slab foundation

_____ 3. T-foundation

_____ 4. Pier and post foundations

_____ 5. Footings

A. Extension of a slab floor.
B. Support for the foundation walls.
C. Used to support a beam.
D. Pressure-treated wood is used.
E. The most common foundation type.

Name _____

SHORT ANSWER
Answer the following questions using short answers.

1. List three methods that might be used to strengthen a concrete block foundation wall when strong earth pressures are present.

   A. _____

   B. _____

   C. _____

2. Identify two methods for dampproofing a cast concrete basement wall.

   A. _____

   B. _____

   _____

3. What are the two types of steel beams commonly used in residential construction?

   A. _____

   B. _____

4. Name the two basic types of loads which are imposed on a structure.

   A. _____

   B. _____

5. Name the four types of lintels generally used in residential building construction.

   A. _____

   B. _____

   C. _____

   D. _____

6. What are the common ingredients in concrete?

   A. _____

   B. _____

   C. _____

   D. _____

7. What are the actual dimensions of an 8" x 8" x 16" concrete block?

   _____

The Foundation Plan

■ OBJECTIVES

After studying this chapter, the student will be able to:
☐ Identify the primary features included in a foundation plan.
☐ Discuss the difference between a foundation plan and a basement plan.
☐ Design and draw a foundation plan for a typical residential structure.

■ DISPLAYS

1. Types of Foundations. Select a foundation plan that includes a basement, crawlspace, and slab construction for display on the bulletin board. Emphasize the different types of foundation construction through the use of titles and different colors.
2. Types of Framing. Display foundation wall details of box sill construction (platform framing) and solid sill and T-sill construction (balloon framing). Label each detail as to the type of framing and sill construction.

■ INSTRUCTIONAL MATERIALS

Text: Pages 183-192
   Review Questions, Suggested Activities
Workbook: Pages 87-91
   Review Questions, Problems/Activities
Teacher's Resource Guide:
   Chapter 10 — Teaching Strategy
   Chapter 10 — Exam

■ TEACHING STRATEGY

* Prepare Display #1.
* Review chapter objectives.

* Discuss the definition and purpose of the foundation plan.
* Draw symbols commonly used on a foundation plan on the chalkboard.
* Present the preliminary steps to drawing a foundation plan.
* Discuss drawing a foundation plan.
* Prepare Display #2.
* Assign workbook Problems 10-1 and 10-2.
* Assign one or more of the Suggested Activities in the text.
* Chapter Review
   —Assign Review Questions in the text. Discuss the correct answers.
   —Assign Review Questions in the workbook. Have students check their own answers.
   —Make a transparency of solution to Problem/Activity 10-1 and use for review.
* Evaluation
   —Administer the Chapter 10 — Exam. Correct the exam and return.
   —Return graded problems with comments.

■ ANSWERS TO REVIEW QUESTIONS, TEXT Page 190

1. The foundation plan is a plan view drawing in section which shows the location and size of footings, piers, columns, foundation walls, and supporting beams.
2. $1/4" = 1'-0"$
3. a. Footings.   e. Drains and sumps.
   b. Foundation walls.   f. Details of
   c. Piers and columns.   construction.
   d. Openings in   g. Notes.
      foundation walls.   h. Scale.
   Also: Beams and pilasters, direction, size, and spacing of joints; bearing wall partitions and dwarf walls.

4. Excavator, mason, and cement worker.
5. floor, plot, elevations.
6. four
7. a. Frost penetration depth.
   b. Building code requirements.
   c. Soil bearing capacity.
8. —— - ——.
9. to provide additional information.
10. show proper materials and add clarity.
11. It has additional features such as interior walls, doors, windows, and permanent fixtures.
12. The footings must be below the frost line. Also it is relatively inexpensive to add a few more feet and excavate the soil under the house to form a basement.

■ ANSWERS TO REVIEW QUESTIONS, WORKBOOK

PART I: SHORT ANSWER/LISTING

1. A. Floor plan.
   B. Plot plan.
   C. Elevations.
2. A. Footings for foundation walls, piers, and columns.
   B. Foundation walls.
   C. Piers and columns.
   D. Dwarf walls.
   E. Partition walls, doors, and bath fixtures if the house has a basement.
   Also: Openings in foundation wall such as windows, doors, and vents; beams and pilasters; direction, size, and spacing of floor joists or trusses; drains and sump; details of foundation and footing construction; complete dimensions and notes; scale of the drawing.
3. Because the dimensions of the foundation may not be the same for different types of exterior walls.
4. Select the scale to be used.
5. A. Foundation plan.
   B. Floor plan.
6. A. Concrete block.   I. Slate.
   B. Cast concrete.   J. Structural clay tile.
   C. Cinder block.   K. Gravel.
   D. Common brick.   L. Sand.
   E. Face brick.   M. Earth.
   F. Firebrick.   N. Rock.
   G. Cut stone.   O. Flashing.
   H. Rubble.
7. It reduces both errors and the time required to make the drawing.
8. C.
9. Center.
10. The basement/foundation plan includes the foundation plan plus interior walls, stairs, doors, and windows. It may also show plumbing fixtures, climate control systems, sump, and floor drains.
11. Examine the drawing to see that all pertinent information is included.
12. Yes, if a basement electrical plan is not drawn.

PART II: COMPLETION

1. split-level
2. columns
3. masons
4. basements.
5. floor
6. 1/4" = 1'-0".
7. hidden
8. center
9. edge
10. footings
11. first

PART III: MULTIPLE CHOICE

1. B. Locate the supporting beam if one is required and draw the beam using a thick center line symbol.
2. A. Mr. Jones' foundation plan will be 8 in. longer and wider than Mr. Smith's because a brick veneer house needs a 4 in. ledge on all four sides.
3. D. All of the above.

PART IV: MATCHING

1. E. Soil bearing test.
2. C. Foundation details.
3. D. Material symbols.
4. A. Dwarf walls.
5. F. Windows or doors.
6. B. Concrete block symbol.

PART V: PROBLEMS/ACTIVITIES

1. Solution on page 119.
2. Solution on page 120.

■ ANSWERS TO CHAPTER 10—EXAM

TRUE—FALSE

1. T		4. F	
2. T		5. T	
3. T			

MULTIPLE CHOICE

1. A		5. C	
2. D		6. B	
3. D		7. B	
4. C		8. A	

1.

DIRECTIONS:
Use the floor plan of the Garden House below to construct a thickened—edge slab foundation in the space provided. Scale is 1/4"=1'-0". Include the following elements in your drawing:
> Thickness of foundation wall (8") and slab floor (4")
> Anchor bolts (1/2" x 8") at least every 4 feet along perimeter
> Cutting plane through one foundation wall. Draw the section and dimension it. Foundation depth should be at least 24" or frost depth for your area.

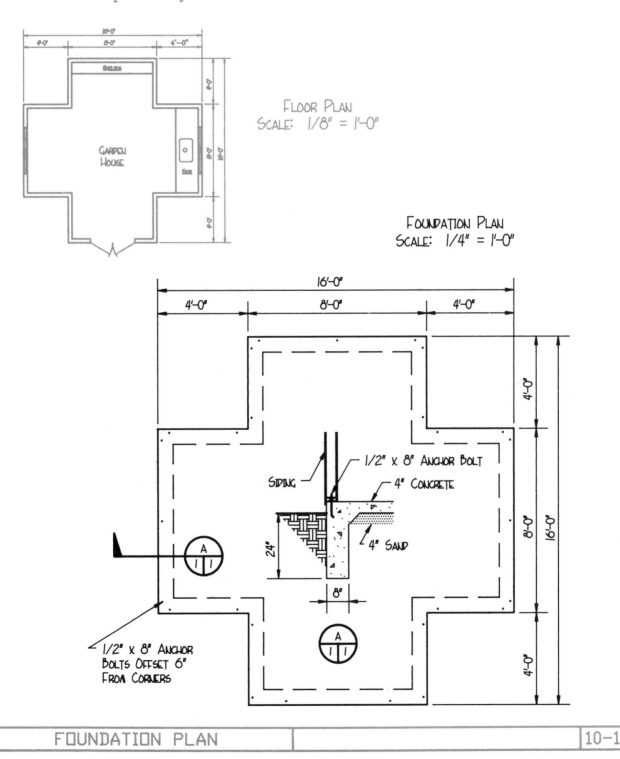

FLOOR PLAN
SCALE: 1/8" = 1'-0"

FOUNDATION PLAN
SCALE: 1/4" = 1'-0"

FOUNDATION PLAN | 10-1

2.

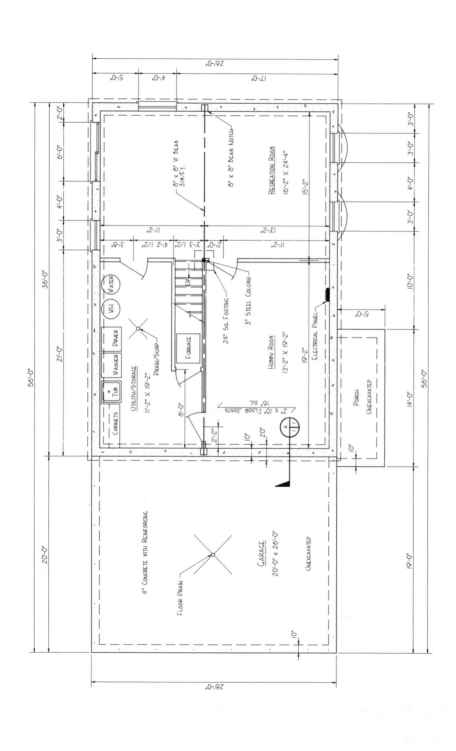

BASEMENT/FOUNDATION PLAN

120   Architecture Resource Guide

Chapter 10—Exam
THE FOUNDATION PLAN

Name _____

Period _____ **Date** _____ **Score** _____

TRUE—FALSE
Circle T if the statement is true or F if the statement is false.

T   F   1. The scale of most residential floor plans is 1/4" = 1'-0".

T   F   2. The face brick section symbol is composed of a series of 45° hatch lines.

T   F   3. Dwarf walls are built to retain an excavation or embankment.

T   F   4. Direction of floor joists or trusses is not shown on the foundation plan.

T   F   5. Footings are represented on the foundation plan using a hidden line symbol.

MULTIPLE CHOICE
Choose the answer that correctly completes the statement. Write the corresponding letter in the space provided.

_____ 1. The foundation plan is a plan view drawing in section showing the location and size of
_____.
   A. footings, piers, columns, foundation walls, and supporting beams
   B. supporting beams, footings, piers, first floor walls and columns
   C. all parts of the structure above the grade
   D. All of the above

_____ 2. The foundation plan is drawn from information presented on the _____.
   A. floor plan
   B. plot plan
   C. elevations
   D. All of the above

_____ 3. When groundwater is present, a _____ is generally required to prevent water in the
basement.
   A. dry well
   B. tight basement wall
   C. thicker footing
   D. sump

_____ 4. The brick ledge is generally _____ inch(es) wide.
   A. 1
   B. 2
   C. 4
   D. 6

_____ 5. A brick veneer structure is dimensioned to the _____.
   A. outside of the brick veneer
   B. inside of the brick veneer
   C. outside of the rough stud wall
   D. inside of the rough stud wall

_____ 6. Floor trusses are generally spaced _____ inches o.c.
   A. 12
   B. 24
   C. 16
   D. 30

_____ 7. One reason that a house may be constructed with a basement is that _____.
   A. basements do not add cost to price of a house
   B. basements are popular in areas where space is crowded and sites are small
   C. some codes require each house to have a basement
   D. heat loss is reduced

_____ 8. The basement plan is _____.
   A. a combination foundation plan and floor plan
   B. no different than a foundation plan
   C. easier to draw than a foundation plan
   D. required for all houses

Sill and Floor Construction

■ OBJECTIVES

After studying this chapter, the student will be able to:
☐ Recognize platform and balloon framing.
☐ Plan the appropriate floor support using joists or trusses for a structure.
☐ Determine proper joist sizes using a typical span data chart.
☐ Describe the components of a floor system.
☐ Demonstrate an understanding of the principles involved in post and beam construction.

■ DISPLAYS

1. Sill Construction. Build a scale model of each of the following types of sill construction: box sill, solid sill, and T-sill. Use a 1" = 1'-0" scale. See Figs. 11-1 and 11-4 in the text.
2. Definition of Terms. Prepare a bulletin board display consisting of terms pertaining to sill and floor construction. Use the terms identified in Suggested Activity #2 at the end of the chapter in the text.

■ INSTRUCTIONAL MATERIALS

Text: Pages 193-208
 Review Questions, Suggested Activities
Workbook: Pages 93-100
 Review Questions, Problems/Activities
Teacher's Resource Guide:
 Chapter 11 — Teaching Strategy
 Chapter 11 — Exam

■ TEACHING STRATEGY

- Prepare Display #1.
- Review chapter objectives.
- Discuss platform and balloon framing.
- Assign workbook Problem 11-1.
- Prepare Display #2.
- Discuss joists and beams.
- Assign workbook Problem 11-2.
- Discuss floor trusses.
- Discuss subfloor, cantilevered joists, and framing under slate or tile.
- Assign workbook Problem 11-3.
- Present post and beam construction.
- Assign one or more of the Suggested Activities in the text.
- Review new terms presented in the chapter.
- Chapter Review
 — Assign Review Questions in the text. Discuss the correct answers.
 — Assign Review Questions in the workbook. Have students check their own answers.
 — Make a transparency of solution to Problem/Activity 11-1 and use for review.
- Evaluation
 — Administer the Chapter 11 — Exam. Correct the exam and return.
 — Return graded problems with comments.

■ ANSWERS TO REVIEW QUESTIONS, TEXT
Page 207

1. platform, balloon
2. sill.
3. 1 1/2" x 5 1/2".
4. box
5. solid, T-
6. a. Less shrinkage.
   b. More vertical stability.
7. joists
8. a. Southern yellow pine.
   b. Fir.
   c. Larch.
   Also: Hemlock and spruce.
9. 16

10. 19
11. 2 x 8.
12. spread the load over a broader area.
13. a. Plywood. d. Oriented strand
    b. Composite board.   board.
    c. Waferboard. e. Structural
                       particleboard.
15. a. Lightweight.
    b. Span great distances.
    c. Reduce sound transmission.
    d. Reduce labor cost.
    Also: Facilities installation of electrical, plumbing, etc.
16. So the floor will be level when loaded.
17. cantilevered
18. a. Post.
    b. Beam.
    c. Plank.
19. a. Solid timber.
    b. Laminated.
    c. Built-up.
    d. Box beams.
20. transverse, longitudinal
21. a. 2".
    b. 3".
    c. 4".
22. Rigid type.

■ ANSWERS TO REVIEW QUESTIONS, WORKBOOK

PART I: SHORT ANSWER/LISTING

1. Platform.
2. A. Plate.
   B. Joists.
   C. Studs.
3. A. It is compatible for both one- and two-story buildings.
   B. It is easy and fast to construct.
   C. Shrinkage is uniform throughout the house.
   Also: A firestop is a built-in feature. The construction is safe because the work is carried out on solid surfaces.
4. The sill.
5. Joists.
6. A. Stairs.
   B. Chimneys.
7. A. Bad surface to work on during construction.
   B. It does not provide a firestop.
8. The wall studs rest directly on the sill plate.
9. A. Solid or standard sill construction.
   B. T-sill construction.
10. Vertical shrinkage is less with balloon framing.
11. A. Length of span.
    B. Load to be supported.
    C. Specie and grade of lumber.
    D. Distance the joists are spaced apart.

12. Span is 22'-5".
13. A. The large size of the sheet.
    B. Sheets can be nailed quickly into place.
14. A. Plywood composite board.
    B. Waferboard.
    C. Oriented strand board.
    D. Structural particleboard.
15. A. Reduce the space between the joists or use larger joists.
    B. Use one or more beams under the section.
16. The maximum allowable span between beams generally is 7'-0".
17. A. Continuous wall.
    B. Series of piers where each post is to be located.
18. A 5 1/4 x 13 1/2 in. beam is needed. It will support 316 lbs./lin. ft. over a span of 24'-0".
19. A. Solid beam.
    B. Horizontal laminated beam.
    C. Vertical laminated beam.
    D. Steel reinforced beam.
    E. Box beam.
20. Normally the subfloor panels are 4' x 8'. This assures that all ends of panels will be supported.
21. A. Southern yellow pine.
    B. Fir.
    Also: Larch, hemlock, spruce, and redwood.

PART II: COMPLETION

1. longitudinal
2. wall
3. floor
4. box
5. header
6. 1 1/2 x 9 1/4 in.
7. header.
8. 4
9. header.
10. vertical
11. 3/4 x 5 1/2 in.
12. trusses
13. wood
14. cold
15. stress
16. 2 x 4
17. support
18. underlayment
19. expansion.
20. beams.
21. 4
22. planks

PART III: MULTIPLE CHOICE

1. A. 1 1/2 x 5 1/2 in.
2. B. Headers are not required.
3. C. 16.
4. D. All of the above.

5. C. 24.
6. C. A squeak-free structure results.
7. A. 25.
8. D. All of the above.
9. C. Posts.
10. B. The soil bearing capacity.

PART IV: MATCHING

1. D. Engineered wood floor trusses.
2. B. Built-in camber.
3. C. Cantilevered joists.
4. E. National Forest Products Association.
5. A. A special type of concrete.
6. G. Post and beam construction.
7. H. Transverse method.
8. F. Metal plates.

PART V: PROBLEMS/ACTIVITIES

1. Solution on page 126.
2. Solution on page 127.
3. Solution on page 128.

■ ANSWERS TO CHAPTER 11—EXAM

TRUE—FALSE

1. T
2. T
3. T
4. F
5. T

MULTIPLE CHOICE

1. D
2. B
3. C
4. D
5. C
6. A
7. A
8. C
9. D
10. C
11. B
12. A
13. B

SHORT ANSWER

1. A. Platform framing.
   B. Balloon framing.
2. A. Plates.
   B. Joists.
   C. Studs.
3. A. Small potential shrinkage.
   B. Vertical stability.
4. A. Length of space.
   B. Load to be supported.
   C. Specie and grade of wood.
   D. Distance the joists are spaced apart.
5. A. To stiffen the floor.
   B. To spread the load over a broader area.
6. A. Ceramic tile.
   B. Slate.
   C. Stone.
7. A. Posts.
   B. Beams.
   C. Planks.

1.

DIRECTIONS:
Using guidelines and proper form, label and dimension the basement wall
section below using the following information:
> Footing is 12" x 24" with two 1/2" re-rods and drain tile in pea gravel
> Basement floor is 4" thick with 4" sand base and 3/8" expansion joint
> Basement wall is 12" concrete block with 1/2" parge coat outside
> Distance from top of footing to grade (224.2' El.) is 8'-8"
> Floor to underside of 24" trusses is 8'-2"
> Anchor bolts are 1/2" x 16" spaced 8'-0" apart
> Flooring material (1st floor) is 3/4" T&G P.W.
> Stud wall is covered with 3/4" RF insulation and panel siding.

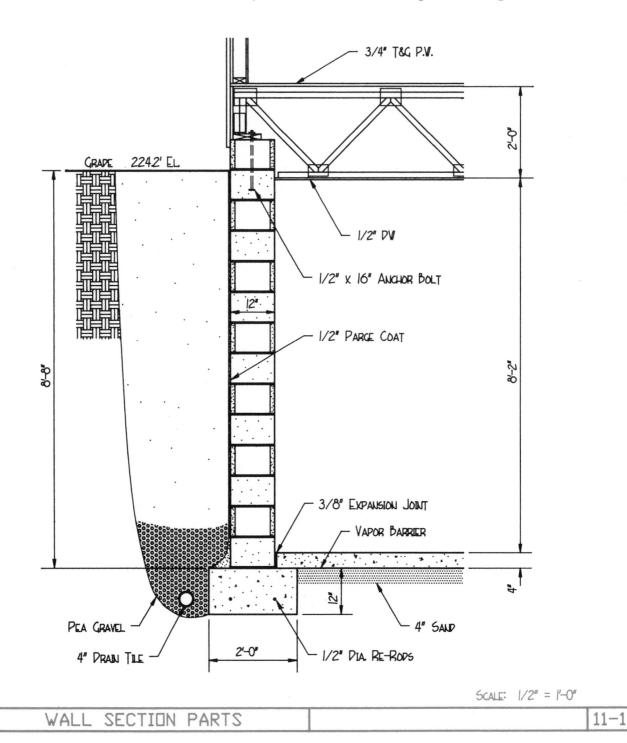

GRADE   224.2' EL

3/4" T&G P.W.

2'-0"

1/2" DW

1/2" x 16" ANCHOR BOLT

12"

1/2" PARGE COAT

8'-8"

8'-2"

3/8" EXPANSION JOINT

VAPOR BARRIER

12"

4"

PEA GRAVEL

4" SAND

4" DRAIN TILE

2'-0"

1/2" DIA. RE-RODS

SCALE: 1/2" = 1'-0"

WALL SECTION PARTS

11-1

2.

DIRECTIONS:
Complete the floor framing problems below as indicated.
- A. Draw the framing to allow for an opening 40" X 36" centered in the floor area. The shortest dimension is parallel to the joist direction. Use double headers and double trimmers. Dimension the opening and label the joists.
- B. Plan the joist layout (16" o.c.) for the area between existing joists and two feet beyond the foundation wall. Label parts and show the dimensions.

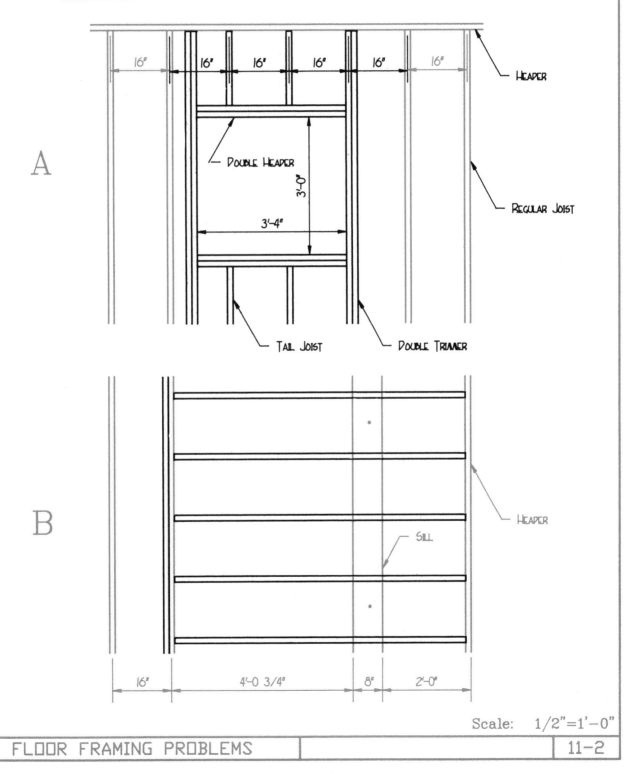

A

16" 16" 16" 16" 16" 16"

HEADER

DOUBLE HEADER

3'-0"

3'-4"

REGULAR JOIST

TAIL JOIST   DOUBLE TRIMMER

B

HEADER

SILL

16"   4'-0 3/4"   8"   2'-0"

Scale: 1/2"=1'-0"

FLOOR FRAMING PROBLEMS   11-2

3.

Floor Framing Plan

Chapter 11—Exam
SILL AND FLOOR CONSTRUCTION

Name _____

Period _____ **Date** _____ **Score** _____

TRUE—FALSE
Circle T if the statement is true or F if the statement is false.

T   F   1. Shrinkage is uniform throughout the structure when platform framing is used.

T   F   2. A sill is the lowest member of the frame of a structure.

T   F   3. Balloon framing was once used extensively, but is not used as frequently today.

T   F   4. Floor joists are generally made from common hardwoods.

T   F   5. Floor joists are usually spaced 12", 16", or 24" o.c.

MULTIPLE CHOICE
Choose the answer that correctly completes the statement. Write the corresponding letter in the space provided.

_____ 1. One advantage of platform framing is _____.
   A. a firestop is automatically provided
   B. construction is safe because the work is performed on solid surfaces
   C. that it is easy and fast to construct
   D. All of the above

_____ 2. The sill plate in most residential construction is _____.
   A. 2" x 4"
   B. 2" x 6"
   C. 2" x 8"
   D. 2" x 10"

_____ 3. Platform framing utilizes a method of sill construction known as _____ construction.
   A. solid sill
   B. T-sill
   C. box sill
   D. None of the above

_____ 4. T-sill construction is used with _____ framing.
   A. platform
   B. barn
   C. Eastern
   D. balloon

_____ 5. The actual size of a 2" x 12" floor joist is _____.
   A. 1 5/8" x 11 5/8"
   B. 1 1/2" x 11 1/2"
   C. 1 1/2" x 11 1/4"
   D. 2" x 12"

_____ 6. A maximum allowable deflection of _____ of the span (with a normal live load) is specified for floor joists.
   A. 1/360th
   B. 1/280th
   C. 1/100th
   D. 1/10th

_____ 7. Floor joists should be _____ under partition walls which run parallel to the joists.
   A. doubled
   B. tripled
   C. omitted
   D. turned on their sides

_____ 8. Wood floor trusses have a built-in _____ so that the floor will be level when the load is applied.
   A. bow
   B. twist
   C. camber
   D. wind

_____ 9. Use _____ lumber for wood floor trusses so that a minimum of material may be used.
   A. hardwood
   B. construction grade
   C. air dried
   D. stress-graded

_____ 10. The spacing of wood floor trusses is usually _____ inches o.c.
   A. 12
   B. 16
   C. 24
   D. 36

_____ 11. A rule of thumb to follow in determining the necessary length of cantilevered joists is to extend the joists inside at least _____ the distance they overhang outside.
   A. the same length as
   B. twice
   C. three times
   D. four times

_____ 12. Most of the weight of a post and beam building is carried by the _____.
   A. posts
   B. beams
   C. sills
   D. curtain walls

_____ 13. Decking planks for the roof and floor of a post and beam structure range in thickness from _____ inches.
   A. 1 to 2
   B. 2 to 4
   C. 4 to 6
   D. 6 to 8

SHORT ANSWER
Answer the following questions using short answers.

1. List the two basic types of floor framing.

   A. _____

   B. _____

2. Identify the three structural members used in floor framing.

   A. _____

   B. _____

   C. _____

3. List two advantages of balloon framing.

    A. _____

    B. _____

4. The size of floor joist required for a given situation will depend on four things. Name them.

    A. _____

    B. _____

    C. _____

    D. _____

5. List two reasons that bridging is used with floor joists.

    A. _____

    B. _____

6. List three floor materials that generally require a substantial base and special joist framing.

    A. _____

    B. _____

    C. _____

7. Identify the three large framing members used in post and beam construction.

    A. _____

    B. _____

    C. _____

Wall and Ceiling Construction

■ OBJECTIVES

After studying this chapter, the student will be able to:
□ Name the members of a typical frame wall.
□ Explain methods of frame wall construction.
□ Interpret information shown on a ceiling joist span data chart.
□ Sketch the various types of exterior walls used in residential construction.

■ DISPLAYS

1. Wall Construction Details. Create a bulletin board arrangement of photos and/or details of frame wall construction which shows construction members.
2. Wall Sections. Display student work from Suggested Activity #1 in the text.
3. Construction Materials. Display a collection of typical materials used in light frame wall and ceiling construction. Label each sample.
4. Brick Bonds. Prepare a bulletin board consisting of photos of brick bonds submitted by students for Suggested Activity #6 in the text.

■ INSTRUCTIONAL MATERIALS

Text: Pages 209-222
  Review Questions, Suggested Activities
Workbook: Pages 101-106
  Review Questions, Problems/Activities
Teacher's Resource Guide:
  Chapter 12 – Teaching Strategy
  Chapter 12 – Exam

■ TEACHING STRATEGY

- Prepare Display #1.
- Review chapter objectives.
- Present frame wall construction. Compare and contrast platform framing and balloon framing.
- Assign one Suggested Activity in the text.
- Prepare Display #2 and/or #3.
- Assign workbook Problem 12-1.
- Discuss ceiling construction.
- Discuss masonry wall construction.
- Assign workbook Problem 12-2.
- Illustrate how the top plate is attached to a masonry wall.
- Prepare Display #4.
- Discuss brick names and sizes.
- Assign one or more of the remaining Suggested Activities in the text.
- Chapter Review
  - Assign Review Questions in the text. Discuss the correct answers.
  - Assign Review Questions in the workbook. Have students check their own answers.
  - Make transparencies of the solutions to Problem/Activities 12-1 and 12-2 and use for review.
- Evaluation
  - Administer the Chapter 12 – Exam. Correct the exam and return.
  - Return graded problems with comments.

■ ANSWERS TO REVIEW QUESTIONS, TEXT Pages 220-221

1. a. Load to be supported.
   b. Span distance.
   c. Wood species.
   d. Spacing of joists.
   e. Grade of lumber.
2. a. Sole plate.
   b. Top plate.
   c. Studs.
   d. Headers.
   e. Braces.

3. a. Good stiffness.
   b. Good nail holding properties.
   c. Freedom from warp.
   d. Easy to work.
4. a. Douglas fir.
   b. Southern yellow pine.
   c. Hemlock.
   Also: Spruce and larch.
5. 15-19
6. 8'-0".
7. header, lintel.
8. Reduces construction time.
9. cripples.
10. 6'-10".
11. 2 x 10.
12. a. Openings for heating ducts.
    b. Wall backing for fixtures.
    c. Extra support for bathtub.
13. Tie the wythes together.
14. 16", 32"
15. 8
16. cavity
17. firecut.
18. ashlar, rubble.
19. 1"
20. anchor bolts.
21. clay.
22. face brick, common brick.
23. running

■ ANSWERS TO REVIEW QUESTIONS, WORKBOOK

PART I: MATCHING

1. J. Sole plate.
2. K. Subfloor.
3. E. Cripples.
4. L. Trimmers.
5. D. Corner bracing.
6. F. Door schedule.
7. B. Ceiling joists.
8. G. Firecut.
9. A. Ashlar stonework.
10. I. Rubble stonework.
11. M. Veneer.
12. H. Flashing.
13. C. Common brick.

PART II: MULTIPLE CHOICE

1. A. Southern yellow pine.
2. B. Sole plate.
3. C. Sufficient support for the building.
4. A. A 2 x 6 fastened to cross blocking.
5. B. The size of the material used.
6. C. Openings wider than 8'-0".
7. D. All of the above.

8. B. The veneer does not support the weight of the wall.
9. A. Face brick.

PART III: COMPLETION

1. prefabrication
2. #2
3. nailer
4. 8
5. shorter
6. floor.
7. header
8. slope
9. double
10. joists
11. 32
12. frame
13. shields
14. 9 x 4 x 2 2/3

PART IV: SHORT ANSWER/LISTING

1. A. Frame.
   B. Masonry.
   C. Combination frame and masonry.
2. A. 1 x 4 stock.
   B. Metal strap.
   C. Plywood sheathing.
3. To allow for the thickness of sheathing, weatherboard, or rigid foam insulation.
4. Solid blocking construction.
5. The length is equal to the width of the opening plus the thickness of the two trimmers.
6. In ceiling joist construction, a header is not placed around the perimeter. Smaller lumber is used in ceiling joist construction than in floor joist construction.
7. Advantages include relatively low expense to construct and the variety of textures and designs possible. The disadvantage is the necessity of using furring strips for interior walls of drywall, plaster, or paneling.
8. A. Better insulation.
   B. Less expensive to construct.
   C. Easier to install electrical and plumbing.
9. A. Running bond.
   B. Common bond.
   C. Stack bond.
   D. Flemish bond.

PART V: PROBLEMS/ACTIVITIES

1. Solution on page 136.
2. Solution on page 137.

■ ANSWERS TO CHAPTER 12—EXAM

TRUE—FALSE

1. F
2. T
3. T
4. T
5. T

MULTIPLE CHOICE

1. C   5. D
2. C   6. C
3. C   7. A
4. B

SHORT ANSWER

1. A. Frame.
   B. Masonry.
   C. Combination frame and masonry.
2. A. Sole plate.
   B. Top plates.
   C. Studs.
   D. Headers.
   E. Braces.
3. A. The load to be supported.
   B. Span distance.
   C. Wood specie.
   D. Spacing of joists.
   E. Grade of lumber used.
4. A. Ashlar.
   B. Rubble.
5. A. Stretcher.
   B. Header.
   C. Shiner.
   D. Soldier.
   E. Rowlock.
   F. Sailor.
6. A. Common brick.
   B. Face brick.
7. A. Flush.
   B. Concave.
   C. Raked.
   D. Flush and rodded.
   E. Struck.
   F. Weathered.
   G. V-shaped.
   H. Beaded.
8. Common bond.

1.

DIRECTIONS:
Complete the wall framing in each of the problems below applying the specific requirements noted.
A. Frame a rough opening which is 52" wide by 40" high. Use a solid (2" x 12") header. Label all framing members and dimension R.O. and height from floor to top of the opening.
B. In these two problems, complete the plan view framing for a corner formed with three full studs (left) and a wall intersecting at a stud (right).

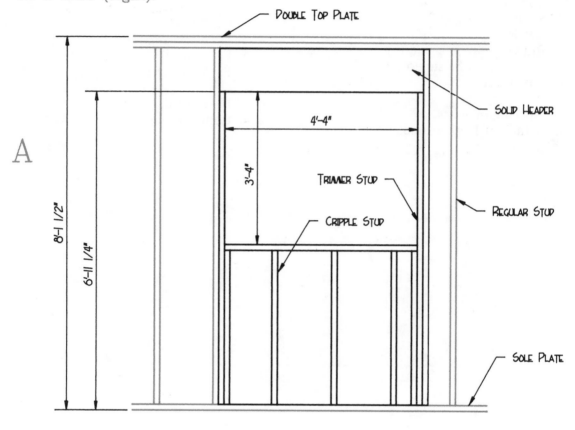

DOUBLE TOP PLATE

SOLID HEADER

4'-4"

TRIMMER STUD

REGULAR STUD

CRIPPLE STUD

3'-4"

8'-1 1/2"

6'-11 1/4"

A

SOLE PLATE

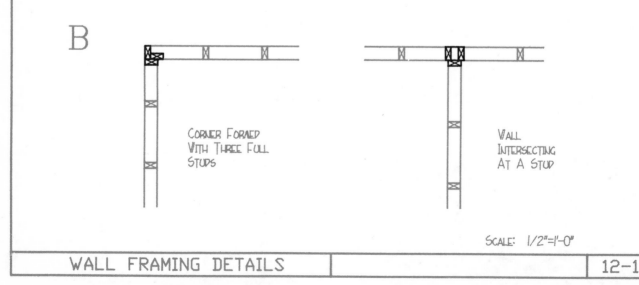

B

CORNER FORMED
WITH THREE FULL
STUDS

WALL
INTERSECTING
AT A STUD

SCALE: 1/2"=1'-0"

WALL FRAMING DETAILS

12-1

DIRECTIONS:
Draw a large scale symbol (elevation view at 1/2"=1'-0") for each of the exterior masonry walls indicated below. Fill the space.

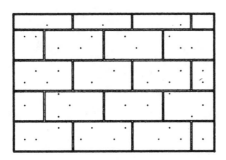

Concrete Block

Brick

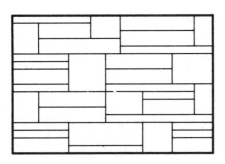

Ashlar Stone

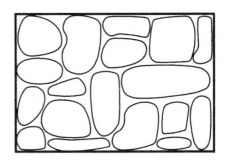

Random Rubble Stone

Stucco

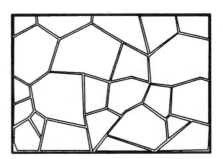

Uncoursed Cobweb

Scale: 1/2"=1'-0"

MASONRY WALL SYMBOLS   12-2

Chapter 12—Exam
WALL AND CEILING CONSTRUCTION

Name _____

Period _____ Date _____ Score _____

TRUE—FALSE
Circle T if the statement is true or F if the statement is false.

T   F   1. The recommended moisture content of construction lumber is 5-15 percent.

T   F   2. Frame wall construction usually begins with the sole plate.

T   F   3. A cripple wall stud may be found under a window opening.

T   F   4. Corner bracing on frame walls is required by most codes.

T   F   5. Trussed headers are generally required for openings wider than 8'-0".

MULTIPLE CHOICE
Choose the answer that correctly completes the statement. Write the corresponding letter in the space provided.

_____ 1. Wall framing lumber is generally Douglas fir, hemlock, spruce, larch, or _____.
A. oak
B. beech
C. Southern yellow pine
D. hickory

_____ 2. The distance from the top of the subfloor to the bottom of the ceiling joists is usually _____.
A. 7'-6"
B. 8'-0"
C. 8'-1 1/2"
D. 8'-6"

_____ 3. The rough opening height of most doors in frame wall construction is _____.
A. 6'-6"
B. 6'-8"
C. 6'-10"
D. 7'-0"

_____ 4. A(n) _____ must be provided in the ceiling to afford entry to the attic.
A. stairway
B. access hole
C. door
D. None of the above

_____ 5. Walls which require more than one thickness of masonry must be _____ together.
A. welded
B. cemented
C. nailed
D. bonded

_____ 6. Solid masonry walls for residential construction are usually _____ inches thick.
A. 4
B. 6
C. 8
D. 10

_____ 7. The term _____ is commonly used to indicate that a less desirable or inexpensive material has been covered up with some type of facing material.
   A. veneer
   B. covering
   C. siding
   D. facing

SHORT ANSWER

Answer the following questions using short answers.

1. Identify the three common types of residential wall construction.

   A. _____

   B. _____

   C. _____

2. Name the basic parts of a conventional frame wall.

   A. _____

   B. _____

   C. _____

   D. _____

   E. _____

3. The size of ceiling joists required is dependent upon what five items?

   A. _____

   B. _____

   C. _____

   D. _____

   E. _____

4. List the two basic types of stonework.

   A. _____

   B. _____

5. List the six brick positions by name.

   A. _____

   B. _____

   C. _____

   D. _____

   E. _____

   F. _____

6. Identify the two types of brick used for wall construction.

   A. _____

   B. _____

7. List eight types of mortar joints that are used in masonry construction.

   A. _____

   B. _____

   C. _____

   D. _____

   E. _____

   F. _____

   G. _____

   H. _____

8. What is the most popular bond used in solid masonry walls?

   _____

13
CHAPTER
Doors and Windows

■ OBJECTIVES

After studying this chapter, the student will be able to:
☐ Recognize the functions that doors and windows perform.
☐ Compare the types of doors used in a residential dwelling.
☐ Draw proper door and window symbols on a typical floor plan.
☐ Interpret the information shown in a window or door detail.

■ DISPLAYS

1. Door and Window Cut-aways. Assemble a collection of door and window cut-away models from door and window manufacturers. Display these models in the classroom.
2. Door and Window Literature. Create a bulletin board display using door and window literature to illustrate products that are available.
3. Windows Add to the Design. Arrange several photos of residential structures that make good design use of modern windows.

■ INSTRUCTIONAL MATERIALS

Text: Pages 223-252
Review Questions, Suggested Activities
Workbook: Pages 107-116
Review Questions, Problems/Activities
Teacher's Resource Guide:
Chapter 13 — Teaching Strategy
Chapter 13 — Exam

■ TEACHING STRATEGY

- Prepare Display #1.
- Review chapter objectives.

- Present interior and exterior doors. Draw typical door symbols on the chalkboard.
- Prepare Display #2.
- Assign workbook Problem 13-1.
- Discuss door schedules.
- Assign workbook Problem 13-3.
- Present windows. Illustrate typical window symbols on the chalkboard.
- Assign workbook Problem 13-2.
- Discuss window schedules.
- Prepare Display #3.
- Assign one or more of the Suggested Activities in the text.
- Chapter Review
  - Assign Review Questions in the text. Discuss the correct answers.
  - Assign Review Questions in the workbook. Have students check their own answers.
  - Make transparencies of the solutions to Problem/Activities 13-1 and 13-2 and use for review.
- Evaluation
  - Administer the Chapter 13 — Exam. Correct exam and return.
  - Return graded problems with comments.

■ ANSWERS TO REVIEW QUESTIONS, TEXT
Page 252

1. a. Keep out the elements.
   b. Add decoration.
   c. Emphasize design.
   d. Admit light and ventilation.
   e. Expand visibility.
2. a. Flush.   f. Double-action.
   b. Panel.   g. Accordion.
   c. Bi-fold.   h. Dutch.
   d. Sliding.   i. French.
   e. Pocket.
3. 1 3/8

4. rails, stiles.
5. for closet doors.
6. 6'-8".
7. pocket
8. double-action
9. a. They are thicker.
   b. They are solid core.
10. 3'-0"
11. a. Overhead sectional.
    b. One-piece overhead.
12. jamb, sill, head.
13. To shed water.
14. 20
15. Picture window or fixed window.
16. a. Double-hung.   e. Hopper.
    b. Horizontal slider.   f. Jalousie.
    c. Casement.   g. Bay or bow.
    d. Awning.   h. Picture.
17. muntins.
18. The rough framed space in a wall required to install the window.
19. Casement.
20. hopper
21. window

■ ANSWERS TO REVIEW QUESTIONS, WORKBOOK

PART I: MULTIPLE CHOICE

1. D. All of the above.
2. A. 1 in.
3. A. Used frequently for large openings.
4. B. Hinged to swing through an arc of 180 degrees.
5. D. All of the above.
6. C. Usually have wood or aluminum frames.
7. B. Composed of two side jambs and a head jamb across the top.
8. C. Glass area which is 20 percent of the floor area should provide adequate natural light.
9. D. All of the above.
10. A. Different specifications from manufacturer to manufacturer.
11. C. Rough opening.
12. D. All of the above.
13. A. Dashed line.
14. B. Hopper windows are more efficient when placed low on the wall because they direct air upward.
15. C. Be large fixed glass units used with other window types.
16. D. Bay.
17. C. 45.
18. B. 4 to 7.
19. A. They can produce striking architectural effects.

PART II: COMPLETION

1. birch
2. kitchens
3. fabric
4. Dutch
5. 6'-8"
6. oak
7. motor
8. manufacturer's
9. casing.
10. sill
11. section
12. placement
13. wide
14. narrow
15. high
16. larger.
17. metal
18. friction
19. basic
20. jalousie
21. single
22. shaped
23. 90
24. rectangular

PART III: SHORT ANSWER/LISTING

1. A. Wood.
   B. Glass.
   C. Metal.
2. An advantage is that they require no wall space along the wall when open. Two disadvantages include being difficult to operate and presenting problems if outlets or cabinets are planned for the wall space outside the pocket cavity.
3. Between rooms or as an opening to a patio or terrace.
4. Interior doors are usually hollow core, while exterior doors are usually solid. Exterior doors are usually thicker than interior doors and are more likely to have glass panels to provide visibility.
5. A. Overhead sectional garage door.
   B. One-piece overhead door.
6. A door schedule would be found with the floor plan, the elevations, or in the details section.
7. The doorjamb supports the door.
8. To provide space for the jambs as well as leveling and squaring.
9. A. Wood.
   B. Metal.
   C. Concrete.
   D. Stone.
10. A. Large areas of glass provide clear view without obstructions.
    B. Use thin horizontal and vertical divisions in the window to curtail obstruction.
    C. Consider the view as well as room arrange-

ment and furniture when planning the sill height.
11. Size, placement, and type should be considered to add to the exterior appearance.
12. Sash opening is the size of the opening inside the frame or outside dimensions of the sash.
13. When several windows are placed together to form a unit.
14. A. Quarter circles.
    B. Half circles.
    C. Ellipses.
    D. Full circle.
15. A. Type of window.
    B. Size.
    C. Identifying symbol.
    D. Manufacturer's number.
    E. Installation.

PART IV: MATCHING

1. L. Stiles.
2. K. Rails.
3. J. Prehung doors.
4. C. Drip cap.
5. B. Brick mold.
6. D. Double-hung.
7. I. Muntins.
8. H. Mullins.
9. F. Glass size.
10. G. Glider.
11. A. Awning.
12. E. Fixed.

PART V: PROBLEMS/ACTIVITIES

1. Solution on page 146.
2. Solution on page 147.
3. Solution on page 148.

■ ANSWERS TO CHAPTER 13—EXAM

TRUE—FALSE

1. T	4. F
2. T	5. F
3. T	6. T

MULTIPLE CHOICE

1. C	8. D
2. C	9. A
3. A	10. B
4. C	11. D
5. B	12. C
6. A	13. B
7. C	

SHORT ANSWER

1. A. Shield an opening from the elements.
   B. Add decoration.
   C. Emphasize the overall design.
   D. Provide light and ventilation.
   E. Expand visibility.
2. A. Interior.
   B. Exterior.
3. A. Flush.
   B. Panel.
   C. Bi-fold.
   D. Sliding.
   E. Pocket.
   F. Double-action.
   G. Accordion.
   H. Dutch.
   I. French.
4. A. Overhead sectional door.
   B. One-piece overhead door.
5. A. Sliding windows.
   B. Swinging windows.
   C. Fixed windows.
6. A. Double-hung windows.
   B. Horizontal sliding windows.
7. A. Double-hung.
   B. Casement.
   C. Fixed panels.
8. A. Quarter circles.
   B. Half circles.
   C. Ellipses.
   D. Full circles.
9. To admit light into areas of the structure that receive little or no natural light.
10. A. Symbol.
    B. Quantity.
    C. Type.
    D. Rough opening.
    E. Sash size.
    F. Manufacturer number.
    G. Remarks.

1.

DIRECTIONS:
Draw a Plan View symbol for each of the door types specified below.

Flush or Panel Door

Bi-Fold Doors

Dutch Door

Accordion Door

Pocket Door

Sliding (Bi-Pass) Doors

Double-Action Door

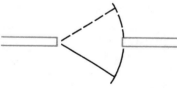

French Doors

Exterior Panel Door

Glass Sliding Door

Garage Door

Scale: 1/4"=1'-0"

PLAN VIEW DOOR SYMBOLS   13-1

DIRECTIONS:
Draw a Plan View symbol for each of the window types specified below.

Double Hung Window

Awning Window

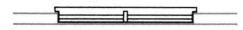

Casement Window (2 Sash)

Fixed Window

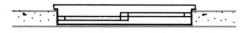

Horizontal Sliding Window

Hopper Window

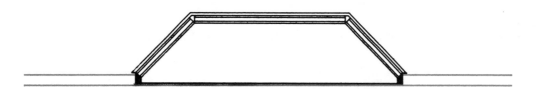

Double Hung 45° Bay Window

Five Unit Casement Bow Window

Scale: 1/4"=1'-0"

PLAN VIEW WINDOW SYMBOLS | | 13-2

3.

DIRECTIONS:
Label the parts indicated on the exterior door details below.

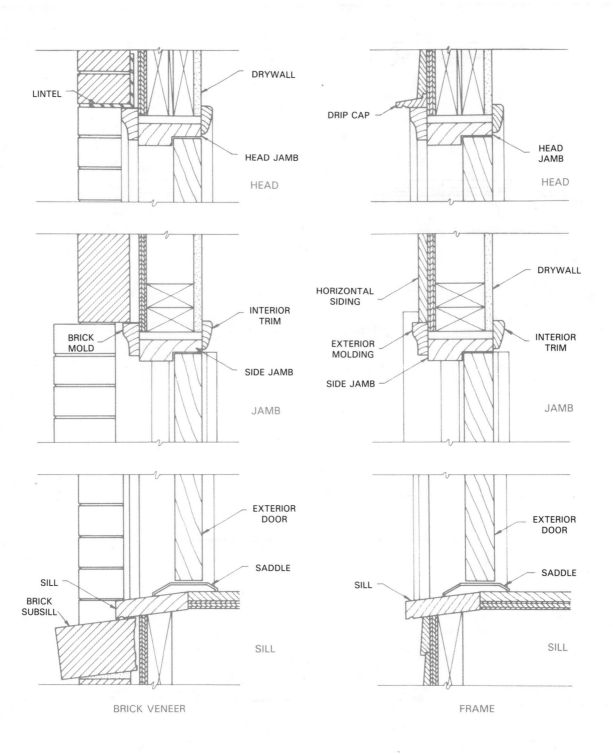

EXTERIOR DOOR DETAIL | 13-3

Chapter 13—Exam
DOORS AND WINDOWS

Name _____

Period _____ **Date** _____ **Score** _____

TRUE—FALSE
Circle T if the statement is true or F if the statement is false.

T   F   1. A panel door has a heavy frame around the outside with cross members.

T   F   2. The pocket door is a variation of the sliding door.

T   F   3. The chief advantage of the pocket door is that it does not require any space along the wall when open.

T   F   4. The accordion door is made of several large panels.

T   F   5. An exterior flush door is usually 6'-6" high.

T   F   6. One large window opening produces less contrast in brightness than several smaller openings.

MULTIPLE CHOICE
Choose the answer that correctly completes the statement. Write the corresponding letter in the space provided.

_____   1. Doors which are smooth on both sides and usually made of wood are called _____ doors.
   A. French
   B. panel
   C. flush
   D. accordion

_____   2. A _____ door has two parts to form the door.
   A. bi-fold
   B. Dutch
   C. All of the above
   D. None of the above

_____   3. A door used when a wide opening exists is a _____ door.
   A. sliding
   B. pocket
   C. French
   D. double-action

_____   4. _____ doors are hinged in such a way that they may swing through an arc of 180 degrees.
   A. Accordion
   B. Dutch
   C. Double-action
   D. Bi-pass

_____   5. A _____ door is composed of two parts—an upper and a lower half.
   A. French
   B. Dutch
   C. double-action
   D. bi-fold

_____ 6. _____ style doors are panel doors with glass panels.
   A. French
   B. Dutch
   C. Bi-fold
   D. Accordion

_____ 7. Exterior doors are generally _____ wide.
   A. 2'-6"
   B. 2'-10"
   C. 3'-0"
   D. 3'-6"

_____ 8. Which of the following is not a standard garage door size?
   A. 6'-6" h x 8'-0" w
   B. 8'-0" h x 8'-0" w
   C. 7'-0" h x 10'-0" w
   D. 8'-0" h x 9'-0" w

_____ 9. A more evenly lighted room will result if the glass area is at least _____ percent of the floor area of the room.
   A. 20
   B. 25
   C. 30
   D. 35

_____ 10. Double-hung windows have two _____.
   A. sills
   B. sashes
   C. muntins
   D. unit sizes

_____ 11. Horizontal sliding windows are also called _____.
   A. casements
   B. walk-throughs
   C. picture windows
   D. glider windows

_____ 12. A _____ window may be opened or closed by using a crank, or push bar on the frame, or handle on the sash.
   A. double-hung
   B. horizontal sliding
   C. casement
   D. hopper

_____ 13. The _____ window directs air upward and should be placed toward the bottom of a wall for best ventilation.
   A. awning
   B. hopper
   C. jalousie
   D. casement

Name _____

SHORT ANSWER
Answer the following questions using short answers.

1. List five functions that windows perform in a residential structure.

   A. _____

   B. _____

   C. _____

   D. _____

   E. _____

2. Name the two general classifications of doors.

   A. _____

   B. _____

3. List nine types of interior doors.

   A. _____

   B. _____

   C. _____

   D. _____

   E. _____

   F. _____

   G. _____

   H. _____

   I. _____

4. Identify the two most common types of garage doors.

   A. _____

   B. _____

5. List the three basic types of windows typically used in residential construction.

   A. _____

   B. _____

   C. _____

6. List the two most common types of sliding windows.

   A. _____

   B. _____

7. Identify three types of windows that are frequently used for bay and bow windows.

   A. _____

   B. _____

   C. _____

8. What four types of circle top windows are generally available?

   A. _____

   B. _____

   C. _____

   D. _____

9. Why are skylights and clerestory windows generally used?

   _____

   _____

10. Identify the categories usually included on a window schedule.

    A. _____

    B. _____

    C. _____

    D. _____

    E. _____

    F. _____

    G. _____

14
CHAPTER
Stairs

■ OBJECTIVES

After studying this chapter, the student will be able to:
- ☐ Define common stair terminology.
- ☐ Discuss the appropriate use of the various stair designs.
- ☐ Design a stairway for a residential structure.
- ☐ Draw structural details for a main stairs.
- ☐ Perform stair calculations for a residential stairway.

■ DISPLAYS

1. Stairs, Stairs, Stairs. Arrange a bulletin board display from photos of well-designed stairs to create interest in the subject.
2. Stair Models. Display scale models of stairs built by students for Suggested Activity #5 in the text.
3. Student Work. Put examples of outstanding student work on the bulletin board. Select examples from the workbook assignments.
4. Stair Materials. Display stair materials—tread, riser, stringer, handrail, etc. Label each part.

■ INSTRUCTIONAL MATERIALS

Text: Pages 253-264
　　Review Questions, Suggested Activities
Workbook: Pages 117-124
　　Review Questions, Problems/Activities
Teacher's Resource Guide:
　　Chapter 14—Teaching Strategy
　　Chapter 14—Exam

■ TEACHING STRATEGY

- Prepare Display #1.
- Review chapter objectives.
- Present types of stairs. Compare and contrast the various types.
- Prepare Display #2.
- Assign workbook Problem 14-1.
- Discuss stair design.
- Prepare Display #3.
- Present stair calculations and drawing procedures.
- Prepare Display #4.
- Assign workbook Problem 14-2.
- Assign one or more of the Suggested Activities in the text.
- Chapter Review
  - Assign Review Questions in the text. Discuss the correct answers.
  - Assign Review Questions in the workbook. Have students check their own answers.
  - Make a transparency of the solution to Problem/Activity 14-1 and use for review.
- Evaluation
  - Administer the Chapter 14—Exam. Correct the exam and return.
  - Return graded problems with comments.

■ ANSWERS TO REVIEW QUESTIONS, TEXT Pages 262-264

1. main
2. a. Straight run.　　　　d. U stairs.
   b. L stairs.　　　　　　e. Winder.
   c. Double-L stairs.　　f. Spiral.
3. Double-L.
4. winder
6. balusters.
7. enclosed or closed, housed, or box
8. 6'-6".
9. plain, housed
10. nosing.
11. open

12. plain
13. The distance from the top surface of one tread to the top surface of the next.
14. The horizontal distance from the face of one riser to the face of the next.
15. total rise.
16. total run.
17. 30, 35
18. 3'-0".
19. oak.
20. 10 1/2, 7 1/4.

■ ANSWERS TO REVIEW QUESTIONS, WORKBOOK

PART I: MATCHING

1. L. Stairway.
2. N. Straight run.
3. C. L.
4. S. U.
5. T. Winder.
6. B. Circular.
7. A. Balusters.
8. D. Landing.
9. E. Newel.
10. F. Nosing.
11. G. Open.
12. H. Plain stringer.
13. I. Rise.
14. J. Riser.
15. K. Run.
16. M. Stairwell.
17. O. Stringer.
18. P. Total rise.
19. Q. Total run.
20. R. Tread.

PART II: COMPLETION

1. safety
2. construction
3. narrow
4. spiral
5. Circular
6. carriage.
7. 3'-0"
8. stringer.
9. nails
10. oak
11. 10 1/2

PART III: SHORT ANSWER/LISTING

1. Long L.
2. The width of the "pie-shaped" steps at midpoint should be the same width as the regular steps.
3. A. The stairs should support the required weight.
   B. They should be wide enough to provide ease of passage and movement of furniture.
   C. The slope of the stairs should be between 30 and 35 degrees.
4. Place the third stringer at midpoint between the outside stringers and under the treads and risers.
5. The advantages are their sturdiness and low construction cost. Disadvantages include an unfinished appearance and they tend to squeak.
6. The stringers normally have 1/2 in. deep routed grooves to hold the treads and risers in place. Wedges are driven into the grooves to keep the treads and risers in place.
7. The ideal riser height is 7 to 7 5/8 in.
8. A. The slope of the stairs (rise-run ratio) should be between 30 and 35 degrees.
   B. The sum of two risers and one tread should equal 25 in.
   C. The product of the riser height multiplied by the tread should equal approximately 75 in.
   D. The sum of one riser and one tread should equal 17 to 18 in.
9. The upper floor serves as the top tread.
10. A. Straight run.
    B. L stairs.
    C. Double-L stairs.
    D. U stairs.
    E. Winder stairs.
    F. Spiral or circular stairs.
11. A. Baluster.
    B. Handrail.
    C. Newel.
    Total run = 94.5 in.
    Number of risers = 10.
    Riser height = 7.2 in.
    Number of treads = 9.
    Run of a step = 10 1/2 in.

PART IV: MULTIPLE CHOICE

1. D. All of the above.
2. B. Straight run.
3. C. Trapezoid.
4. D. All of the above.
5. B. Service stairs.
6. D. All of the above.
7. C. 1 1/6 in.
8. A. 30 in. along the incline and 34 in. at the landing.
9. B. 6'-6".

PART V: PROBLEMS/ACTIVITIES

1. Solution on page 156.
2. Solution on page 157.

■ ANSWERS TO CHAPTER 14—EXAM

TRUE—FALSE

1. T
2. F
3. T
4. T
5. T

MULTIPLE CHOICE

1. B
2. C
3. D
4. A
5. C
6. B
7. D

MATCHING

1. H
2. C
3. J
4. A
5. E
6. B
7. I
8. G
9. L
10. F
11. D
12. K
13. E
14. A
15. G
16. B
17. D
18. F
19. C

SHORT ANSWER

1. A. Straight run stairs.
   B. L stairs.
   C. Double-L stairs.
   D. U stairs.
   E. Winder stairs.
   F. Spiral stairs.
   Also: Circular stairs.
2. total rise.
3. total run.
4. 7 1/4" to 10 1/2".
5. A. 34".
   B. 30".
6. 14

1.

DIRECTIONS:

Problem A——Draw the Plan View and Elevation in Section of a plain stringer stairs which meet the following specifications: width = 36", tread width = 11 1/2", riser height = 7 1/4", nosing = 1", stringer is 2" x 12", number of risers is 6, and the total run is 52.5".

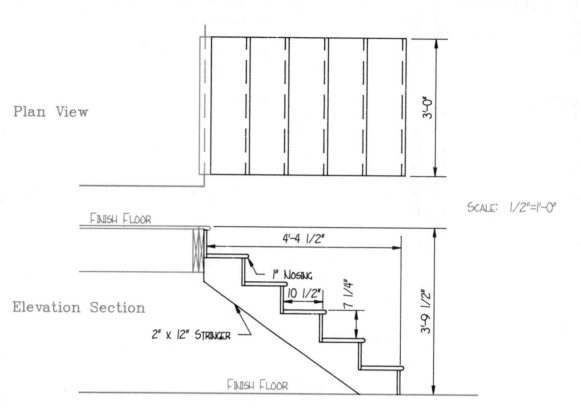

Plan View

SCALE: 1/2"=1'-0"

Elevation Section

Problem B——Draw a detail (Scale: 1"=1'-0") of a housed stringer stairs showing 5/4" oak treads, 1" pine risers, 2" x 12" vertical grain fir stringers, and wedges. Label and show dimensions.

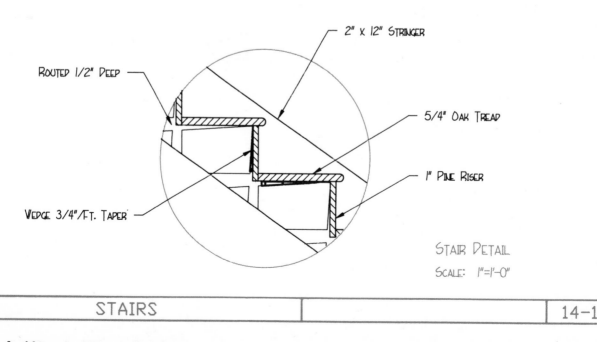

STAIR DETAIL

SCALE: 1"=1'-0"

| STAIRS | | 14-1 |

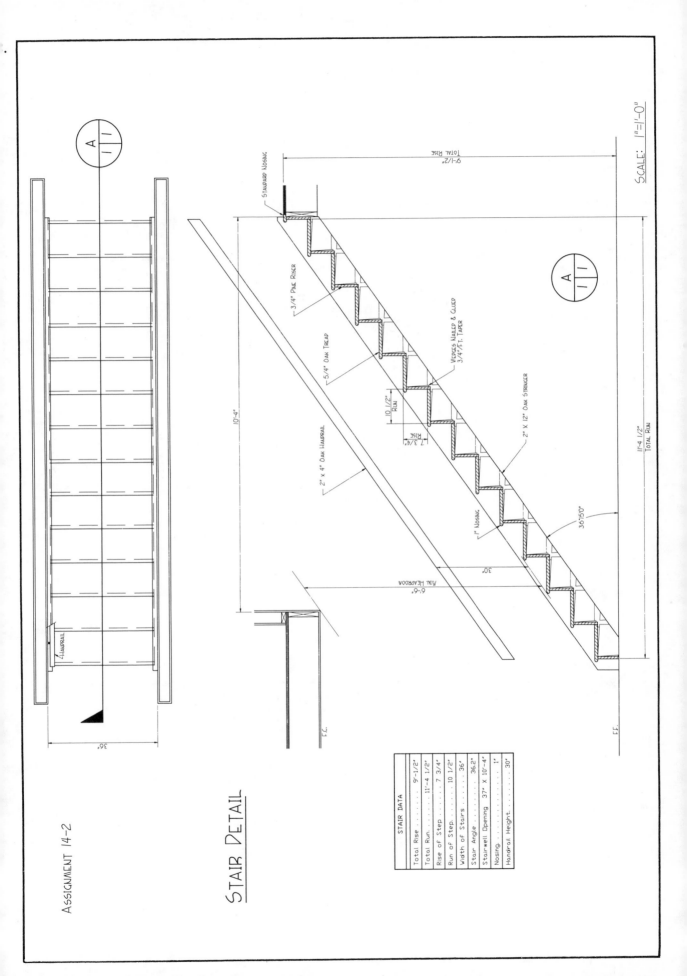

ASSIGNMENT 14-2

STAIR DETAIL

SCALE: 1"=1'-0"

Standard Nosing

Total Rise
9'-1/2"

3/4" Pine Riser

5/4" Oak Tread

Wedges Nailed & Glued
3/4"/Ft. Taper

10 1/2"
Run

2" x 12" Oak Stringer

10'-4"

7 3/4"
Rise

2" x 4" Oak Handrail

1" Nosing

36°50'

Min. Headroom
6'-9"

30"

11'-4 1/2"
Total Run

Handrail

36"

STAIR DATA	
Total Rise	9'-1/2"
Total Run	11'-4 1/2"
Rise of Step	7 3/4"
Run of Step	10 1/2"
Width of Stairs	36"
Stair Angle	36.2°
Stairwell Opening	37" X 10'-4"
Nosing	1"
Handrail Height	30"

Chapter 14—Exam
STAIRS

Name _____

Period _____ **Date** _____ **Score** _____

TRUE—FALSE
Circle T if the statement is true or F if the statement is false.

T   F   1. Prime considerations in stair design should be easy ascent or descent and safety.

T   F   2. Double-L stairs require one 90° turn along the flight.

T   F   3. There are two types of U stairs.

T   F   4. Two stringers are usually sufficient to support a 3 foot wide stairs.

T   F   5. Wedges are generally used with housed stringer stairs.

MULTIPLE CHOICE
Choose the answer that correctly completes the statement. Write the corresponding letter in the space provided.

_____ 1. _____ stairs are usually made of hardwoods such as oak, maple, or birch.
     A. Service
     B. Main
     C. Side
     D. Open stringer

_____ 2. The type of stairs which has one landing at some point along the flight of steps is a(n) _____.
     A. straight run stairs
     B. winder stairs
     C. L stairs
     D. U stairs

_____ 3. Winder stairs have _____ steps which are substituted for a landing.
     A. trapezoid
     B. rectangular
     C. square
     D. pie-shaped

_____ 4. Most spiral stairs are made from _____.
     A. steel
     B. wood
     C. stone
     D. aluminum

_____ 5. A well-designed set of main stairs should have an angle of _____ degrees.
     A. 15-20
     B. 20-30
     C. 30-35
     D. 35-40

_____ 6. The main supporting members of the stairs are the _____.
     A. handrails
     B. stringers
     C. steps
     D. balusters

_____ 7. Plain stringers are generally cut from _____ straight-grain fir.
                  A. 2" x 4"
                  B. 2" x 6"
                  C. 2" x 8"
                  D. 2" x 12"

MATCHING
Select the answer that correctly matches each term. Place your answer in the space provided.

_____ 1. Balusters

_____ 2. Enclosed stairs

_____ 3. Headroom

_____ 4. Housed stringer

_____ 5. Newel

_____ 6. Nosing

_____ 7. Open stairs

_____ 8. Plain stringer

_____ 9. Rise

_____ 10. Riser

_____ 11. Run

_____ 12. Tread

A. A stringer which has been routed to receive the treads and risers.
B. The routed projection of the tread which extends past the face of the riser.
C. Stairs which have a wall on both sides.
D. The distance from the face of one riser to the face of the next.
E. The main posts of the handrail at the top, bottom, or at points where the stairs change directions.
F. The vertical face of a step.
G. A stringer which has been cut or notched to fit the profile of the stairs.
H. Vertical members which support the handrail on open stairs.
I. Stairs which have no wall on one or both sides.
J. The shortest clear vertical distance measured between the nosing of the treads and the ceiling.
K. The horizontal member of each step.
L. The distance from the top surface of one tread to the top surface of the next tread.

_____ 13. Rise of a step

_____ 14. Run of a step

_____ 15. Total Rise

_____ 16. Total Run

_____ 17. Nosing

_____ 18. Standard tread width

_____ 19. Tread thickness

A. 10.5".
B. 12'-3".
C. 1 1/16".
D. 1".
E. 7.15".
F. 11 1/2".
G. 8'-11 1/4".

Name _____

SHORT ANSWER

Answer the following questions using short answers.

1. List the six general types of stairs commonly used in residential construction.

   A. _____

   B. _____

   C. _____

   D. _____

   E. _____

   F. _____

   Also: _____

2. The total floor-to-floor vertical height of the stairs is the definition of _____.

3. The total horizontal length of the stairs is the definition of _____.

4. What is the ideal ratio of rise to run for a stair step?

   _____

5. What are the standard heights of a handrail at a landing (A) and along the stairs (B)?

   A. _____

   B. _____

6. A stair that has 15 risers will have _____ treads.

Fireplaces and Chimneys

■ OBJECTIVES

After studying this chapter, the student will be able to:
- ☐ Compare the various types of fireplaces appropriate for a modern residence.
- ☐ Identify the parts of a standard masonry fireplace and chimney.
- ☐ Apply the appropriate principles to design a typical fireplace.
- ☐ Use a fireplace design data chart.
- ☐ Recognize the difference between a radiant and circulating stove.

■ DISPLAYS

1. Fireplace Styles. Collect photos of various styles of fireplaces. Create a bulletin board arrangement using the photos.
2. Fireplace Materials and Parts. Display typical fireplace materials and parts. Examples might include a damper, firebrick, ash dump, flue liner, etc.
3. Fireplace Models. Display fireplace models built by students for Suggested Activity #2 in text.

■ INSTRUCTIONAL MATERIALS

Text: Pages 265-282
  Review Questions, Suggested Activities
Workbook: Pages 125-133
  Review Questions, Problems/Activities
Teacher's Resource Guide:
  Chapter 15 — Teaching Strategy
  Chapter 15 — Exam

■ TEACHING STRATEGY

- Prepare Display #1.
- Review chapter objectives.
- Discuss fireplace design considerations.
- Present hearth and fire chamber and damper and smoke shelf.
- Prepare Display #2.
- Assign workbook Problem 15-1.
- Discuss framing around the fireplace and chimney.
- Assign Suggested Activity #2 in the text.
- Prepare Display #3.
- Present fireplace specifications for other designs.
- Discuss prefabricated metal fireplaces and stoves.
- Review fireplace/chimney terms.
- Assign one or more of the remaining Suggested Activities in the text.
- Chapter Review
  - Assign Review Questions in the text. Discuss the correct answers.
  - Assign Review Questions in the workbook. Have students check their own answers.
- Evaluation
  - Administer the Chapter 15 — Exam. Correct the exam and return.
  - Return graded problems with comments.

■ ANSWERS TO REVIEW QUESTIONS, TEXT Pages 281-282

1. a. Single-face.   d. Three-face.
   b. Two-face opposite. e. Prefabricated metal.
   c. Two-face adjacent.
2. hearth.
3. the fireplace will smoke.
4. it is designed to circulate the air better.
5. smoke shelf
6. smoke chamber.
7. 1/10
8. increase
9. 2

10. A warmer chimney will work better.
11. 2
12. shed water from the chimney roof area.
13. angle steel.
14. single-face fireplace.
15. two-face adjacent fireplace.
16. prefabricated metal.
17. local
18. a. Radiant.
    b. Circulating.
19. a. Baffles.
    b. Long smoke paths.
    c. Heat exchange devices.

■ ANSWERS TO REVIEW QUESTIONS, WORKBOOK

PART I: COMPLETION

1. focal
2. wood
3. noncombustible
4. deep.
5. shallow.
6. cleanout.
7. wall
8. throat.
9. damper
10. chimney.
11. flue
12. draft
13. large, small.
14. warm
15. free-standing
16. 2
17. noncombustible
18. decreases
19. saddle
20. efficiently
21. three-way
22. building
23. Circulating
24. 35
25. 2

PART II: MULTIPLE CHOICE

1. C. 16 in.
2. A. 8 in.
3. B. Very efficient.
4. D. All of the above.
5. C. Basically a pyramid with the back side usually vertical.
6. A. Clay.
7. C. 4 in.
8. A. 8 in.
9. B. 16 x 16.
10. A. 2 ft.
11. D. Angle steel.

12. B. Opens on the front and either left or right sides.
13. C. A and B.
14. C. Heat exchange devices.
15. A. 11 1/2 x 11 1/2 in.

PART III: SHORT ANSWER/LISTING

1. A. Single face.
   B. Two-face opposite.
   C. Two-face adjacent.
   D. Three-face.
   E. Prefabricated metal.
2. Firebrick.
3. Fireclay is a bonding agent between the firebrick in the fire chamber of a fireplace.
4. It must be designed properly so that smoke and hot gases will go into the throat and up the chimney.
5. A. Firebox.
   B. Heating chamber.
   C. Throat.
   D. Damper.
   E. Smoke shelf.
   F. Smoke chamber.
6. Cool air is drawn into the chamber where it is heated and then returned through registers located high on the fireplace.
7. The smoke shelf causes cold air flowing down the chimney to be deflected upward into the rising warm air.
8. Smoke chambers are usually constructed of masonry such as brick.
9. Select a flue which has at least 1/10 the sectional area of the fireplace opening.
10. A. When the height of the flue is less than 14 ft.
    B. When the flue is sheltered by trees and buildings.
11. Yes, a chimney may have several flues.
12. A. Gas furnace.
    B. Gas water heater.
    C. Incinerator.
    D. Each fireplace.
13. A. Double headers.
    B. Trimmers.
14. A saddle or cricket should be built on the high side of the chimney to shed water. Flashing can be placed around the chimney.
15. They are placed in existing fireplaces to circulate warmed air.
16. Stoves use wood and coal to generate heat.
17. Radiant stoves pass heat through the air with no assistance. Circulating stoves use radiation and air flow to distribute heat.
18. Circulating.
19. A. Simple box stoves.
    B. Franklin stoves.
    C. Potbelly stoves.
    D. Some parlor stoves.

20. Cover the opening with a piece of sheet metal.
21. Increasing the height of the chimney increases the agent.
22. 29 in.

PART IV: MATCHING

1. F. Hearth.
2. D. Fireclay.
3. C. Ash dump.
4. A. Ash chamber.
5. B. Damper.
6. K. Smoke shelf.
7. J. Smoke chamber.
8. E. Flue.
9. H. Saddle.
10. G. Lintel.
11. I. Single-face.
12. O. Two-face (opposite).
13. N. Two-face (adjacent).
14. M. Three-face.
15. L. Stove.

PART V: PROBLEMS/ACTIVITIES

1. Solution on page 166.
2. A. 40"   H. 48"
   B. 29"   I. 20"
   C. 16"   J. 29"
   D. 27"   K. 16"
   E. 14"   L. 12"
   F. 21"   M. 12"
   G. 8 3/4"
3. Solution on page 167.

■ ANSWERS TO CHAPTER 15—EXAM

TRUE—FALSE

1. T   4. F
2. T   5. T
3. T   6. T

MULTIPLE CHOICE

1. C   5. A
2. B   6. C
3. D   7. B
4. C

SHORT ANSWER

1. A. Single-face.
   B. Two-face (opposite).
   C. Two-face (adjacent).
   D. Three-face.
   E. Wall-hung prefabricated.
   F. Free-standing prefabricated.
2. Little heat will be reflected out into the room.
3. The fireplace is likely to smoke.
4. Below the fireplace floor.
5. Choose a flue which is at least 1/10th the cross-sectional area of the fireplace opening.
6. It increases the draft.
7. 2 feet.
8. A. Fireplace.
   B. Gas furnace.
   C. Gas water heater.
   D. Incinerator.
9. A. Radiant stoves.
   B. Circulating stoves.

2.

DIRECTIONS:
Study the pictorial section of a fireplace and chimney below and identify each of the materials, parts, etc. indicated by the leaders. Use these specific notes:

> Ash pit
> Ash dump
> Clean—out door
> Damper
> Double header
> Face brick
> Fire brick
> Floor joist

> Smoke chamber
> Smoke shelf
> Steel lintel
> Stone hearth
> 4" Reinforced concrete inner hearth
> Minimum thickness of walls of fire chamber is 8"
> Flue lining

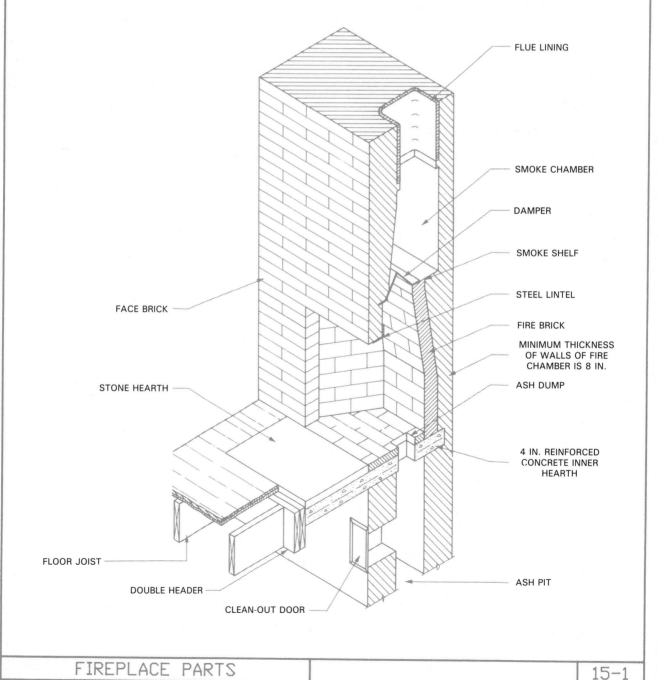

FLUE LINING

SMOKE CHAMBER

DAMPER

SMOKE SHELF

STEEL LINTEL

FIRE BRICK

MINIMUM THICKNESS OF WALLS OF FIRE CHAMBER IS 8 IN.

ASH DUMP

4 IN. REINFORCED CONCRETE INNER HEARTH

ASH PIT

FACE BRICK

STONE HEARTH

FLOOR JOIST

DOUBLE HEADER

CLEAN-OUT DOOR

FIREPLACE PARTS   15—1

FIREPLACE/CHIMNEY
DETAIL

ASSIGNMENT 15-3

PLAN VIEW

7'-0"
5'-0"
4'-4"
2'-4"
12" TYP.
23"
36"
9"
FIREBRICK
SANDSTONE

FRONT ELEVATION

6"
2'-0"
6'-0 1/2"
8'-0"
2'-11 1/8"
12"
FLASHING
CAST IRON DAMPER
C.O.

PROFILE SECTION

4" CONCRETE CAP
FLASHING
12"
9"
21"
14"
18"
2'-3"
6"
2'-5"
12"X12" C.O.
WIRE MESH

SCALE: 1/2"=1'-0"

Chapter 15—Exam
FIREPLACES AND CHIMNEYS

Name _____

Period _____ **Date** _____ **Score** _____

TRUE—FALSE
Circle T if the statement is true or F if the statement is false.

T   F   1. The function of the outer hearth is to protect the floor from sparks.

T   F   2. Fireclay is a fire-resistant mortar.

T   F   3. The smoke chamber is the area just above the smoke shelf and damper.

T   F   4. Flue liners are available in square and rectangular shapes only.

T   F   5. Each flue requires at least 4" of brick on all sides.

T   F   6. The chimney is a free-standing structure.

MULTIPLE CHOICE
Choose the answer that correctly completes the statement. Write the corresponding letter in the space provided.

_____   1. The hearth should extend at least _____ inches in front of the fireplace.
      A. 8
      B. 12
      C. 16
      D. 20

_____   2. A hearth should be constructed from a _____ material.
      A. sturdy
      B. noncombustible
      C. cementitious
      D. fireclay

_____   3. Every modern fireplace should have a _____ to regulate the flow of air and to stop cold drafts when the fireplace is not in operation.
      A. throat
      B. lintel
      C. flue liner
      D. damper

_____   4. The damper is placed _____ inches above the top of the fireplace opening.
      A. 2 or 4
      B. 4 or 6
      C. 6 or 8
      D. 8 or 10

_____   5. Dampers are produced in both _____.
      A. steel and cast iron
      B. steel and aluminum
      C. cast iron and aluminum
      D. cast iron and slate

_____   6. Each fireplace must have its own _____.
      A. foundation
      B. flue
      C. All of the above
      D. None of the above

_____ 7. Low-efficiency stoves range from _____ percent efficiency.
     A. 10 to 20
     B. 20 to 30
     C. 30 to 40
     D. 40 to 50

SHORT ANSWER
Answer the following questions using short answers.

1. Identify six types of fireplaces that are used in homes.

   A. _____

   B. _____

   C. _____

   D. _____

   E. _____

   F. _____

2. What is the expected result when a fire chamber is too deep?

_____

3. What is the expected result if the fire chamber is too shallow?

_____

4. Where is the ash dump usually located?

_____

5. What is the rule of thumb to follow in selecting the proper flue size for a particular fireplace opening?

_____

_____

6. How will increasing the height of a flue affect the draft of a fireplace?

_____

7. How high should the flue generally extend above the roof?

_____

8. List four devices that require a flue.

   A. _____

   B. _____

   C. _____

   D. _____

9. What are the two main types of wood or coal burning stoves?

   A. _____

   B. _____

16
CHAPTER
The Floor Plan

■ OBJECTIVES

After studying this chapter, the student will be able to:

☐ List the information required on a typical floor plan.

☐ Represent typical materials using standard architectural symbols.

☐ Design and draw a residential floor plan using accepted symbols and techniques.

☐ Dimension a floor plan in a clear and precise manner.

☐ Recognize the difference between a good and poor drawing of a floor plan.

■ DISPLAYS

1. Sample Floor Plan. Select a well-designed floor plan for display on the bulletin board. Be sure the plan illustrates proper techniques described in the text.
2. Student Work. Display student work on the bulletin board. Select samples from the workbook assignments.

■ INSTRUCTIONAL MATERIALS

Text: Pages 283-301
Review Questions, Suggested Activities
Workbook: Pages 135-144
Review Questions, Problems/Activities
Teacher's Resource Guide:
Chapter 16—Teaching Strategy
Chapter 16—Exam

■ TEACHING STRATEGY

- Prepare Display #1.
- Review chapter objectives.

- Present the definition and purpose of the floor plan.
- Identify the required information on a floor plan.
- Discuss location and size of walls.
- Present location and size of windows and doors, cabinets, appliances, and permanent fixtures.
- Cover stairs and fireplaces, walks, patios, and decks.
- Discuss room names and material symbols.
- Assign workbook Problem 16-1.
- Cover dimensioning floor plans, scale, and sheet identification.
- Assign workbook Problem 16-2.
- Prepare Display #2.
- Discuss the procedure for drawing the floor plan.
- Assign workbook Problem 16-3.
- Assign one or more of the Suggested Activities in the text.
- Chapter Review
  —Assign Review Questions in the text. Discuss the correct answers.
  —Assign Review Questions in the workbook. Have students check their own answers.
  —Make a transparency of the solution for Problem/Activity 16-1 and use for review.
- Evaluation
  —Administer the Chapter 16—Exam. Correct the exam and return.
  —Return graded problems with comments.

■ ANSWERS TO REVIEW QUESTIONS, TEXT
Page 297

1. section
2. To show the location of interior and exterior walls, windows, doors, major appliances, cabinets, fireplaces, and stairs.

3. 1/4" = 1'-0".
4. 6"
5. center
6. each side
7. ![diagram of stairs symbol]

8. a. Width.
   b. Direction of flight.
   c. Number of risers.
9. a. Plaster.
   b. Aluminum.
   c. Rigid insulation.
   d. Dimension lumber.
   e. Common brick.
   f. Cast concrete.
10. a. 0'-4".
    b. 4".

■ ANSWERS TO REVIEW QUESTIONS, WORKBOOK

PART I: SHORT ANSWER/LISTING

1. A. Location and dimensions of interior and exterior walls.
   B. Location of windows and doors.
   C. Built-in cabinets and appliances.
   D. Permanent fixtures.
   E. Stairs and fireplaces.
   F. Walks, patios, and decks.
   G. Room names and material symbols.
   H. Location and size dimensions.
   I. Scale.
2. Use the manufacturer's information given for each of the cabinets, appliances, and permanent fixtures. Dimensions, specifications, and installation requirements should be indicated.
3. A. Basic size.
   B. Location.
   C. Direction of flight.
   D. Number of risers.
   E. Width of the stairs.
4. A. Basic width.
   B. Length.
   C. Location.
   D. Fireplace opening shape.
   E. Additional chimney flues.
5. It is not necessary to list the sizes of the rooms, but it is helpful to have them. The size should be placed below the name of the room.
6. They should be placed at least 3/4 in. from the view.
7. At the bottom of each drawing.
8. The number of the sheet should be placed in the lower-right corner.
9. It lets the person reading the plans know how many sheets are in the set and the position of each sheet in the set.
10. Decide the requirements (the specific rooms desired, sizes, etc.) and make some rough sketches.
11. Lay out the exterior walls.
12. Yes.
13. Find the finished floor to finished floor height as well as the tread width and riser height.
14. Dimensions, notes, and room names should be added after the kitchen and bathroom fixtures are drawn, but before the material and identification symbols are added.
15. A. Sheet number.
    B. Name of drawing.
    C. Scale.
    D. Data.
    E. The name of the person for whom the drawing is made.
    F. Who made the drawing.
16. A. If the expansion is planned in the initial drawing, the overall appearance of the completed structure is more pleasing.
    B. The number of changes required are minimized when the expansion takes place.
17. No.
18. 1/2 + 3 1/2 + 3/4 + 1/2 = 5 1/4 in.

PART II: MULTIPLE CHOICE

1. A. First.
2. C. Section view.
3. B. 5 in.
4. B. Sash.
5. A. Actual.
6. C. Hidden line.
7. D. All of the above.
8. C. 3/16 in.
9. B. Above the line.
10. A. 1/4 or 3/8.
11. C. All of the above.
12. C. Center.
13. A. 4 ft.
14. D. 1/4" = 1'-0".
15. B. Interior walls.
16. A. The doors, windows, stairs, and fireplaces have been drawn.
17. C. Before the kitchen cabinets, appliances, and bathroom fixtures have been drawn.
18. A. 24 and 12.
19. D. When the drawing is almost complete.
20. C. Black and vary in width.
21. D. Hidden line.

PART III: MATCHING

1. B. Floor plan.
2. E.

3. G.

4. H.

5. F.

6. C. Hidden line.

7. I.

8. K.

9. N.

10. M.

11. L.

12. J.

13. A. Dimensions.
14. D. Solid or Object.

PART IV: COMPLETION

1. plumbing
2. 8
3. dividers
4. center
5. windows
6. swing
7. symbols
8. parallel
9. 2
10. outside
11. outside
12. width
13. construction
14. center
15. outline
16. type
17. hidden
18. exterior
19. construction
20. accuracy
21. edge
22. center

PART V: PROBLEMS/ACTIVITIES

1. Solution on page 174.
2. Solution on page 175.
3. Solution on page 176.

■ ANSWERS TO CHAPTER 16—EXAM

TRUE—FALSE

1. T
2. T
3. T
4. F
5. F

MULTIPLE CHOICE

1. D
2. C
3. A
4. C
5. B
6. C
7. A

SHORT ANSWER

1. A. Exterior and interior walls
   B. Size and location of windows and doors
   C. Built-in cabinets and appliances
   D. Permanent fixtures
   E. Stairs
   F. Fireplaces
   G. Walks, patios, and decks
   H. Room names
   I. Material symbols
   J. Location and size dimensions
   K. Scale
2. Because building material sizes are keyed to this dimension.
3. When information cannot be represented by a conventional dimension or symbol.
4. 1/8" high or slightly smaller.
5. 1/4" = 1'-0".
6. Check the entire drawing for accuracy and completeness.

1.

DIRECTIONS:
Complete the Plan View of the following symbols which are used on typical residential floor plans:

BRICK VENEER ON FRAME

SOLID BRICK WALL

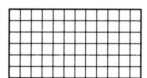

CONCRETE BLOCK WALL

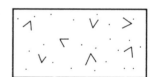

CAST CONCRETE WALL

ARCHWAY OR PLAIN OPENING

TERRA COTTA TILE
Plan View

TERRAZZO
Section

SLATE
Section

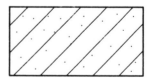

RUBBLE STONE
Section

Scale: 1/4"=1'-0"

FLOOR PLAN SYMBOLS   16-1

DIRECTIONS:
Using the procedure discussed in the text, properly dimension the
frame wall structure (upper) and the concrete wall structure (lower)
examples.   Note: The scale is 1/4"=1'-0".

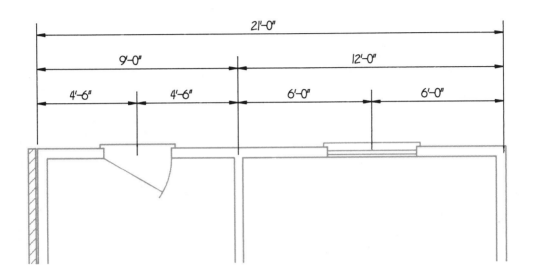

FRAME WALL CONSTRUCTION

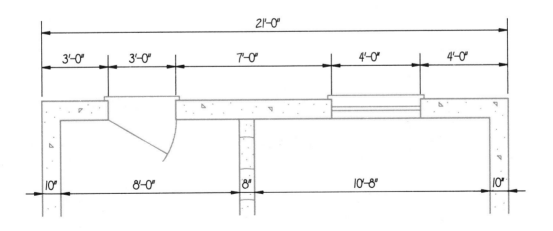

CONCRETE WALL CONSTRUCTION

DIMENSIONING FLOOR PLANS

16-2

3.

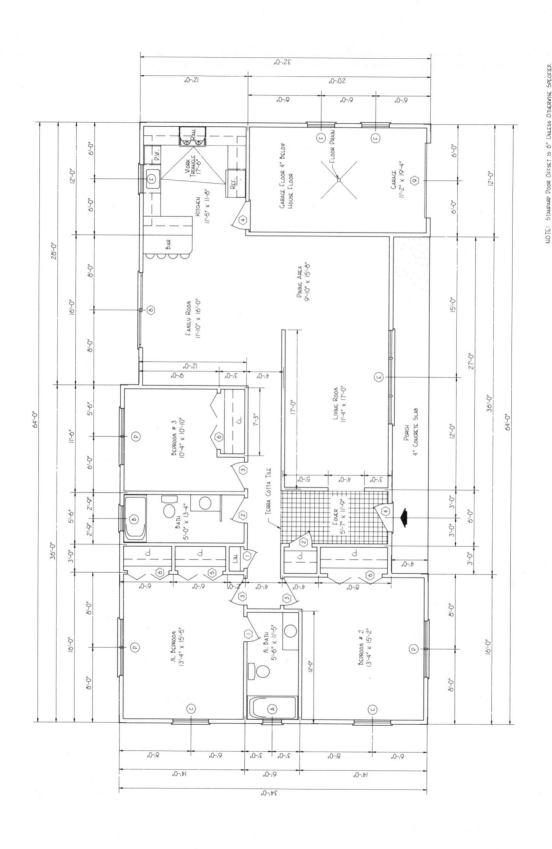

FLOOR PLAN

SCALE: 1/4"=1'-0"

NOTE: STANDARD DOOR OFFSET IS 6" UNLESS OTHERWISE SPECIFIED.

ASSIGNMENT 16-3

Chapter 16—Exam
THE FLOOR PLAN

Name _____

Period _____ **Date** _____ **Score** _____

TRUE—FALSE
Circle T if the statement is true or F if the statement is false.

T   F   1. The floor plan is referred to by all tradeworkers.

T   F   2. Beams are shown using a hidden line symbol on a floor plan.

T   F   3. Exterior frame walls are dimensioned to the outside of the stud wall.

T   F   4. Windows in a masonry wall are dimensioned to the center of the opening.

T   F   5. Dimensions on a floor plan should read from the bottom and left side.

MULTIPLE CHOICE
Choose the answer that correctly completes the statement. Write the corresponding letter in the space provided.

_____ 1. The floor plan is actually a(n) _____ drawing.
A. elevation
B. pictorial
C. top view
D. section

_____ 2. An exterior frame wall that includes the following materials—5/8" siding, 3/4" insulation board, 2" x 4" studs, and 1/2" drywall—would be exactly _____ inches thick.
A. 3 7/8
B. 6
C. 5 3/8
D. 5 7/8

_____ 3. Some symbols are simplified while others are _____.
A. detailed
B. abbreviated
C. described
D. None of the above

_____ 4. A good policy to follow when locating dimensions on a floor plan is to _____.
A. group them all together in one corner
B. leave out everything that may be obvious
C. locate dimensions where one would logically look for them
D. follow your hunches

_____ 5. Dimensions should not be closer than _____ inch(es) from the floor plan.
A. 1/2
B. 3/4
C. 1
D. 2

_____ 6. Which of the following dimension formats are correct for floor plans?
A. 0'-1/2"
B. 6.125"
C. 1'-6"
D. 10.6'

_____ 7. One of the most frequent errors in dimensioning is that _____.
  A. partial dimensions do not add up to the total distance
  B. the numbers cannot be read
  C. dimensions face the wrong direction
  D. dimensions are too close together

SHORT ANSWER
Answer the following questions using short answers.

1. List eleven basic features commonly shown on a floor plan.

  A. _____

  B. _____

  C. _____

  D. _____

  E. _____

  F. _____

  G. _____

  H. _____

  I. _____

  J. _____

  K. _____

2. Why should the overall lengths of major wall segments be multiples of 4 feet?

  _____

3. When are notes used in some cases instead of dimensions?

  _____

  _____

4. What is the standard height of lettering for notes?

  _____

5. What is the usual scale of a residential floor plan?

  _____

6. What is the very last thing to do when drawing a floor plan?

  _____

17 CHAPTER
Roof Design

■ OBJECTIVES

After studying this chapter, the student will be able to:
☐ Sketch ten different types of basic roof designs.
☐ Describe the construction of a typical frame roof.
☐ Draw a roof using a typical roof slope or pitch.
☐ Interpret information found on a rafter span chart.
☐ Explain the importance of proper ventilation and flashing.
☐ Compile the appropriate information to order roof trusses for a specific dwelling.

■ DISPLAYS

1. Roof Styles. Create a bulletin board display of interesting roof designs using photos or pictures cut from magazines. Identify each roof design.
2. Roofing Materials. Display typical roof covering products such as asphalt shingles, cedar shakes, terra cotta tile, slate, and metal roofing.
3. Cornice Models. Show cornice models built by students for Suggested Activity #3 in the text.
4. Roof Trusses. Build scale models of various roof trusses for display in the classroom.

■ INSTRUCTIONAL MATERIALS

Text: Pages 301-318
   Review Questions, Suggested Activities
Workbook: Pages 145-155
   Review Questions, Problems/Activities
Teacher's Resource Guide:
   Chapter 17 — Teaching Strategy
   Chapter 17 — Exam

■ TEACHING STRATEGY

• Prepare Display #1.
• Review chapter objectives.
• Compare and contrast the different types of roofs.
• Discuss traditional frame roof construction.
• Assign workbook Problems 17-1 and 17-2.
• Cover rake or gable end.
• Prepare Display #2.
• Assign workbook Problem 17-3.
• Prepare Display #3.
• Discuss roof trusses, ventilation, and flashing.
• Assign workbook Problem 17-4.
• Discuss gutters and downspouts, roof sheathing, and roofing.
• Prepare Display #4.
• Assign one or more of the Suggested Activities in the text.
• Chapter Review
   —Assign Review Questions in the text. Discuss the correct answers.
   —Assign Review Questions in the workbook. Have students check their own answers.
   —Make a transparency of the solution to Problem/Activity 17-3 and use for review.
• Evaluation
   —Administer the Chapter 17 — Exam. Correct the exam and return.
   —Return graded problems with comments.

■ ANSWERS TO REVIEW QUESTIONS, TEXT Page 318

1. a. Gable.   f. Gambrel.
   b. Hip.   g. Butterfly.
   c. Flat.   h. A-frame.
   d. Shed.   i. Folded plate.
   e. Mansard.   j. Curved panel.
   Also: Parasol, warped, and freeform.
2. to support the roof covering materials.
3. rafter.
4. 24

5. inside of exterior wall, inside of opposite wall.
6. run
7. P = rise/span.
8. 12:12 or 1/2.
9. a. Span.
   b. Spacing.
   c. Weight.
10. 4
11. cornice
12. a. Open cornice.
    b. Box cornice.
    c. Close cornice.
13. a. Reducing moisture damage.
    b. Cool the house in summers.
14. 1/300
15. a. Aluminum.
    b. Copper.
    Also: Galvanized metal and roll roofing.
16. 1/2
17. a. Asphalt shingles.   d. Tile.
    b. Asbestos shingles.   e. Slate.
    c. Wood shingles.
    Also: Roll roofing, copper, aluminum, tin, gal-
    vanized steel, and built-up roof.
18. 235
19. a. Support heavier loads.
    b. Span greater distances.
    Also: Less expensive and faster.
20. a. W-type.
    b. King post.
    c. Scissors.
21. a. Span.
    b. Pitch.
    c. Spacing.
    d. Load.
22. A gusset is a flat piece of wood or metal used
    to provide a connection at the intersection of
    wood members.

■ ANSWERS TO REVIEW QUESTIONS, WORKBOOK

PART I: MULTIPLE CHOICE

1. D. All of the above.
2. A. Flat.
3. C. Common rafters extend from the plate or
      beyond to the ridge of the roof.
4. B. Asphalt shingles.
5. C. 6 and 12 in.
6. A. Close.
7. B. Generally, 2 x 4 lumber is used in lightweight
      wood roof trusses.
8. A. At least 6 sq. ft.
9. D. All of the above.
10. C. 3/4 in.
11. A. Asphalt.
12. C. 12 ft.

PART II: MATCHING

1. H. Gable.
2. L. Hip.
3. G. Flat.
4. U. Shed.
5. M. Mansard.
6. I. Gambrel.
7. B. Butterfly.
8. A. A-frame.
9. O. Rafters.
10. N. Pitch.
11. C. Clear span.
12. Q. Rise.
13. S. Run.
14. D. Cornice.
15. P. Rake.
16. R. Roof trusses.
17. J. Gusset.
18. F. Flashing.
19. E. Drip edge.
20. K. Gutters.
21. T. Sheathing.

PART III: SHORT ANSWER/LISTING

1. It is made of layers of roofing felt and tar, or
   some other material such as rubber topped with
   gravel.
2. A. Ridge cut.
   B. Seat cut.
   C. Plumb cut.
   D. Tail cut.
3. A. Distance to be spanned.
   B. Spacing of the rafters.
   C. Weight to be supported.
4. In low-pitched roofs, rafters may also serve as
   a base for the finished ceiling.
5. A. Exposed beam construction.
   B. Contemporary designs.
   C. Rustic designs.
6. Where the overhangs are very wide.
7. It is nailed to the underside of the rafters.
8. A. Wide overhangs protect the sidewall.
   B. Wide overhangs decrease the frequency of
      painting.
9. A narrow box cornice is suited for a Colonial
   or Cape Cod.
10. A. Span.
    B. Roof pitch.
    C. Spacing of trusses.
    D. Anticipated roof load.
11. A. Added ceiling insulation.
    B. Added ventilation.
    Also: Less moisture condensation.
12. A. Louvered openings in gable ends and
       overhangs.
    B. Ridge ventilators.

13. A. Planks.
    B. Individual boards.
    C. 1 x 3 in. strips.

PART IV: COMPLETION

1. flat.
2. 3:12.
3. gambrel.
4. curved panel.
5. pitches
6. 4
7. gable
8. open
9. narrow
10. lookouts
11. sloped
12. rake
13. King Post
14. moisture
15. 18
16. ogee.
17. perpendicular
18. felt
19. Flashing
20. cornice.

PART V: PROBLEMS/ACTIVITIES

1. Solution on page 182.
2. Solution on page 183.
3. Solution on page 184.
4. Solution on page 185.

■ ANSWERS TO CHAPTER 17—EXAM

TRUE—FALSE

1. T
2. T
3. T
4. F
5. T

MULTIPLE CHOICE

1. B
2. A
3. D
4. D
5. B
6. C
7. A
8. D
9. C
10. A
11. B
12. D

SHORT ANSWER

1. A. Open cornice.
   B. Box cornice.
   C. Close cornice.
2. A. Narrow box.
   B. Wide box with lookouts.
   C. Wide box without lookouts.
3. A. Where the roof comes in contact with a wood or masonry wall.
   B. Where the roof comes in contact with a chimney.
   C. Where the roof comes in contact with a roof valley.
   D. At the edge of a roof.
4. A. Aluminum.
   B. Copper.
   C. Galvanized sheet steel.
   D. Roll roofing.
   E. Vinyl plastic (drip edge).
5. A. Planks (as in post and beam construction).
   B. Individual boards.
   C. Plywood.
   D. Other approved panel products.

1.

DIRECTIONS:
Identify the elements indicated in the partial roof framing plan below.

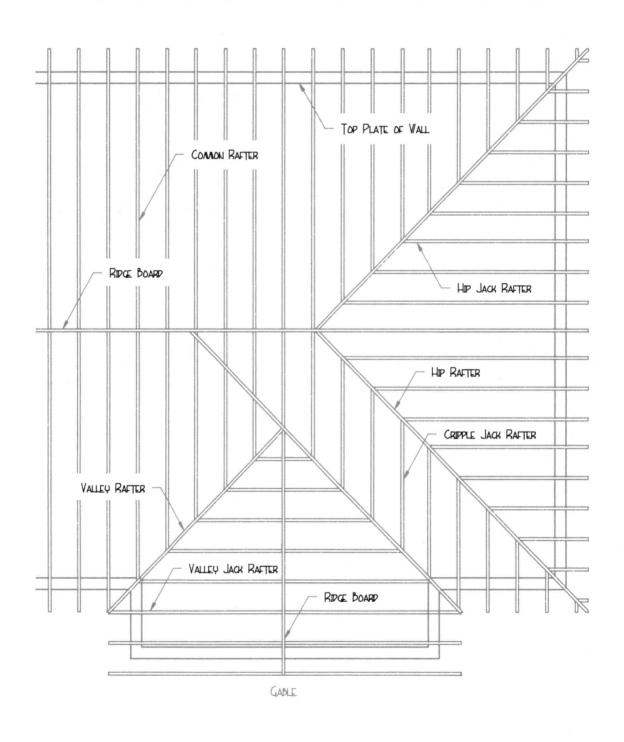

Top Plate of Wall

Common Rafter

Ridge Board

Hip Jack Rafter

Hip Rafter

Cripple Jack Rafter

Valley Rafter

Valley Jack Rafter

Ridge Board

Gable

Scale: 1/4"=1'-0"

| ROOF FRAMING PARTS | | 17-1 |

2.

DIRECTIONS:
A.   Construct the ceiling joist (2" x 6") and rafter (2" x 4") layout for a cottage which has a clear span of 19'–3 1/2", a roof slope of 6:12, and an 18" overhang.   Dimension the rise and run and show the roof slope triangle.
B.   Instead of ceiling joists and rafters, show the roof structure using roof trusses ("W" or "Kingpost").   Dimension as above.

A

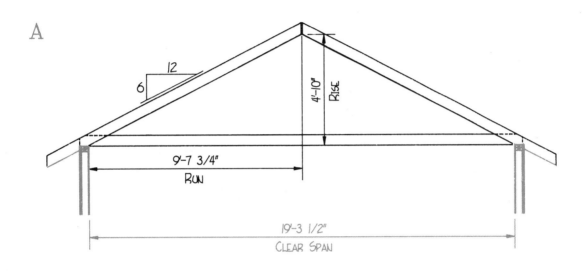

B

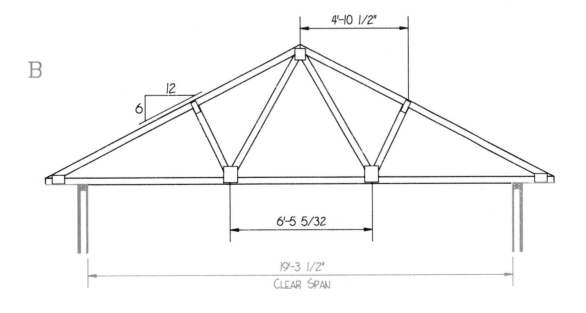

SCALE: 1/4"=1'–0"

ROOF SLOPE — 17–2

3.

DIRECTIONS:
Draw a large scale (1"=1'-0") section through a wide box cornice with lookouts. Incorporate the following dimensions, materials, etc. in your drawing:
> 2" x 4" stud wall with 3/4" RF insulation and horizontal siding on the outside and 1/2" DW inside
> 24" overhang (outside of insulation to end of rafters) with ventilation
> 2" x 6" rafters and 2" X 8" ceiling joists
> 1/2" plywood roof sheathing, redwood fascia board, and asphalt shingles.

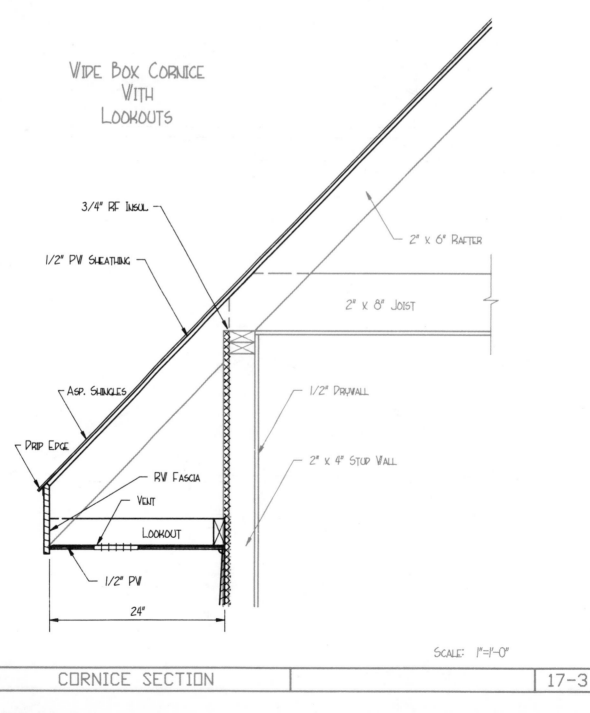

WIDE BOX CORNICE
WITH
LOOKOUTS

3/4" RF INSUL

1/2" PW SHEATHING

2" X 6" RAFTER

2" X 8" JOIST

ASP. SHINGLES

1/2" DRYWALL

DRIP EDGE

2" X 4" STUD WALL

RW FASCIA

VENT

LOOKOUT

1/2" PW

24"

SCALE: 1"=1'-0"

CORNICE SECTION		17-3

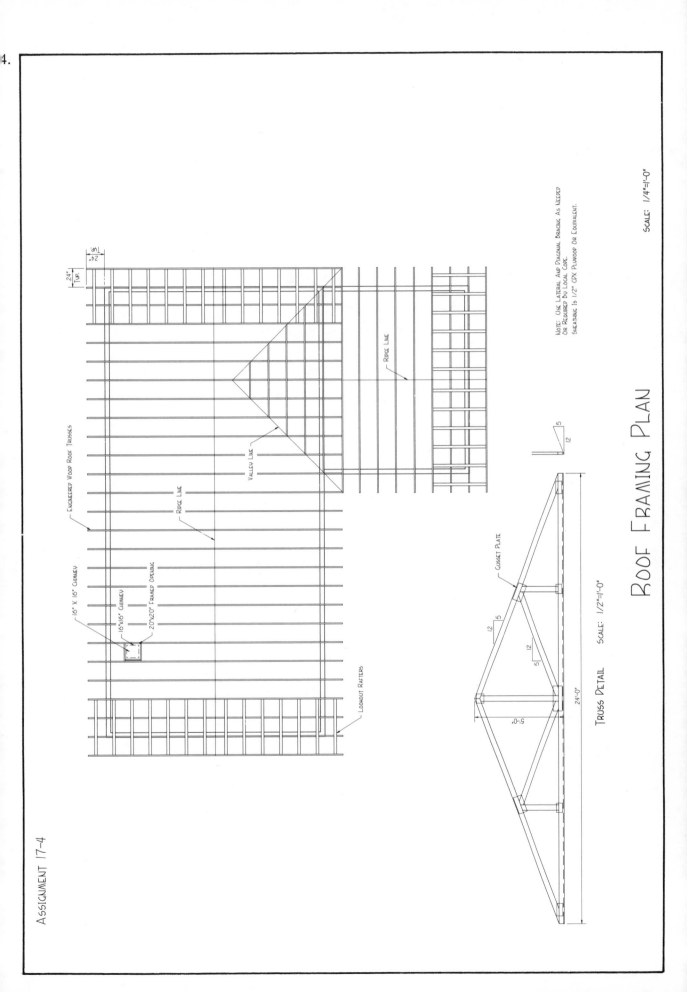

ASSIGNMENT 17-4

ENGINEERED WOOD ROOF TRUSSES

24" TYP.

18" TYP.

16" X 16" CHIMNEY

16"X16" CHIMNEY

20"X20" FRAMED OPENING

RIDGE LINE

VALLEY LINE

RIDGE LINE

LOOKOUT RAFTERS

NOTE: USE LATERAL AND DIAGONAL BRACING AS NEEDED OR REQUIRED BY LOCAL CODE.
SHEATHING IS 1/2" CDX PLYWOOD OR EQUIVALENT.

SCALE: 1/4"=1'-0"

ROOF FRAMING PLAN

GUSSET PLATE

5
12

5
12

5
12

5-0"

24'-0"

TRUSS DETAIL   SCALE: 1/2"=1'-0"

Chapter 17—Exam
ROOF DESIGNS

Name _____

Period _____ **Date** _____ **Score** _____

TRUE—FALSE
Circle T if the statement is true or F if the statement is false.

T   F   1. A flat roof is the most economical roof to construct.

T   F   2. The run of a roof is one-half the clear span.

T   F   3. The slope diagram represents the rise/run ratio.

T   F   4. An 8:12 slope is steeper than a 12:12 slope.

T   F   5. A gable roof has a cornice on two sides.

MULTIPLE CHOICE
Choose the answer that correctly completes the statement. Write the corresponding letter in the space provided.

_____ 1. The _____ roof is a very popular type of roof because it is easy to build, sheds water well, provides for ventilation, and is applicable to a variety of house shapes and designs.
A. folded plate
B. gable
C. A-frame
D. flat

_____ 2. A _____ roof is similar to a flat roof, but has more pitch.
A. shed
B. gable
C. mansard
D. butterfly

_____ 3. A gambrel roof is sometimes called a _____ roof.
A. French
B. winged gable
C. folded plate
D. barn

_____ 4. The _____ roof is an example of a modern roof that is experimental for residential housing structures.
A. parasol
B. warped
C. freeform
D. All of the above

_____ 5. In typical gable roof construction, the _____ support the roof covering.
A. top plates
B. rafters
C. ceiling joists
D. soffits

_____ 6. The _____ of a roof is one-half of the span.
  A. pitch
  B. rise
  C. run
  D. slope

_____ 7. The fractional pitch of a roof is calculated by dividing the _____.
  A. rise by the span
  B. span by the rise
  C. run by the span
  D. None of the above

_____ 8. A light-weight roofing is one that weighs less than _____ pound(s) per square foot.
  A. 1
  B. 2
  C. 3
  D. 4

_____ 9. A roof covering of _____ is an example of heavy roofing.
  A. roll roofing
  B. asphalt shingles
  C. slate
  D. cedar shakes

_____ 10. The _____ is the extension of a gable roof beyond the end wall of the house.
  A. rake
  B. soffit
  C. overhang
  D. fascia

_____ 11. If sufficient _____ is not provided in the attic, moisture will probably form on the underside of the roof sheathing.
  A. headroom
  B. ventilation
  C. insulation
  D. number of heating ducts

_____ 12. Wood trusses commonly used in residential construction include _____ trusses.
  A. W-type and King-post
  B. King-post and scissors
  C. W-type and scissors
  D. All of the above

SHORT ANSWER
Answer the following questions with short answers.

1. List the three types of cornices frequently used in residential buildings.

  A. _____

  B. _____

  C. _____

2. Identify the three types of box cornices.

  A. _____

  B. _____

  C. _____

3. Where should flashing be used on a roof?

    A. _____

    B. _____

    C. _____

    D. _____

4. What common materials are frequently used as roof flashing?

    A. _____

    B. _____

    C. _____

    D. _____

    E. _____

5. What materials are generally used as roof sheathing?

    A. _____

    B. _____

    C. _____

    D. _____

Elevations

■ OBJECTIVES

After studying this chapter, the student will be able to:
- [ ] List features that should be included on an exterior elevation.
- [ ] Identify the dimensions commonly shown on elevations.
- [ ] Illustrate symbols that are often found on elevations.
- [ ] Draw a typical exterior elevation which demonstrates proper techniques.

■ DISPLAYS

1. Front Elevations. Select a well-designed front elevation of a residential structure and display it on the bulletin board. Include the floor plan if available.
2. Student Work. Display student work on the bulletin board. Use completed workbook assignments.

■ INSTRUCTIONAL MATERIALS

Text: Pages 319-330
   Review Questions, Suggested Activities
Workbook: Pages 157-164
   Review Questions, Problems/Activities
Teacher's Resource Guide:
   Chapter 18—Teaching Strategy
   Chapter 18—Exam

■ TEACHING STRATEGY

- Prepare Display #1.
- Review chapter objectives.
- Discuss the definition and purpose of exterior elevations.
- Present required information, elevation identification, and grade line, floors, and ceilings.
- Discuss walls, windows, and doors.
- Assign workbook Problem 18-1.

- Discuss roof features.
- Prepare Display #2.
- Assign workbook Problems 18-2 and 18-3.
- Present dimensions, notes, and symbols.
- Discuss the procedure for drawing an elevation.
- Assign workbook Problem 18-4.
- Assign one or more of the Suggested Activities in the text.
- Chapter Review
  - Assign Review Questions in the text. Discuss the correct answers.
  - Assign Review Questions in the workbook. Have students check their own answers.
  - Make transparencies of solutions to Problems/Activities 18-1 and 18-3 and use for review.
- Evaluation
  - Administer the Chapter 18—Exam. Correct the exam and return.
  - Return graded problems with comments.

■ ANSWERS TO REVIEW QUESTIONS, TEXT Page 329

1. To show the finished appearance of a given side of the building and furnish vertical height dimensions.
2. Front elevation, rear elevation, right side elevation and left side elevation.
3. grade line.
4. hidden
5. 8'-0".
6. 7'-6".
7. 6'-2".
8. 8
9. it provides accurate height dimensions.
10. 6'-10".
11. Where the roof slope is shown as in the gable end.
12. 2'-0".

ANSWERS TO REVIEW QUESTIONS, WORKBOOK

PART I: COMPLETION

1. details.
2. first
3. hidden
4. 4
5. center
6. section
7. slope triangle
8. flashing
9. 1/4" = 1'-0".
10. floor
11. horizontal
12. Sweets Architectural File.
13. scale

PART II: SHORT ANSWER/LISTING

1. A. To show the finished appearance of each side of the house as well as exterior materials desired.
   B. To illustrate the vertical height dimensions about basic features of the house.
2. A. Grade lines.
   B. Finished floor and ceiling levels.
   C. Location of exterior wall corners.
   D. Windows and doors.
   Also: Roof features; vertical dimensions of important features; porches, decks, and patios; and material symbols.
3. In the finished floor-to-finished ceiling distance, the first floor measurement is 8'-0", while the second floor measurement is 7'-6" or 8'-0". The construction dimension is measured from the top of the subfloor to the top of the wall plate — the first floor is usually 8'-1 1/2" while the second floor is usually 7'-7 1/2" or 8'-1 1/2". The latter method usually does not require any calculations and is generally preferred by carpenters.
4. This practice protects the framing members from moisture.
5. The tops of the windows and doors should measure 6'-10" from the top of the subfloor to the top of the lower face of the head jamb.
6. Highest.
7. B. Lay out the desired slope from the top inside corner of the plate.
   D. Measure the amount of desired overhang, include the thickness of the roof sheathing.
   E. Repeat the procedure for the other side of the roof.
   A. Locate the top of the upper wall plate and center line of the proposed ridge location.
   C. Measure the width of the rafter perpendicular to the bottom edge and draw the top edge parallel to the bottom edge of the rafter.
8. A. Thickness of the footing.

B. Distance from the footing to the grade.
C. Finished floor-to-finished ceiling distance.
D. Overhang width.
Also: Height of the top of the windows and doors and height of the chimney above the roof.
9. Light construction lines.
10. The dimensions, notes, and symbols are the last details added to the elevation drawing. They are added after the details and before the title block.

PART III: MULTIPLE CHOICE

1. B. Plot or site plan.
2. A. 8'-0".
3. C. Object.
4. D. All of the above.
5. B. Roof pitch symbol.
6. B. Section drawing.
7. D. After the vertical and horizontal lines have been drawn and the features have been darkened.

PART IV: PROBLEMS/ACTIVITIES

1. Solution on page 193.
2. Solution on page 194.
3. Solution on page 195.
4. Solution on page 196.

ANSWERS TO CHAPTER 18—EXAM

TRUE—FALSE

1. T	4. T
2. F	5. T
3. T	

MULTIPLE CHOICE

1. D	5. C
2. B	6. B
3. A	7. A
4. A	8. B

SHORT ANSWER

1. A. Identification of the side of the house shown.
   B. Grade lines.
   C. Finished floors and ceiling levels.
   D. Location of exterior wall corners.
   E. Windows and doors.
   F. Roof features.
   G. Vertical dimensions of important features.
   H. Porches, decks, and patios.
   I. Material symbols.
2. A. Front, rear, right side, left side.
   B. North, south, east, west.
3. They are projected down from the floor plan.
4. Because they may interfere with the other information if drawn earlier.

DIRECTIONS:
Draw an Elevation View of each of the exterior wall materials indicated below. Symbols should be drawn at 1/4"=1'-0" scale.

Brick

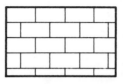

Concrete Block

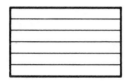

Horizontal Siding

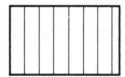

Vertical Siding

Stucco

Rubble Stone

Cast Concrete

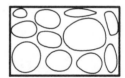

Glass Panel

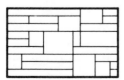

Ashlar Stone

12" Square Tile

EXTERIOR ELEVATION SYMBOLS   18-1

2.

DIRECTIONS:
Complete the partial Front Elevation of the two-story colonial below.
See Figures 18-1 and 18-2 for ideas.

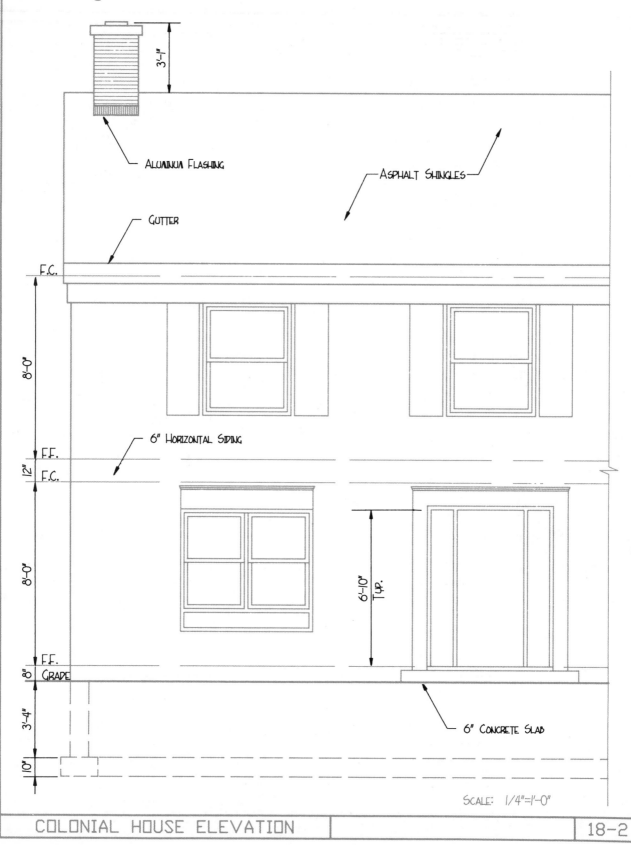

COLONIAL HOUSE ELEVATION | 18-2

B.

DIRECTIONS:
Draw a complete Front Elevation for the Garden House shown below using the following information: Thickened—edge slab 24" deep, floor to ceiling height of 8'—0", 6'—10" to top of windows and doors, 12" overhang with bottom of soffit level with finished ceiling (truss construction), floor 4" above the grade, 12:12 roof slope, asphalt shingles, 6" fascia, vertical siding (rough sawn 12" boards with 1" channel, four—panel doors. Follow the procedure described in Chapter 18 in the text.

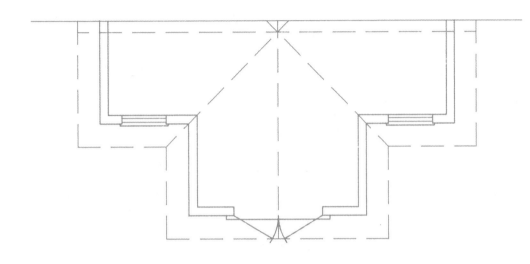

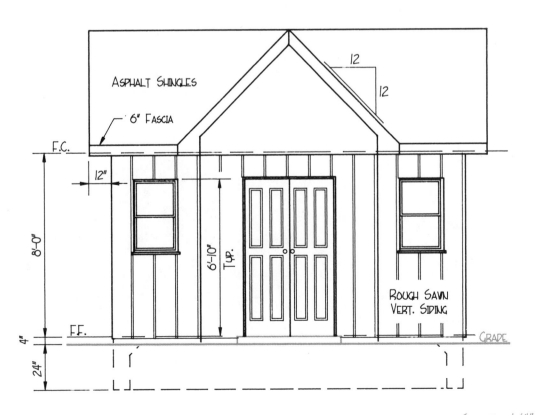

SCALE: 1/4"=1'-0"

GARDEN HOUSE ELEVATION | 18-3

4.

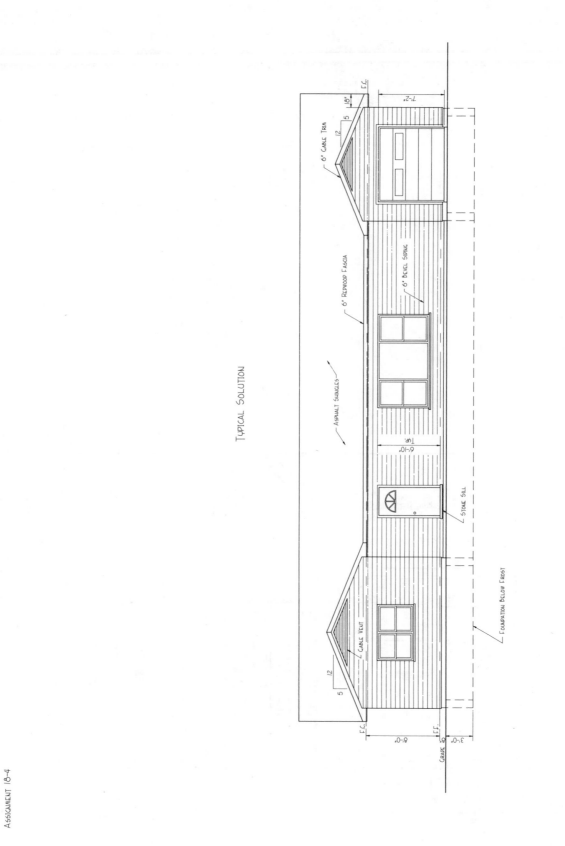

TYPICAL SOLUTION

FRONT ELEVATION

SCALE: 1/4"=1'-0"

Chapter 18—Exam
ELEVATIONS

Name _____

Period _____ **Date** _____ **Score** _____

TRUE—FALSE
Circle T if the statement is true or F if the statement is false.

T   F   1. Elevation drawings provide height information about basic features of the house.

T   F   2. The minimum recommended height for garage ceilings is 9'-0".

T   F   3. All visible wall corners are shown on the elevation using object lines.

T   F   4. Tops of exterior doors are usually the same height as tops of windows.

T   F   5. Window swing is shown on an elevation.

MULTIPLE CHOICE
Choose the answer that correctly completes the statement. Write the corresponding letter in the space provided.

_____ 1. The reference point of most elevations is the _____.
A. finish floor level
B. eaves line
C. top of the foundation wall
D. grade line

_____ 2. Features on an elevation which are below the grade line are shown as _____.
A. center lines
B. hidden lines
C. object lines
D. phantom lines

_____ 3. Most codes require that the top of the foundation wall be at least _____ inches above the grade.
A. 8
B. 10
C. 12
D. 14

_____ 4. The usual height of the lower face of the head jamb of an exterior door is _____ from the top of the subfloor.
A. 6'-10"
B. 6'-8"
C. 6'-6"
D. 6'-4"

_____ 5. Roof angle is shown on the elevation using the _____.
A. slope triangle
B. fractional pitch
C. slope triangle or fractional pitch
D. None of the above

_____ 6. Dimensions on the elevation drawing are primarily _____ dimensions.
   A. location
   B. vertical height dimensions
   C. size
   D. dimensions are not used on the elevation

_____ 7. Material symbols are shown extensively on the _____ elevation(s).
   A. front
   B. four
   C. front and right side
   D. front and rear

_____ 8. The usual scale of an exterior elevation is _____.
   A. 1/8" = 1'-0"
   B. 1/4" = 1'-0"
   C. 3/8" = 1'-0"
   D. 1/2" = 1'-0"

SHORT ANSWER
Answer the following questions using short answers.

1. List the features that are commonly included on elevation drawings.

 A. _____
 B. _____
 C. _____
 D. _____
 E. _____
 F. _____
 G. _____
 H. _____
 I. _____

2. What are the two methods commonly used to identify a particular elevation?

 A. _____
 B. _____

3. How is the placement (location) of windows, doors, and walls located on an elevation?

_____

4. Why are material symbols usually drawn last on an elevation?

_____

_____

19
CHAPTER

Residential Electrical

■ OBJECTIVES

After studying this chapter, the student will be able to:
□ Define typical residential electrical terms.
□ Plan for the electrical needs of a modern home.
□ Identify and explain the three types of electrical circuits used in a residential structure.
□ Calculate circuit requirements for a residence.

■ DISPLAYS

1. Electrical Hardware. Show a collection of electrical, such as switches, boxes, and outlets commonly used in residential electrical systems.
2. Electrical Circuits. Prepare a bulletin board illustrating the circuits in a house and the equipment, appliances, and lighting they serve.

■ INSTRUCTIONAL MATERIALS

Text: Pages 331-342
Review Questions, Suggested Activities
Workbook: Pages 165-172
Review Questions, Problems/Activities
Teacher's Resource Guide:
Chapter 19—Teaching Strategy
Chapter 19—Exam

■ TEACHING STRATEGY

- Prepare Display #1.
- Review chapter objectives.
- Review electrical terms.
- Discuss the service entrance and distribution panel.
- Discuss branch circuits.
- Prepare Display #2.
- Assign workbook Problem 19-1.

- Discuss circuit requirements and outlets and switches.
- Assign workbook Problem 19-2.
- Discuss signal and communication systems.
- Present low-voltage switching.
- Assign one or more of the Suggested Activities in the text.
- Chapter Review
  —Assign Review Questions in the text. Discuss the correct answers.
  —Assign Review Questions in the workbook. Have students check their own answers.
  —Make transparencies of solutions to Problems/Activities 19-1 and 19-2 and use for review.
- Evaluation
  —Administer the Chapter 19—Exam. Correct the exam and return.
  —Return graded problems with comments.

■ ANSWERS TO REVIEW QUESTIONS, TEXT Page 341

1. voltage.
2. fuses, circuit breakers.
3. conductor.
4. watts.
5. Three.
6. 12
7. copper.
8. No. 12.
9. Fire, blow fuse, or use too much electricity.
10. 14
11. to stop the flow of electricity to all parts of the house.
12. 100
13. circuit breaker.
14. a. Lighting.
    b. Special appliance.
    c. Individual appliance.

15. 2.
16. 15
17. 3
18. 600
19. 2 or 3
20. 12, 20
21. 2400.
22. a. Range.   d. Countertop oven.
    b. Water heater.   e. Clothes dryer.
    c. Dishwasher.
    Also: Clothes washer, garbage disposal, furnace blower, attic fan, and water pump.
23. a. Size of house.
    b. Appliances and lighting to be installed.
    c. Planning for the future.
24. 3.
25. 6
26. three-way
27. There is less danger of shock and any or all of the outlets may be controlled from a single location.

■ ANSWERS TO REVIEW QUESTIONS, WORKBOOK

PART I: MULTIPLE CHOICE

1. C. 3.
2. D. 12.
3. B. Circuit breakers.
4. A. 120.
5. C. 2400.
6. D. All of the above.
7. B. 8 ft.
8. C. Ground-fault interrupters.
9. B. 2.
10. A. 24.

PART II: SHORT ANSWER/LISTING

1. Two voltages are available.
2. The amount of current may cause a fire.
3. Main disconnect switch.
4. A. To accommodate switches and outlets which are not designed for large wires.
   B. If one branch loses service, the remaining branches are available to provide service to other parts of the house.
   Also: So that appliances which use smaller amounts of current have the proper fuse protection.
5. A. Range.
   B. Dryer.
   C. Dishwasher.
   Also: Some air conditioners.
6. 40 x 56 = 2240 sq. ft.
   Six lighting circuits should be adequate.

7. 40 x 56 = 2240 sq. ft.
   Lighting circuits:
   2240 sq. ft. x 3 watts per sq. ft.   = 6720 watts
   Special appliance circuit:
   3 circuits (2400 watts each) = 7200 watts
   Individual appliance circuit:

Electric range with oven	= 12,000 watts
Refrigerator	= 12,000 watts
Washer	= 700 watts
Dryer (electric)	= 5000 watts
Dishwasher	= 1200 watts
Garbage disposal	= 300 watts
Furnace	= 800 watts
Water heater	= 2000 watts
TOTAL	= 36,220 watts

   $36,220/240 = 150.91$ or 150 amp. service.
8. Lighting fixtures, convenience outlets, switches, and joints where wire is spliced should be housed in electrical boxes.
9. A. Entrances.
   B. Garages.
   C. Stairs.
   D. Hallways.
   E. Rooms with more than one entrance.
10. A. Fire detection.
    B. Intrusion detection.
11. Low voltage switching.

PART III: COMPLETION

1. service
2. larger
3. 200
4. appliance
5. 20
6. 240
7. waterproof
8. 48
9. bathtub.
10. dimmer

PART IV: MATCHING

1. J. Receptacle.
2. B. Circuit.
3. O. Watt.
4. A. Ampere.
5. F. Fuse.
6. N. Voltage.
7. I. Ohm.
8. C. Circuit breaker.
9. L. Service entrance.
10. M. Service panel.
11. D. Conductor.
12. K. Service drop.
13. G. Lighting outlet.
14. E. Convenience outlet.
15. H. Low voltage switching.

PART V: PROBLEMS/ACTIVITIES

1. Solution on page 202.
2. Solution on page 203.

■ ANSWERS TO CHAPTER 19—EXAM

TRUE—FALSE

1. T	4. T
2. F	5. T
3. T	

MULTIPLE CHOICE

1. C	5. C
2. B	6. A
3. C	7. B
4. C	8. B

SHORT ANSWER

1. A. Familiarization with related terms.
   B. Electrical requirements for lighting and appliances.
   C. Code restrictions.
   D. Safety considerations.
2. A. Lighting circuits.
   B. Special appliance circuits.
   C. Individual appliance circuits.
3. 2.
4. When it uses a large amount of electricity (over 1400 watts), is permanently connected, or has an automatically-starting electric motor.
5. Weatherproof outlets.
6. 48".
7. Bathroom or other area that is likely to be wet.
8. To control a fixture from two locations.
9. A. Signal that a visitor is present.
   B. Enable persons within the home to communicate with one another
   C. Permit the owner to monitor the various systems within the dwelling and property.

MATCHING

1. J	7. K
2. D	8. B
3. L	9. G
4. A	10. E
5. H	11. I
6. C	12. F

1.

DIRECTIONS:
Label each of the electrical circuits below as to wire size, voltage, and amperage (fuse protection). See the completed example for format.

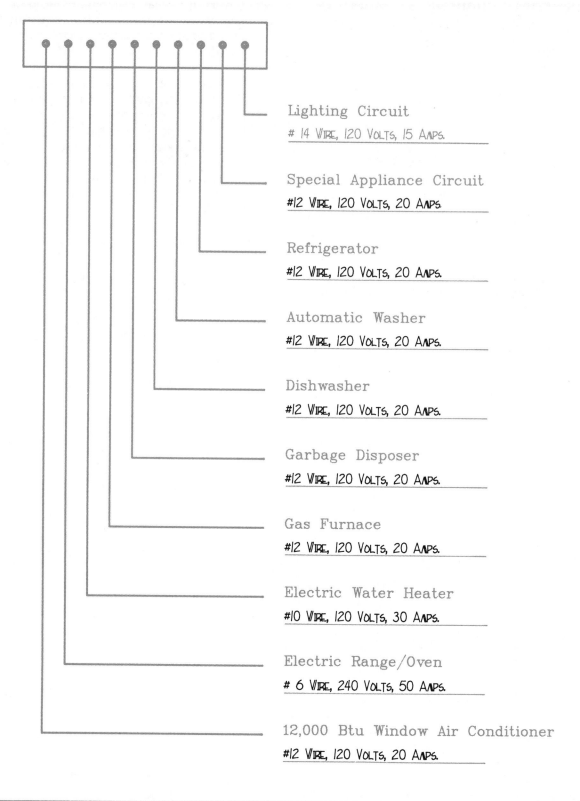

Lighting Circuit
14 Wire, 120 Volts, 15 Amps.

Special Appliance Circuit
#12 Wire, 120 Volts, 20 Amps.

Refrigerator
#12 Wire, 120 Volts, 20 Amps.

Automatic Washer
#12 Wire, 120 Volts, 20 Amps.

Dishwasher
#12 Wire, 120 Volts, 20 Amps.

Garbage Disposer
#12 Wire, 120 Volts, 20 Amps.

Gas Furnace
#12 Wire, 120 Volts, 20 Amps.

Electric Water Heater
#10 Wire, 120 Volts, 30 Amps.

Electric Range/Oven
6 Wire, 240 Volts, 50 Amps.

12,000 Btu Window Air Conditioner
#12 Wire, 120 Volts, 20 Amps.

RESIDENTIAL ELECTRICAL CIRCUITS | 19-1

DIRECTIONS:
Plan the location of switches and outlets for each of the situations below.

A. Ceiling outlet fixture with single pole switch.

B. Ceiling outlet fixture switched from two locations.

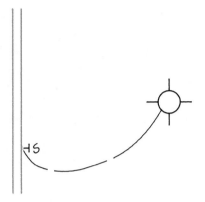
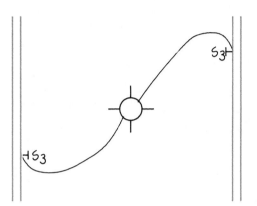

C. Room with switched ceiling outlet fixture and duplex outlets approximately 6 feet apart along the walls.

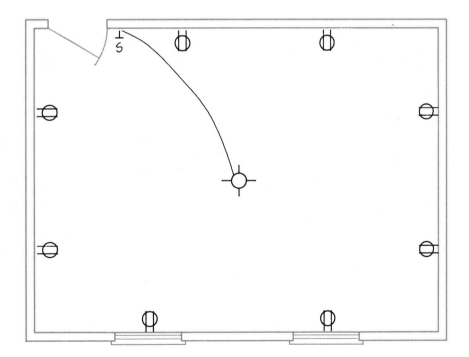

SWITCHES AND OUTLETS   19-2

Chapter 19—Exam
RESIDENTIAL ELECTRICAL

Name _____

Period _____ **Date** _____ **Score** _____

TRUE—FALSE
Circle T if the statement is true or F if the statement is false.

T   F   1. Voltage is the pressure which forces current through a wire.

T   F   2. A residence may have 120 or 340 volt service.

T   F   3. The service drop must be at least 10' above the ground at all points.

T   F   4. No. 2 wire is larger than No. 4.

T   F   5. No. 12 wire is recommended for branch lighting circuits.

MULTIPLE CHOICE
Choose the answer that correctly completes the statement. Write the corresponding letter in the space provided.

_____ 1. A 240 volt service requires _____ conductor(s).
     A. 1
     B. 2
     C. 3
     D. 4

_____ 2. The most common arrangement of electrical service to a house is with the service conductors first terminating at the _____.
     A. service panel
     B. meter
     C. distribution box
     D. ground post

_____ 3. The main disconnect switch is usually located _____.
     A. in the meter
     B. at the last utility pole
     C. in the distribution panel
     D. at the service drop

_____ 4. The National Electrical Code recommends that a minimum of _____ amp. service be provided for all residences.
     A. 50
     B. 75
     C. 100
     D. 150

_____ 5. How many watts of lighting capacity will a #12 copper wire with a 20 amp. fuse provide?
     A. 1200
     B. 1800
     C. 2400
     D. 3000

_____ 6. The Code requires a minimum of _____ watts of lighting power for each square foot of floor space.
A. 3
B. 6
C. 9
D. 12

_____ 7. All convenience outlets, switches, and joints where wires are spliced must be housed in a(n) _____.
A. fuse box
B. electrical box
C. distribution panel
D. conduit

_____ 8. The height of most convenience outlets is _____ inches above the floor.
A. 6 or 12
B. 12 or 18
C. 18 or 24
D. 24 or 36

SHORT ANSWER
Answer the following questions using short answers.

1. Planning for the electrical needs of a modern home requires a basic understanding of several factors. Name them.

A. _____

B. _____

C. _____

D. _____

2. Name the three types of branch circuits used in a residence.

A. _____

B. _____

C. _____

3. How many special appliance circuits should be provided (minimum) in the kitchen?

_____

4. When does an appliance require an individual appliance circuit?

_____

_____

_____

5. What type of outlets are used outside the house?

_____

6. What is the typical height of switches on the wall?

_____

7. Where might a ground fault interrupter circuit be installed?

_____

8. Why would two, three-way switches be used?

_____

9. What are the functions of a signal and communication system?

A. _____

B. _____

C. _____

MATCHING
Select the answer that correctly matches each term. Place your answer in the space provided.

_____ 1. Ampere

_____ 2. Circuit

_____ 3. Circuit breaker

_____ 4. Conductor

_____ 5. Convenience outlet

_____ 6. Fuse

_____ 7. Lighting outlet

_____ 8. Receptacle

_____ 9. Service drop

_____ 10. Service entrance

_____ 11. Service panel

_____ 12. Watt

A. A material which permits the flow of electricity.

B. A contact device installed at an outlet for the connection of an attachment plug and flexible cord.

C. A safety device which breaks the circuit when it is overloaded by melting a fusible link.

D. A path through which electricity flows from a source to one or more outlets and then returns to the source.

E. The fittings and conductors that bring electricity into the building.

F. One ampere under one volt of pressure.

G. The overhead service conductors between the last pole and the first point of attachment to the house.

H. A device attached to a circuit to allow electricity to be drawn off for appliances or lighting.

I. The main distribution box.

J. The unit of current used to measure the amount of electricity flowing through a conductor per unit of time.

K. An outlet intended for the use of a lighting fixture.

L. A device designed to open and close a circuit by nonautomatic means, and then to open the circuit automatically on a predetermined overload of current.

20 CHAPTER
The Electrical Plan

■ OBJECTIVES

After studying this chapter, the student will be able to:

☐ Describe an electrical plan and identify its features.

☐ Represent typical electrical symbols found on a residential electrical plan.

☐ Compile a circuit data chart.

☐ Draw an electrical plan for a residential structure.

■ DISPLAYS

1. Electrical Plan. Select an outstanding example of a residential electrical plan. Display it on the bulletin board for the class to study.
2. Code Requirements. Display the National Electrical Code book and other local requirements that affect the design of a residential electrical system.

■ INSTRUCTIONAL MATERIALS

Text: Pages 343-348
   Review Questions, Suggested Activities
Workbook: Pages 173-178
   Review Questions, Problems/Activities
Teacher's Resource Guide:
   Chapter 20 — Teaching Strategy
   Chapter 20 — Exam

■ TEACHING STRATEGY

- Prepare Display #1.
- Review chapter objectives.
- Discuss the definition and purpose of the electrical plan.
- Present required information on an electrical plan.

- Discuss the service entrance.
- Assign workbook Problem 20-1.
- Cover switches, convenience outlets, and lighting.
- Prepare Display #2.
- Discuss branch circuits.
- Assign workbook Problem 20-2.
- Discuss the procedure for drawing an electrical plan.
- Assign workbook Problem 20-3.
- Assign one or more of the Suggested Activities in the text.
- Chapter Review
  - Assign Review Questions in the text. Discuss the correct answers.
  - Assign Review Questions in the workbook. Have students check their own answers.
  - Make transparencies of solutions to Problems/Activities 20-1 and 20-2 and use for review.
- Evaluation
  - Administer the Chapter 20 — Exam. Correct the exam and return.
  - Return graded problems with comments.

■ ANSWERS TO REVIEW QUESTIONS, TEXT Page 347

1. An electrical plan is a plan view drawing that shows the meter, distribution panel, outlets, switches, and fixtures.
2. It should be close to the point of incoming service and should be near the point where the most electricity will be used.
3. outside
4. a. Flush mounted distribution panel. ▄▄
   b. Three-way switch. s_3
   c. Push button. ⊡
   d. Telephone. ▼
   e. Duplex convenience outlet. ⊕

5. a. Toggle switch.
   b. Quiet switch.
   c. Mercury switch.
   Also: Push button, dimmer and delayed action.
6. shock.
7. to describe each fixture to be used.
8. three-way

■ ANSWERS TO REVIEW QUESTIONS, WORKBOOK

PART I: SHORT ANSWER/LISTING

1. The electrical plan shows the location and type of electrical equipment to be used.
2. A. Service entrance capacity.
   B. Meter and distribution panel location.
   C. Placement and type of switches.
   D. Location and type of lighting fixtures.
   E. Special electrical equipment.
   F. Number and types of circuits.
   G. Electrical fixture schedule.
   H. Symbols and legend.
   I. Notes which help to describe the system.
3. Toggle switch.
4. A regular outlet remains "hot" all the time, while a switched outlet may be switched from open to closed.
5. A ceiling fixture may be used above an eating area or in an entry. Fluorescent tubes may be used above a suspended ceiling and are functional for kitchens, bathrooms, and workshops. Recessed lighting fixtures are convenient for foyers, hallways, and closets.
6. Near the meter and distribution panel.
7. A. Weatherproof outlet.
   B. Appliance receptacle.
   C. Split-wired outlet.
   D. 240 volt outlet.
   E. Telephone junction box.
   F. Electric service meter.
   G. Electrical distribution meter.
   H. Duplex receptacle outlet.
   I. Telephone.
   J. Single-pole switch.
   K. Three-way switch.
   L. Fluorescent fixture.

PART II: COMPLETION

1. plan
2. National Electrical Code.
3. patterns
4. two
5. fluorescent.
6. lighting

PART III: MULTIPLE CHOICE

1. B. Floor plan.
2. A. It is less expensive and more efficient.
3. C. Hidden line symbol or center line symbol drawn with an irregular curve.
4. D. Exterior fixtures.
5. A. Lighting fixture schedule.

PART IV: PROBLEMS/ACTIVITIES

1. Solution on page 211.
2. Solution on page 212.
3. Solution on page 213.

■ ANSWERS TO CHAPTER 20—EXAM

TRUE—FALSE

1. T	4. F
2. T	5. T
3. T	

MULTIPLE CHOICE

1. A
2. C
3. B

SHORT ANSWER

1. A. Meter.
   B. Distribution panel box.
   C. Electrical outlets.
   D. Switches.
   E. Special electrical features.
2. A. Thin hidden line symbol.
   B. Center line symbol.
3. A. Incandescent.
   B. Fluorescent.
4. A. Type.
   B. Manufacturer.
   C. Catalog #.
   D. Number required.
   E. Mounting height.
   F. Watts.
   G. Remarks.

MATCHING

1. I		7. E	
2. D		8. B	
3. L		9. K	
4. A		10. H	
5. F		11. C	
6. J		12. G	

DIRECTIONS:
Draw each of the electrical symbols specified below as shown in the
completed example.   Scale is 1/4'=1'-0".

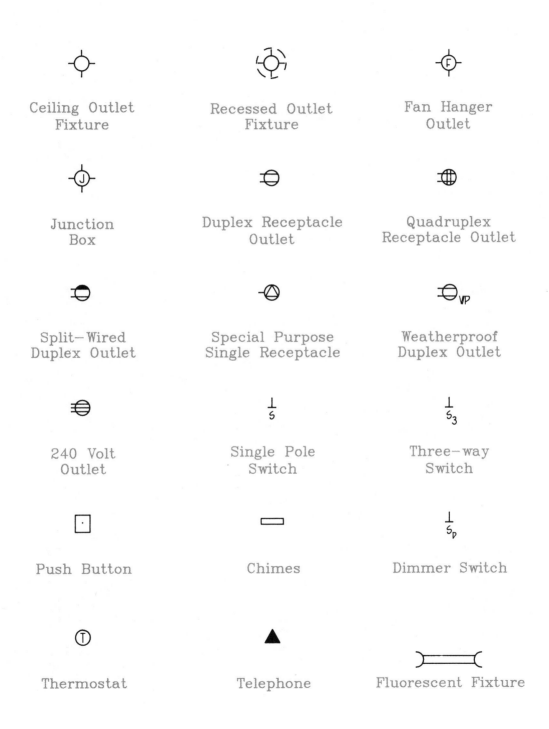

Ceiling Outlet
Fixture

Recessed Outlet
Fixture

Fan Hanger
Outlet

Junction
Box

Duplex Receptacle
Outlet

Quadruplex
Receptacle Outlet

Split—Wired
Duplex Outlet

Special Purpose
Single Receptacle

Weatherproof
Duplex Outlet

240 Volt
Outlet

Single Pole
Switch

Three—way
Switch

Push Button

Chimes

Dimmer Switch

Thermostat

Telephone

Fluorescent Fixture

ELECTRICAL SYMBOLS

20-1

2.

DIRECTIONS:
Using the Garage Floor Plan below, prepare an Electrical Plan which includes the following features:
> Three—way switch for two ceiling outlet fixtures
> Switch for two outside lights on either side of the garage door
> Four duplex outlets on garage side walls (two each side)
> Two duplex outlets above the work bench
> Garage door opener outlet and switch.

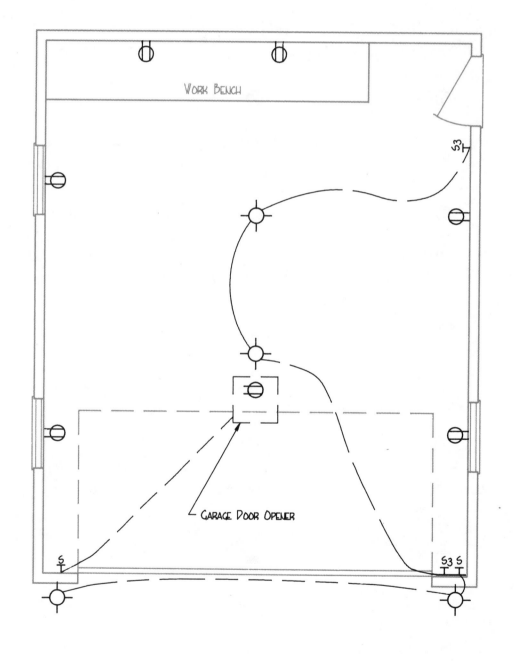

WORK BENCH

GARAGE DOOR OPENER

GARAGE ELECTRICAL PLAN | 20—2

3.

ASSIGNMENT 20-3

TYPICAL SOLUTION

TELEPHONE JUNCTION BOX
ELECTRIC SERVICE METER 240 VOLTS, 150 AMPS.
ELECTRICAL DISTRIBUTION PANEL

GARAGE DOOR OPENER

GARAGE 11'-2" x 19'-4"

KITCHEN 11'-5" x 11'-8"

REF.

BAR

PATIO

FAMILY ROOM 11'-10" x 16'-0"

DINING AREA 9'-10" x 15'-8"

HEAT PUMP

BEDROOM #3 10'-4" x 10'-10"

CL.

LIVING ROOM 11'-4" x 17'-0"

PORCH 4" CONCRETE SLAB

TO DRIVEWAY LIGHTS

BATH 5'-0" x 13'-4"

CL.

CL.

LIN.

FOYER 5'-7" x 11'-0"

CHIMES

CL.

CL.

M. BEDROOM 13'-4" x 15'-5"

M. BATH 5'-6" x 11'-5"

BEDROOM #2 13'-4" x 15'-2"

ELECTRICAL PLAN

SCALE: 1/4"=1'-0"

CIRCUIT DATA

LIGHTING CIRCUITS:
4 PROVIDING 1800 WATTS EACH = 7200 WATTS
SPECIAL APPLIANCE CIRCUITS:
2 PROVIDING 2400 WATTS EACH = 4800 WATTS
INDIVIDUAL APPLIANCE CIRCUITS:
1 FOR REFRIGERATOR = 2400 WATTS
1 FOR GARBAGE DISPOSER = 2400 WATTS
1 FOR DISHWASHER = 2400 WATTS
1 FOR WASHER AND GAS DRYER = 2400 WATTS
1 FOR HEAT PUMP = 7200 WATTS
1 FOR ELECTRIC RANGE = 12000 WATTS
1 FOR ELECTRIC HOT WATER HEATER = 5000 WATTS
1 FOR FUTURE USE = 2400 WATTS
DISTRIBUTION PANEL:
150 AMP, 16 CIRCUIT CAPACITY

Chapter 20—Exam
THE ELECTRICAL PLAN

Name _____

Period _____ **Date** _____ **Score** _____

TRUE—FALSE
Circle T if the statement is true or F if the statement is false.

T   F   1. The electrical plan is usually traced from the floor plan.

T   F   2. The main breaker should be as close as possible to the meter.

T   F   3. Voltage drops over a long distance.

T   F   4. Electric meters are not weatherproof.

T   F   5. Convenience outlets may be switched.

MULTIPLE CHOICE
Choose the answer that correctly completes the statement. Write the corresponding letter in the space provided.

_____ 1. The least expensive type of switch used to switch lights is the _____ switch.
   A. toggle
   B. quiet
   C. mercury
   D. dimmer

_____ 2. Most outlets in the home are 120 volt _____ type which have two receptacles.
   A. simplex
   B. quiet
   C. duplex
   D. mercury

_____ 3. Lighting fixtures which are located outside the house must be _____ fixtures.
   A. high quality
   B. exterior
   C. typical
   D. brass

SHORT ANSWER
Answer the following questions using short answers.

1. List the features commonly shown on the electrical plan.

   A. _____

   B. _____

   C. _____

   D. _____

   E. _____

Name _____

2. What two symbols are used to show the connection of switches to fixtures?

    A. _____

    B. _____

3. What two types of lights are generally used in homes?

    A. _____

    B. _____

4. What information is generally shown on a lighting fixture schedule?

    A. _____

    B. _____

    C. _____

    D. _____

    E. _____

    F. _____

    G. _____

MATCHING

Select the answer that correctly matches each symbol. Place your answer in the space provided.

_____ 1.

_____ 2.

_____ 3.

_____ 4.

_____ 5.

_____ 6.

_____ 7.

_____ 8.

_____ 9.

_____ 10.

_____ 11.

_____ 12.

A. Telephone.
B. 230-volt outlet.
C. Push button.
D. Recessed outlet fixture.
E. Split-wired duplex receptacle outlet.
F. Thermostat.
G. Chimes.
H. Single-pole switch.
I. Ceiling outlet fixture.
J. Duplex receptacle outlet.
K. Weatherproof duplex outlet.
L. Fluorescent fixture.

21
CHAPTER

Residential Plumbing

■ OBJECTIVES

After studying this chapter, the student will be able to:
☐ Discuss the purpose of a residential plumbing system.
☐ Identify the elements contained in a residential water supply system.
☐ Prepare a schematic diagram of a residential water and waste removal system.
☐ Draft a residential water supply system.
☐ Explain the layout of a sewage disposal system.

■ DISPLAYS

1. Plumbing Supplies. Collect examples of galvanized steel, copper, and plastic pipe and fittings which are used in residential plumbing systems. Display these for examination by the class.
2. Code Requirements. Prepare a bulletin board display using excerpts from the plumbing code enforced in your area. Highlight areas of particular importance.

■ INSTRUCTIONAL MATERIALS

Text: Pages 349-358
   Review Questions, Suggested Activities
Workbook: Pages 179-184
   Review Questions, Problems/Activities
Teacher's Resource Guide:
   Chapter 21 — Teaching Strategy
   Chapter 21 — Exam

■ TEACHING STRATEGY

• Prepare Display #1.
• Review chapter objectives.
• Discuss the water supply system.

• Assign workbook Problem 21-1.
• Discuss the water and waste removal systems.
• Assign workbook Problem 21-2.
• Discuss fixtures.
• Present the private sewage disposal system.
• Assign workbook Problem 21-3.
• Discuss the septic tank and disposal field.
• Present calculation of disposal field size.
• Assign one or more of the Suggested Activities in the text.
• Chapter Review
   — Assign Review Questions in the text. Discuss the correct answers.
   — Assign Review Questions in the workbook. Have students check their own answers.
   — Make transparencies of the solutions to Problems/Activities 21-1 and 21-2 and use for review.
• Evaluation
   — Administer the Chapter 21 — Exam. Correct the exam and return.
   — Return graded problems with comments.

■ ANSWERS TO REVIEW QUESTIONS, TEXT
Page 357

1. a. Water supply.
   b. Water and waste removal.
   c. Fixtures.
2. building main.
3. hose bibb.
4. cold water branch.
5. a. Threaded galvanized steel pipe.
   b. Copper tubing.
6. 3/4
7. to reduce noise and cushion water flow.
8. a. Each main line.
   b. Each branch line.
   c. Each fixture.
9. gravity.

10. 4
11. soil stack.
12. secondary
13. house
14. traps.
15. cleanout
16. stack wall.
17. sump pump
18. fixture
19. a. The septic tank.
    b. Disposal field.
20. a. Adequate area.
    b. Proper soil.
21. 50-75
22. 750
23. a garbage disposal.
24. to allow waste water to seep into the ground.
25. dry and porous soil (sand and gravel).
26. 1"/50'.
27. percolation

■ ANSWERS TO REVIEW QUESTIONS, WORKBOOK

PART I: MATCHING

1. B. Building main.
2. D. Hot water branch.
3. G. Main stacks.
4. H. Secondary stacks.
5. A. Branch main.
6. E. House sewer.
7. C. Cleanout.
8. K. Vent stack.
9. I. Stack wall.
10. J. Sump.
11. F. Percolation test.

PART II: COMPLETION

1. Water treatment devices
2. blocked
3. shutoff
4. 6
5. turns
6. secondary
7. disposal
8. bedrooms
9. 2

PART III: SHORT ANSWER/LISTING

1. A. Water supply.
   B. Water and waste removal.
   C. Fixtures.
2. A. When pipes are installed along exterior walls, they should be insulated to prevent freezing.
   B. Frost-free hose bibbs should be used.
3. Special heavy-duty copper tubing with soldered or flare-type joints.
4. A small electric heating element is placed under the sink or lavatory and requires only a cold water line. The heater produces hot water instantly and is effective where only small amounts of hot water are needed, such as shaving, etc.
5. One main drain.
6. It is removed through the soil/vent stack which protrudes about 12 in. above the roof.
7. A. It removes about 75 percent of the solids from the sewage by bacterial action before discharging it into the disposal field.
   B. It provides storage space for the settled solids while they undergo digestive action.
8. It receives liquid sewage from the septic tank and allows it to seep into the soil.
9. $3 \times 500 = 1500$ sq. ft.

PART IV: MULTIPLE CHOICE

1. A. Are smaller than cold water main lines.
2. B. 3/4 in.
3. D. Cushion the water flow and reduce pipe noise during use.
4. C. Gravity.
5. B. 4 in.
6. B. Fixtures.
7. A. 1 acre.
8. C. 750.
9. C. Water supply well.

PART V: PROBLEMS/ACTIVITIES

1. Solution on page 220.
2. Solution on page 221.
3. Solution on page 222.

■ ANSWERS TO CHAPTER 21—EXAM

TRUE—FALSE

1. T	4. F
2. T	5. T
3. F	

MULTIPLE CHOICE

1. B	8. B
2. D	9. D
3. A	10. A
4. C	11. C
5. B	12. A
6. D	13. B
7. A	

SHORT ANSWER

1. A. The water supply system.
   B. The water and waste removal system.
   C. The fixtures which facilitate the use of water.
2. A. Threaded galvanized steel pipe.
   B. Plastic pipe.
   C. Copper pipe (tubing) with soldered joints or flare fittings.
3. A. Each main line.
   B. Each branch line.
   C. At each fixture.
4. A. Cast iron pipe.
   B. Copper and brass alloy pipes.
   C. Fiber pipe.
   D. Plastic pipe.
5. The fixtures.
6. A. Septic tank.
   B. Disposal field.
7. 75 percent.

1.

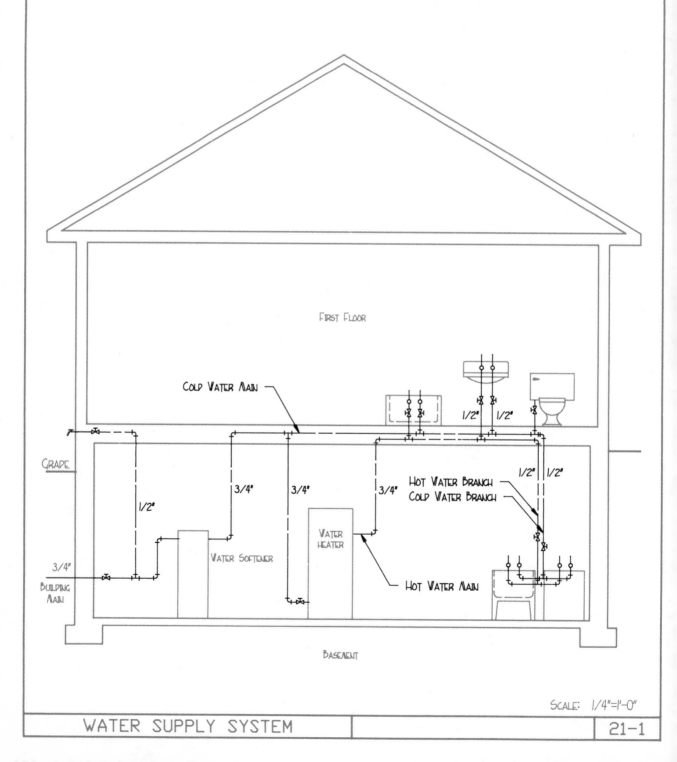

DIRECTIONS:
Using the simplified house section below, draw the schematic of a residential water supply system. Connect each fixture to the cold water and hot water mains (where appropriate). Complete the system to the building main. Label each pipe as to size and name. Include shutoff valves for each branch line and fixture. Provide a hose bib and air chamber at each faucet. See Fig. 21-1 in the text for typical layout.

FIRST FLOOR

COLD WATER MAIN

1/2"   1/2"

GRADE

3/4"   3/4"   3/4"   HOT WATER BRANCH
COLD WATER BRANCH   1/2"   1/2"

1/2"

VATER SOFTENER   VATER HEATER

3/4"
BUILDING MAIN   HOT WATER MAIN

BASEMENT

SCALE: 1/4"=1'-0"

WATER SUPPLY SYSTEM   21-1

2.

DIRECTIONS:
Using the simplified house section below, draw the schematic of a
residential water and waste removal system. Connect each fixture
to the house drain and connect the house drain to the house sewer.
Provide a 4" vent stack through the roof and label each part of
the system showing size of pipe used. Study Fig. 21-8 in your
text for layout. Remember this is a gravity system.

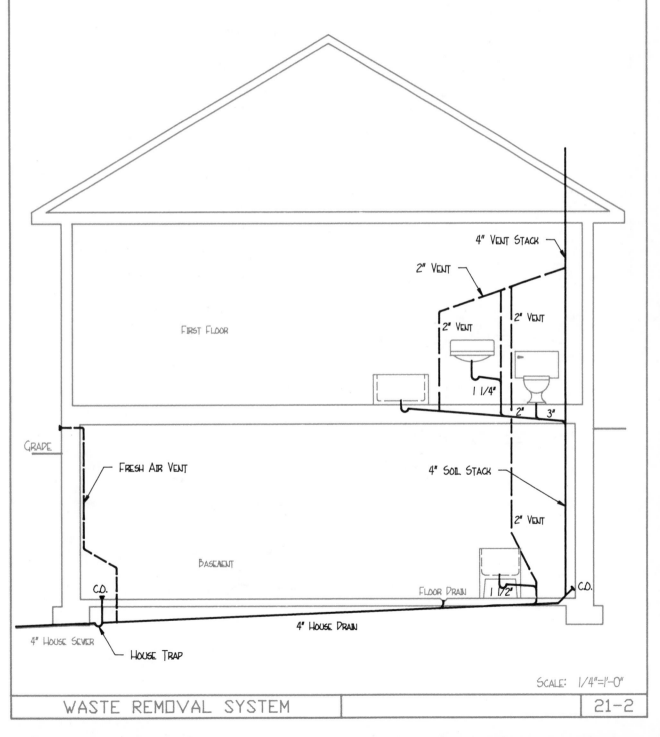

WASTE REMOVAL SYSTEM

21-2

3.

DIRECTIONS:
Suppose you purchased Lot #2 in the subdivision below and wished to install a private well for household use. The surrounding lots have wells and septic systems already and your lot has the septic tank and disposal field in place. The local code specifies a minimum distance of 150' from the disposal field and 75' from the septic tank to the well. Indicate the area on your lot where your well could be placed.

SCALE: 1"=50'-0"

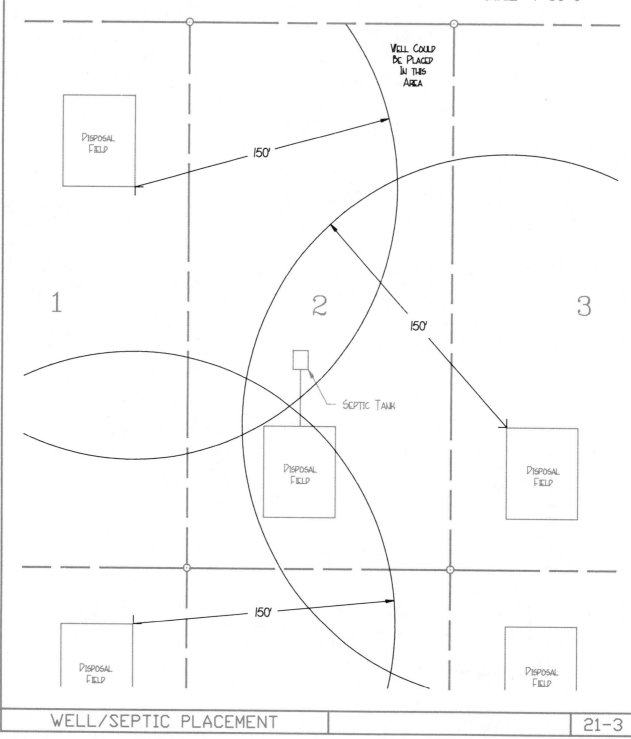

WELL/SEPTIC PLACEMENT

21-3

Chapter 21—Exam
RESIDENTIAL PLUMBING

Name _____

Period _____ **Date** _____ **Score** _____

TRUE—FALSE
Circle T if the statement is true or F if the statement is false.

T   F   1. A residential water supply system begins at the city water main or private water source.

T   F   2. Branch lines are smaller than mains.

T   F   3. Frost-free hose bibbs are not available.

T   F   4. Blocking should be used when large pipes pass through the bottom of a joist.

T   F   5. Lead-free solder should be used to join copper pipe in water distribution systems.

MULTIPLE CHOICE
Choose the answer that correctly completes the statement. Write the corresponding letter in the space provided.

_____ 1. In the water supply system, the pipe which enters the house is known as the _____.
A. branch main
B. building main
C. water supply line
D. branch line

_____ 2. The hot water main emerges from the _____.
A. water storage tank
B. hot water branch line
C. hose bibb
D. water heater

_____ 3. Many codes require that a(n) _____ chamber be located at each faucet.
A. air compression
B. water storage
C. water purification
D. noise

_____ 4. Generally, cold and hot water branch lines are placed about _____ inches apart.
A. 2
B. 4
C. 6
D. 8

_____ 5. Small, on-demand water heaters are located _____.
A. in the basement
B. under the vanity
C. in a closet
D. near the water storage tank

_____ 6. Drain lines are generally _____ inside with minimum projections and sharp turns.
A. glazed
B. rubber lined
C. zinc coated
D. smooth

_____ 7. Unlike the water supply system, the drainage system is _____.
   A. not under pressure
   B. not so important
   C. last thing to be planned
   D. installed by apprentices

_____ 8. A vertical drain pipe which collects waste from one or more fixtures is called a _____.
   A. house sewer
   B. soil stack
   C. vent pipe
   D. cleanout

_____ 9. Once the house drain passes outside of the house it is called a _____.
   A. septic line
   B. secondary stack
   C. main stack
   D. house sewer

_____ 10. Traps are installed below each fixture (except the water closet) to _____.
   A. prevent gases from escaping through the fixture drain into the house
   B. aid in draining the water
   C. reduce sound
   D. slow the flow of water

_____ 11. Each stack requires a _____ located at the base of the stack.
   A. 45 degree elbow
   B. closet bend
   C. cleanout
   D. trap

_____ 12. When 2" x 6" studs are required to enclose a 4" cast iron pipe, this wall is called a _____ wall.
   A. stack
   B. soil
   C. vent
   D. sewer

_____ 13. The suitability of the soil for a disposal field must be determined by _____.
   A. well drilling records
   B. soil percolation tests
   C. compaction tests
   D. history of the area

SHORT ANSWER
Answer the following questions using short answers.

1. List the three principle parts of a residential plumbing installation.

   A. _____

   B. _____

   C. _____

2. Identify three types of pipes that are commonly used in the water supply system.

   A. _____

   B. _____

   C. _____

3. Where should shutoff valves be used in a water supply system?

   A. _____

   B. _____

   C. _____

4. Identify the types of pipe that are commonly used for the waste removal system in a residential structure.

   A. _____

   B. _____

   C. _____

   D. _____

5. What is the most obvious part of the plumbing system?

   _____

6. What are the two parts of a private sewage disposal system?

   A. _____

   B. _____

7. Bacterial action removes approximately what percentage of the solids in the septic tank?

   _____

22
CHAPTER

The Plumbing Plan

■ OBJECTIVES

After studying this chapter, the student will be able to:
- ☐ Explain the purpose and components of a residential plumbing plan.
- ☐ Draw plumbing symbols and fixtures on a plumbing plan using proper techniques.
- ☐ Develop a residential plumbing plan.
- ☐ Compile a plumbing fixture schedule.

■ DISPLAYS

1. Plumbing Plan. Select a residential plumbing plan which illustrates good layout and design. Display the plan on the bulletin board.
2. Student Work. Display some of the best student work on the bulletin board using assignments from the workbook.

■ INSTRUCTIONAL MATERIALS

Text: Pages 359-366
   Review Questions, Suggested Activities
Workbook: Pages 185-190
   Review Questions, Problems/Activities
Teacher's Resource Guide:
   Chapter 22 — Teaching Strategy
   Chapter 22 — Exam

■ TEACHING STRATEGY

- Prepare Display #1.
- Review chapter objectives.
- Review the definition, purpose, and required information for the plumbing plan.
- Discuss waste lines and vent stacks.
- Present water supply lines.
- Discuss drain and fixture locations and size and type of pipe.

- Present the plumbing fixture schedule.
- Discuss the use of symbols, legends, and notes.
- Assign workbook Problem 22-1.
- Present the procedure for drawing a plumbing plan.
- Assign workbook Problems 22-2 and 22-3.
- Prepare Display #2.
- Assign one or more of the Suggested Activities in the text.
- Chapter Review
  - Assign Review Questions in the text. Discuss the correct answers.
  - Assign Review Questions in the workbook. Have students check their own answers.
  - Make transparencies of solutions to Problems/Activities 22-1 and 22-2 and use for review.
- Evaluation
  - Administer the Chapter 22 — Exam. Correct the exam and return.
  - Return graded problems with comments.

■ ANSWERS TO REVIEW QUESTIONS, TEXT
Pages 364-365

1. To show the location, size, and type of plumbing.
2. a. Proper location.
   b. Sufficient size.
3. the waste system.
4. a water closet.
5. 3
6. gravity.
7. sewer.
8. 3/4
9. storm sewer.
10. a. Average amount of water used.
    b. Peak loads.
    c. Water pressure on the line.
    d. Length of pipe run.

11. inside
12. DWV.
13. plumbing fixture schedule.

■ ANSWERS TO REVIEW QUESTIONS, WORKBOOK

PART I: COMPLETION

1. plan
2. electrical
3. 1/4
4. wider
5. shutoff
6. larger
7. heavier
8. standard
9. manufacturers'
10. cleanout

PART II: SHORT ANSWER/LISTING

1. A. Water supply lines.
   B. Waste disposal lines.
   C. Fixtures.
2. The National Plumbing Code.
3. They should be connected to the building main before it reaches the softener.
4. At least two plans; one for each level.
5. Plumbing for fixtures should be located in order to provide access for servicing.
6. It refers to the approximate inside diameter of the pipe.
7. A. Identifying symbol.
   B. Name of the fixture.
   C. Number of fixtures required.
   D. Manufacturer and catalog number.
   E. Pipe connection sizes.
   F. Remarks.
8. These notes are often located in a prominent place such as above the title block.
9. Hidden line symbol.
10. A. ——— S ——— S ——— S ——

PART III: MULTIPLE CHOICE

1. B. Floor plan.
2. C. Waste lines.
3. A. Building main.
4. D. Fixtures.
5. A. Storm sewer or dry well.

6. B. 3/8 in.
7. C. Thinner than.
8. B. Legend.
9. A. Plot.
10. B. Parallel.
11. B. Floor drain—plan view.

PART IV: PROBLEMS/ACTIVITIES

1. Solution on page 229.
2. Solution on page 230.
3. Solution will be evaluated based on principles presented in the text.

■ ANSWERS TO CHAPTER 22—EXAM

TRUE—FALSE

1. T	4. T
2. T	5. T
3. T	

MULTIPLE CHOICE

1. B	5. D
2. B	6. D
3. C	7. B
4. C	

SHORT ANSWER

1. A. Waste lines and vent stacks.
   B. Water supply lines.
   C. Drain and fixture locations.
   D. Size and type of pipe to be used.
   E. Plumbing fixture schedule.
   F. Symbols and legend.
   G. Notes required to describe the system.
   H. Scale of the drawing.
2. A. Split-level houses.
   B. Two-story houses.
3. A. Storm sewer.
   B. Dry well.
4. Local code or National Plumbing Code.
5. A. The average amount of water used.
   B. Peak loads.
   C. Water pressure on the line.
   D. Length of the pipe run.
6. Drain, waste, and vent.

1.

DIRECTIONS:
Draw the Plan View symbol for each of the plumbing elements specified below.   The scale for these symbols is 1/4"=1'-0".

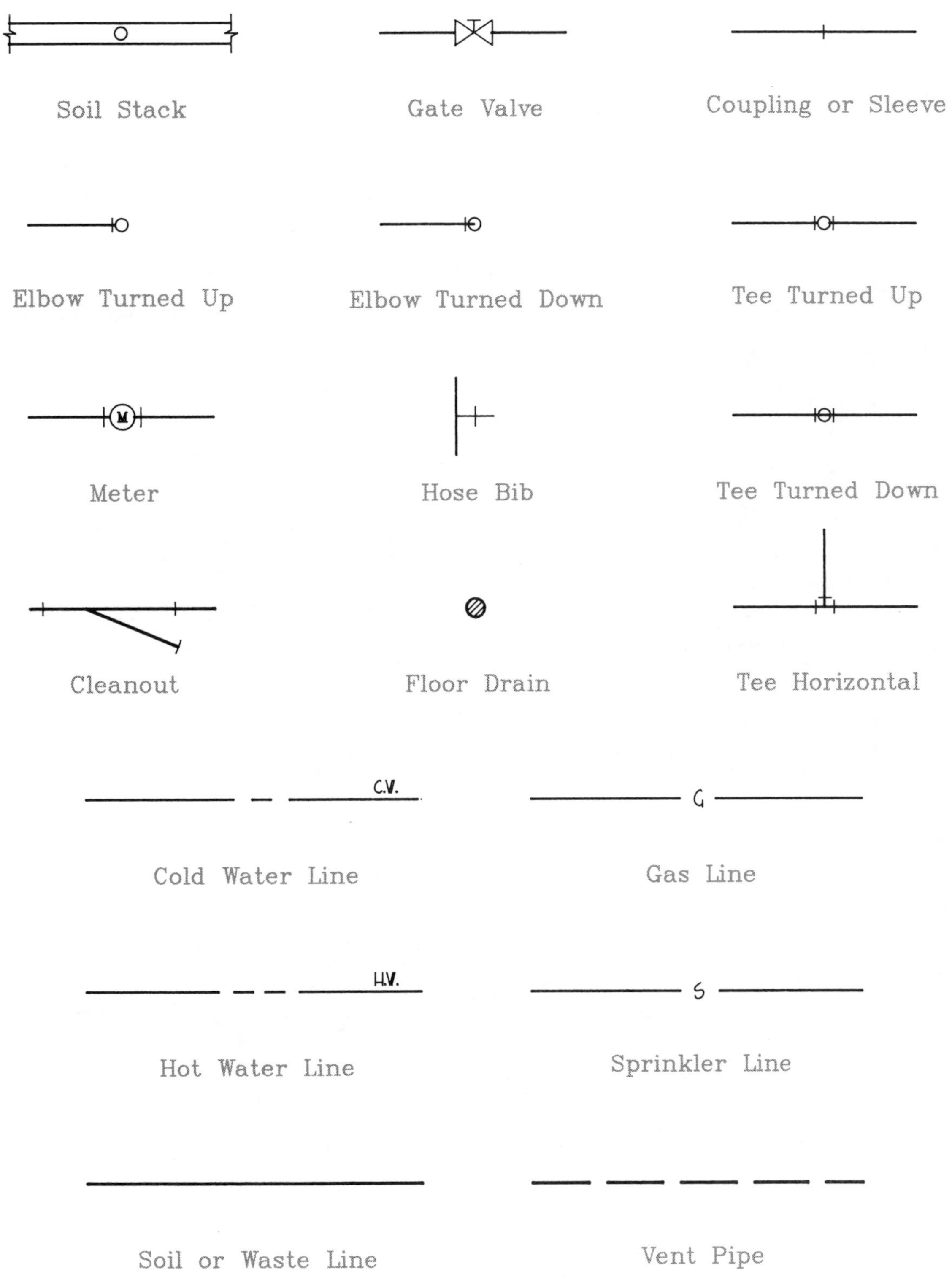

Soil Stack

Gate Valve

Coupling or Sleeve

Elbow Turned Up

Elbow Turned Down

Tee Turned Up

Meter

Hose Bib

Tee Turned Down

Cleanout

Floor Drain

Tee Horizontal

C.V.

Cold Water Line

G

Gas Line

H.V.

Hot Water Line

S

Sprinkler Line

Soil or Waste Line

Vent Pipe

PLUMBING SYMBOLS

22-1

2.

DIRECTIONS:
Show the typical piping arrangement for the two situations below.
Use proper symbols and show tees, elbows, etc.

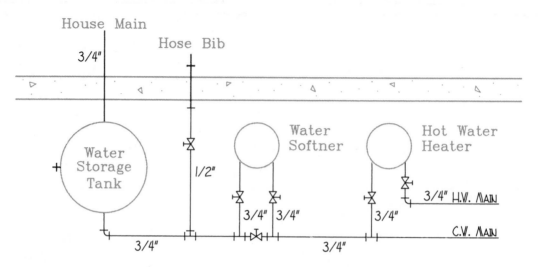

Water Supply Lines

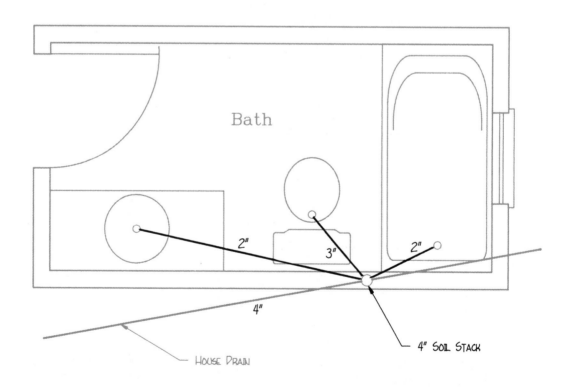

Waste Lines and Vent Stack

SCALE: VARIES

PIPING ARRANGEMENTS		22-2

Chapter 22—Exam
THE PLUMBING PLAN

Name _____

Period _____ **Date** _____ **Score** _____

TRUE—FALSE
Circle T if the statement is true or F if the statement is false.

T   F   1. Gas lines and built-in vacuum systems are shown on the plumbing plan.

T   F   2. The plumbing system should be coordinated with the electrical and climate control systems.

T   F   3. Proper location and sufficient pipe size are the major considerations in planning the waste lines.

T   F   4. A main stack must be designated for each water closet.

T   F   5. Waste line symbols are wider line symbols than water supply lines.

MULTIPLE CHOICE
Choose the answer that correctly completes the statement. Write the corresponding letter in the space provided.

_____ 1. The entire plumbing system is usually planned around the _____.
   A. water supply system
   B. water and waste removal system
   C. heating system
   D. kitchen

_____ 2. The minimum waste line size for a water closet is _____ inches.
   A. 2
   B. 3
   C. 4
   D. 6

_____ 3. Waste lines depend on _____ to move the waste.
   A. vacuum
   B. pressure
   C. gravity
   D. lots of water

_____ 4. Waste lines are usually sloped about _____ inch per foot to facilitate even flow.
   A. 1/16
   B. 1/8
   C. 1/4
   D. 1/2

_____ 5. Hose bibbs and other fixtures that do not require softened or filtered water should be connected to the _____ before it reaches the water softener.
   A. house main
   B. cold water main
   C. cold water branch line
   D. building main

_____ 6. Minimum recommended pipe sizes are given by the _____.
    A. Federal Housing Administration
    B. textbook
    C. National Plumbing Code
    D. All of the above

_____ 7. The usual scale of a plumbing plan is _____.
    A. 1/8" = 1'-0"
    B. 1/4" = 1'-0"
    C. 3/8" = 1'-0"
    D. 1/2" = 1'-0"

SHORT ANSWER
Answer the following questions using short answers.

1. List the required information on a plumbing plan.

    A. _____

    B. _____

    C. _____

    D. _____

    E. _____

    F. _____

    G. _____

    H. _____

2. What types of house designs may require two plumbing plans?

    A. _____

    B. _____

3. What are floor drains usually connected to?

    A. _____

    B. _____

4. Where can the clearance dimensions and minimum space requirements for fixtures be found?

    _____

5. What factors determine the proper pipe size required in a water supply system for a given installation?

    A. _____

    B. _____

    C. _____

    D. _____

6. What does a DWV designation on copper pipe mean?

    _____

23

Residential Climate Control

■ OBJECTIVES

After studying this chapter, the student will be able to:
- [ ] Discuss the components of a complete climate control system.
- [ ] List the advantages and disadvantages of various types of residential heating systems.
- [ ] Perform heat loss calculations for a typical residential structure.
- [ ] Select building materials that will provide the best insulation properties.

■ DISPLAYS

1. Typical Residential Climate Control Systems. Create a bulletin board display from manufacturer's literature showing typical residential climate control systems. Identify each system.
2. Advantages and Disadvantages of Climate Control Systems. Using charts developed by students in response to Suggested Activity #5 in the text, show the advantages and disadvantages of each of the typical residential climate control systems.

■ INSTRUCTIONAL MATERIALS

Text: Pages 367-386
   Review Questions, Suggested Activities
Workbook: Pages 191-196
   Review Questions, Problems/Activities
Teacher's Resource Guide:
   Chapter 23 — Teaching Strategy
   Chapter 23 — Exam

■ TEACHING STRATEGY

- Prepare Display #1.
- Review chapter objectives.

- Discuss temperature control.
- Assign workbook Problem 23-1.
- Discuss humidity control and air circulation and cleaning.
- Discuss forced warm air systems.
- Present hydronic systems.
- Discuss electric radiant systems.
- Discuss heat pumps.
- Present heat loss calculations.
- Assign workbook Problem 23-2.
- Assign one or more of the Suggested Activities in the text.
- Chapter Review
   - Assign Review Questions in the text. Discuss the correct answers.
   - Assign Review Questions in the workbook. Have students check their own answers.
   - Make transparencies of the solutions to Problems/Activities 23-1 and 23-2 and use for review.
- Evaluation
   - Administer the Chapter 23 — Exam. Correct the exam and return.
   - Return graded problems with comments.

■ ANSWERS TO REVIEW QUESTIONS, TEXT
Pages 384-385

1. a. Temperature control.
   b. Humidity control.
   c. Air circulation.
   d. Air cleaning.
2. a. Adequate insulation.
   b. Ventilation.
   c. Solar orientation.
   d. Weatherstripping.
   e. Color of roofing materials.
   Also: Length of overhang, landscaping, and insulating glass.

3. humidity.
4. 50
5. a. Throat and skin irritation.
   b. Cracking furniture.
6. a. "Sticky," uncomfortable air.
   b. More infectious germs.
   Also: Tight doors and windows and water on windows and walls.
7. dehumidifier.
8. a. Forced warm air.
   b. Hydronic.
   c. Electric radiant.
   d. Heat pump.
9. The furnace heats the air. The blower pushes the warm air through the registers to various parts of the house and returns cool air to be reheated again.
10. a. Upflow.
    b. Downflow.
    c. Horizontal.
11. An automatic sensing device that may be set to a predetermined level to activate the furnace.
12. a. Boiler.
    b. Pipes.
    c. Radiator.
13. a. Temperature control of an individual room or area.
    b. Quiet.
    c. Hidden.
    Also: A hydronic system is clean.
14. resistance wires.
15. refrigeration

■ ANSWERS TO REVIEW QUESTIONS, WORKBOOK

PART I: SHORT ANSWER/LISTING

1. A. In the ceiling.
   B. In the exterior walls.
   C. Under the floor.
2. A. Crawl space.
   B. Attic.
3. Dehumidifier.
4. A. Forced warm air systems.
   B. Hydronic systems.
   C. Electric radiant systems.
   D. Heat pump.
5. A. Relatively inexpensive to purchase and install.
   B. Provides a sufficient amount of heat quickly.
   C. A central air cooling system may use the same air ducts.
   D. Humidification is easily added.
6. Consider zoned heating system with a separate furnace and thermostat for each zone.
7. A. Forced warm air system.
   B. Hydronic system.

8. Heat pump, because it is not efficient in areas where the temperature drops below 30 degrees F.

PART II: MULTIPLE CHOICE

1. C. Rigid foam.
2. B. Landscaping.
3. A. Humidifiers.
4. B. A forced warm air system.
5. A. Thermostat.
6. C. One-pipe.
7. A. The temperature of each room may be controlled individually.
8. C. All of the above.
9. D. Heat pump.

PART III: COMPLETION

1. insulation
2. solar
3. more
4. Air
5. horizontal
6. radiant
7. Resistance
8. heat

PART IV: MATCHING

1. G. Relative humidity.
2. A. BTU.
3. H. Resistivity.
4. I. U factor.
5. C. Heat loss.
6. D. Infiltration.
7. B. Design temperature difference.
8. E. Inside design temperature.
9. F. Outside design temperature.

PART V: PROBLEMS/ACTIVITIES

1. Solution on page 236.
2. Solution on page 237.

■ ANSWERS TO CHAPTER 23—EXAM

TRUE—FALSE

1. T	3. T	5. F
2. T	4. F	

MULTIPLE CHOICE

1. D	7. A	13. B
2. B	8. D	14. A
3. A	9. B	15. C
4. C	10. A	16. C
5. B	11. C	
6. B	12. C	

SHORT ANSWER

1. A. Temperature control.
   B. Humidity control.
   C. Air circulation.
   D. Air cleaning.
2. To prevent the transfer of heat or cold from one location to another.
3. The amount of moisture in the air related to the temperature level.
4. Throat and skin irritations are likely.
5. A. Forced warm air.
   B. Hydronic.
   C. Electric radiant.
   D. Heat pumps.
6. A. Standard upflow.
   B. Counterflow.
   C. Horizontal.
7. A. Boiler.
   B. Water pipes.
   C. Radiators or radiant panels.
8. A. Availability of fuels.
   B. Temperature variations.
   C. Cost of installation and maintenance.
   D. Type of house.
   E. Personal preference of the owner.

1.

DIRECTIONS:
Add insulation to the Crawl Space/First Floor section below to maximize resistance to heat loss. The following areas are suggested for consideration: RF insulation on the outside of the stud wall, blanket insulation between the studs and between the floor joists, sill sealer, and RF insulation either inside or outside of the foundation wall.

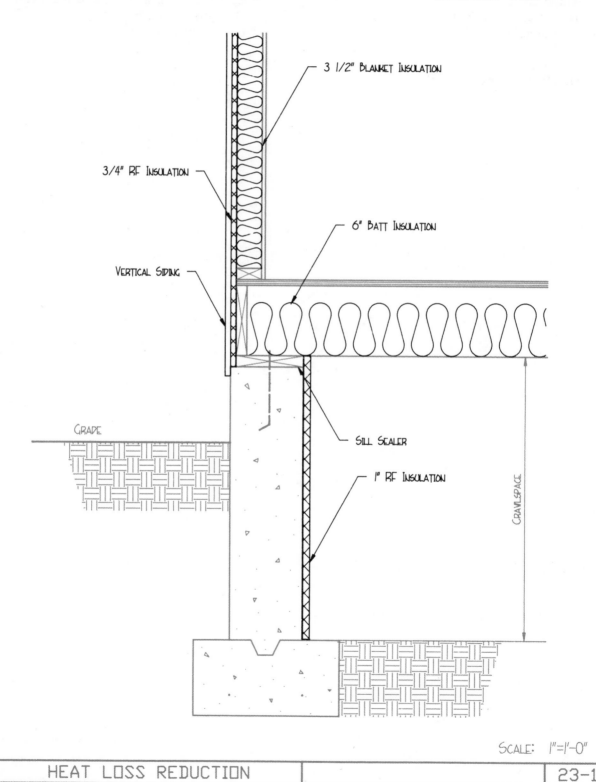

SCALE: 1"=1'-0"

HEAT LOSS REDUCTION   23-1

2.

DIRECTIONS:
Calculate the heat loss for the exterior wall below and fill in the
values as indicated.   The wall has no windows or doors.

WALL AREA CALCULATION:
  Total Wall Area = 8'–0" x 12'–0" = 96 Sq. Ft.
  Window and Door Area = 0 Sq. Ft.
  Net Wall Area = 96 Sq. Ft.

Air Film, R = 0.68
1/2" Drywall, R = 0.45
3 1/2" Blanket Insulation R = 11.0
3/4" RF Insulation R = 2.88
1" Air Space, R = 1.01
Face Brick, R = 0.45
Outside Air Film R = 0.17

RESISTIVITY OF WALL MATERIALS:
  4" Face Brick   =   0.45
  1" Air Space   =   1.01
  3/4" RF Insulation   =   2.88
  3 1/2" Blanket Insulation =   11.00
  1/2" Drywall   =   0.45
  Outside Air Film   =   0.17
  Inside Air Film   =   0.68
    Total Resistivity   =   16.64

U FACTOR FOR NET WALL AREA:
  1.00 Divided by Total Resistivity = 0.060
  Therefore, U Factor for Net Wall = 0.060

DESIGN TEMPERATURE DIFFERENCE:
  Inside Design Temperature   =   70°
  Outside Design Temperature   =   5°
  Design Temperature Difference   =   65°

BTU/H FOR NET WALL:
  Net Wall Area X U Factor X Temperature Difference
  96 Sq. Ft. X 0.060 X 65° = 374/4 BTU/H

Therefore, the heat loss for the 8'–0" x 12'–0" wall is 374.4 BTU/H.

HEAT LOSS CALCULATIONS   23-2

Chapter 23—Exam
RESIDENTIAL CLIMATE CONTROL

Name _____

Period _____ **Date** _____ **Score** _____

TRUE—FALSE
Circle T if the statement is true or F if the statement is false.

T   F   1. Temperature control includes both heating and cooling.

T   F   2. Ventilation reduces the temperature and moisture content in the house.

T   F   3. Color of roofing may affect the efficiency of the temperature control system.

T   F   4. Weather stripping has no effect on heat loss.

T   F   5. Landscaping has no effect on heat loss.

MULTIPLE CHOICE
Choose the answer that correctly completes the statement. Write the corresponding letter in the space provided.

_____ 1. The efficiency of the heating or cooling system is affected by the _____ of the house.
   A. solar orientation
   B. ventilation provided
   C. installation of insulation
   D. All of the above

_____ 2. In cold climates, an attempt should be made to place all large areas of glass on the _____ side of the house away from the cold winter winds, and in a position to take advantage of the winter sun.
   A. north
   B. south
   C. east
   D. west

_____ 3. Air will hold _____ water when the temperature is high than when it is low.
   A. more
   B. less
   C. about the same
   D. Temperature makes no difference

_____ 4. A comfortable humidity level is around _____ percent when the temperature is about 75 degrees.
   A. 25
   B. 35
   C. 50
   D. 60

_____ 5. When water condenses on the inside of windows it generally indicates that the _____.
   A. temperature is too low in the house
   B. moisture content is too high in the house
   C. furnace needs repair because carbon dioxide is being produced
   D. heating system is working well

_____ 6. A _____ may be used to remove water from the air in a house.
   A. humidifier
   B. dehumidifier
   C. air filtering system
   D. hydrometer

_____ 7. Air cleaning devices remove _____ from the air in the house.
   A. dust and foreign particles
   B. viruses
   C. moisture
   D. All of the above

_____ 8. The _____ heating system is popular because it is relatively inexpensive to purchase and install, provides heat in adequate amounts quickly, the heating ducts may be used in a central air cooling system, and humidification is simple.
   A. hydronic
   B. solar warm water
   C. electric radiant
   D. forced warm air

_____ 9. Furnace operation is controlled by the use of a _____.
   A. manometer
   B. thermostat
   C. multiflow valve
   D. timer

_____ 10. One of the major advantages of a hydronic heating system is that _____.
   A. each room may be controlled individually
   B. humidification is easy
   C. it is the least expensive to operate
   D. the system is inexpensive to install

_____ 11. Electric radiant systems use _____ to produce heat.
   A. radio waves
   B. atomic energy
   C. resistance wiring
   D. evaporation units

_____ 12. Heat pumps are essentially _____ units which pump or transfer natural heat from air or water to heat or cool the house.
   A. hot air engine
   B. condensing
   C. refrigeration
   D. None of the above

_____ 13. Heat pumps are highly efficient in _____.
   A. very cold climates
   B. mild climates
   C. all climates
   D. the climate is not a factor

_____ 14. Before determining the proper size heating or cooling unit, heat loss calculations are required for _____.
   A. exposed surfaces
   B. all interior spaces
   C. the heating unit itself
   D. None of the above

_____ 15. Ability of a material to resist the transfer of heat or cold is called its _____.
   A. U factor
   B. infiltration
   C. resistivity
   D. design temperature difference

_____ 16. The U factor for one square foot of material that has a resistivity of 16.63 is _____.
   A. 1.00 x 16.63 = 16.63
   B. 16.63 ÷ 100 = .1663
   C. 1.00 ÷ 16.63 = .060
   D. 16.63 x 100 = 1663

SHORT ANSWER
Answer the following questions using short answers.

1. Identify the four elements of a complete climate control system.

   A. _____

   B. _____

   C. _____

   D. _____

2. What is the function of insulation?

   _____

3. What is humidity?

   _____

4. What is the human effect when the humidity is too low in a house?

   _____

5. Name the four basic types of heating systems most commonly used in residential structures.

   A. _____

   B. _____

   C. _____

   D. _____

6. Identify the three basic kinds of forced warm air furnaces available for residential installations.

   A. _____

   B. _____

   C. _____

7. What are the three main parts of a hydronic system?

   A. _____

   B. _____

   C. _____

8. List five factors which should be considered in choosing the appropriate heating system for a particular home.

A. _____

B. _____

C. _____

D. _____

E. _____

24
CHAPTER

Climate Control Plan

■ OBJECTIVES

After studying this chapter, the student will be able to:

☐ List features included on a residential climate control plan.

☐ Plan the ductwork for a typical forced warm air system.

☐ Select an appropriate heating or cooling unit for a given structure.

☐ Draw a climate control plan using proper symbols and conventions.

■ DISPLAYS

1. Climate Control Plan. Display a complete climate control plan on the bulletin board which illustrates the procedure described in the text.
2. Student Work. Display samples of student work from workbook assignments on the bulletin board.

■ INSTRUCTIONAL MATERIALS

Text: Pages 387-394
   Review Questions, Suggested Activities
Workbook: Pages 197-200
   Review Questions, Problems/Activities
Teacher's Resource Guide:
   Chapter 24 — Teaching Strategy
   Chapter 24 — Exam

■ TEACHING STRATEGY

- Prepare Display #1.
- Review chapter objectives.
- Discuss the definition, purpose, and information required on a climate control plan.
- Discuss the distribution system.

- Assign workbook Problems 24-1 and 24-2.
- Discuss thermostats and climate control equipment.
- Prepare Display #2.
- Discuss schedules, calculations, and notes.
- Present the procedure for drawing a climate control plan.
- Assign one or more of the Suggested Activities in the text.
- Chapter Review
  - Assign Review Questions in the text. Discuss the correct answers.
  - Assign Review Questions in the workbook. Have students check their own answers.
  - Make a transparency of the solution to Problem/Activity 24-1 and use for review.
- Evaluation
  - Administer the Chapter 24 — Exam. Correct the exam and return.
  - Return graded problems with comments.

■ ANSWERS TO REVIEW QUESTIONS, TEXT
Page 393

1. To show the location and size of the climate control equipment.
2. a. Size and location of ducts or pipes.
   b. Location of thermostats and registers.
   c. Location and type of climate control equipment.
   d. Heat loss calculations.
3. ducts, pipes.
4. $1/4" = 1'-0"$.
5. It distributes heat along the exterior wall where it is needed most.
6. When it is large (over 180 sq. ft.) or when it has more than 15 ft. of exterior wall.
7. a. Radial.
   b. Exterior plenum.

8. 6, 8
9. 8" x 10" (4 x 2 = 8 + 2 = 10).
10. wall stack.
11. 3
12. a. Equipment schedule.
    b. Register schedule.
    Also: Heat loss schedule.

■ ANSWERS TO REVIEW QUESTIONS, WORKBOOK

PART I: MULTIPLE CHOICE

1. C. Floor plan.
2. B. Location of thermostats and registers or baseboard convectors.
3. A. Concentrates heating or cooling along outside walls.
4. C. Cool air moves slower than warm air.
5. A. The total area of the round register pipes.
6. B. The size of the baseboard unit or convector cabinet.
7. C. On an inside wall away from any lamps or heat-producing equipment.
8. C. All of the above.

PART II: COMPLETION

1. climate
2. pipes
3. outlets
4. extended plenum
5. 8 x 26 in.
6. outlets
7. schedules.
8. hidden
9. 1/4" = 1'-0".

PART III: SHORT ANSWER/LISTING

1. A. Piping or heating ducts.
   B. Furnace and other climate control equipment.
   C. Location, size, and type of heating, cooling, ventilating, humidifying, and air cleaning equipment.
2. Ducts are drawn as near to scale as possible while pipes are shown as single lines.
3. At least one inlet for each level.
4. Extended plenum system.
5. 1 1/2 in. main.
6. One.
7. Heat loss calculations.

PART IV: PROBLEMS/ACTIVITIES

1. Solution on page 245.
2. Solution on page 246.

■ ANSWERS TO CHAPTER 24—EXAM

TRUE—FALSE

1. T	4. F
2. T	5. T
3. T	

MULTIPLE CHOICE

1. B	6. C
2. A	7. B
3. C	8. D
4. B	9. B
5. A	

1.

DIRECTIONS:
Draw the climate control symbols indicated below. The scale is
1/4"=1'-0".

Warm Air Supply

Cold Air Return

Second Floor Supply

Second Floor Return

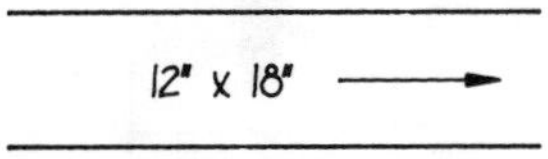

12" x 18" →

12" x 18" Duct/Flow

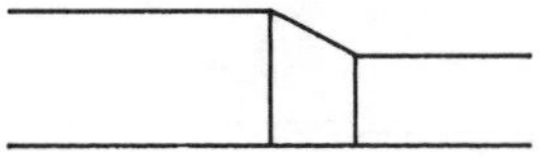

Duct Change in Size

T

Thermostat

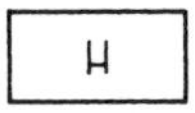

H

Humidistat

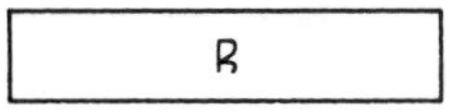

R

Radiator

CONVECTOR

Convector

REGISTER

Register

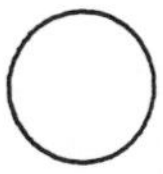

Ceiling Duct Outlet

Scale: 1/4'=1'-0"

CLIMATE CONTROL SYMBOLS

24-1

2.

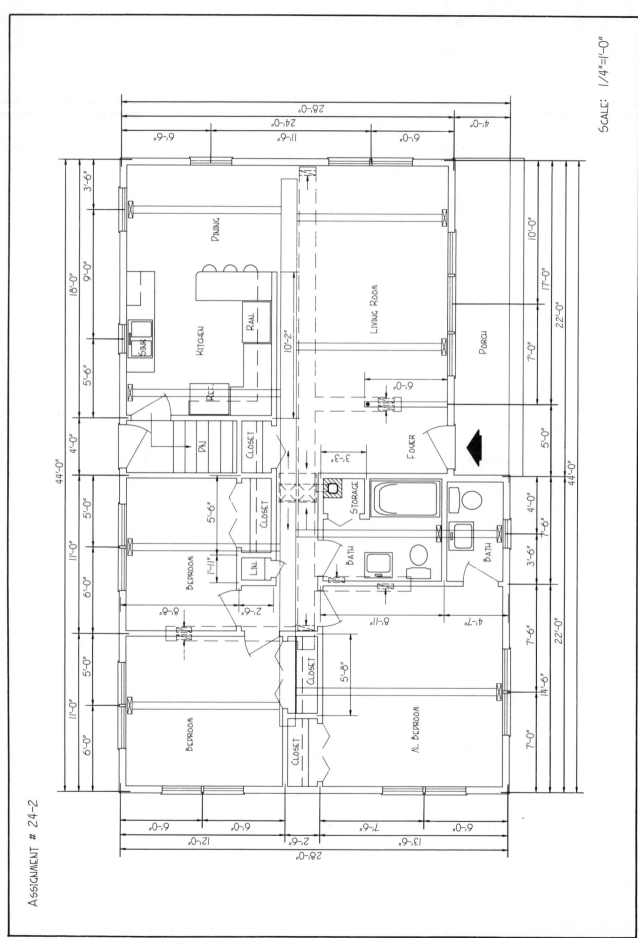

Chapter 24—Exam
CLIMATE CONTROL PLAN

Name _____

Period _____ **Date** _____ **Score** _____

TRUE—FALSE

Circle T if the statement is true or F if the statement is false.

T   F   1. The climate control plan should be closely coordinated with the structural, plumbing, and electrical aspects of the home.

T   F   2. A perimeter system of outlets provides uniform heating or cooling.

T   F   3. A 6" or 8" round pipe may be used to supply a register in the extended plenum system.

T   F   4. Inlets are required for all types of heating systems.

T   F   5. In a hydronic heating system, the size baseboard unit or convector cabinet required depends on the heat loss calculated for a given area.

MULTIPLE CHOICE

Choose the answer that correctly completes the statement. Write the corresponding letter in the space provided.

_____ 1. The scale of a residential climate control plan is generally _____.
A. 1/8" = 1'-0"
B. 1/4" = 1'-0"
C. 3/8" = 1'-0"
D. 1/2" = 1'-0"

_____ 2. There should be at least _____ outlet(s) (register or baseboard unit) in each large area to be heated or cooled.
A. one
B. two
C. three
D. four

_____ 3. If a room has more than _____ feet of exterior wall, then two or more registers should be used.
A. 5
B. 10
C. 15
D. 20

_____ 4. Two basic types of ductwork systems are the radial system and the _____ system.
A. round pipe
B. extended plenum
C. perimeter
D. underground

_____ 5. A vertical duct designed to fit between the studs is called a _____.
A. wall stack
B. feeder duct
C. stack wall
D. thin duct

_____ 6. Each automatic climate control system requires at least one _____.
   A. automatic timer
   B. relief valve
   C. thermostat
   D. resistance hydrastat

_____ 7. A thermostat should be located _____ in a place where the temperature will be representative of the room as a whole.
   A. on an outside wall
   B. on an inside partition
   C. in a closet
   D. in the basement

_____ 8. A complete climate control plan will show a summary of the _____.
   A. length of pipe/ductwork required
   B. number of fittings required for the job
   C. hours needed to install the system
   D. heat loss calculations

_____ 9. A reasonable amount of heat loss for a 1500 square foot house might be _____ BTUs/H.
   A. 5,000
   B. 50,000
   C. 500,000
   D. 5,000,000

25
CHAPTER

Solar Space Heating

■ OBJECTIVES

After studying this chapter, the student will be able to:
- [ ] Describe the two basic types of solar space heating.
- [ ] Explain how a passive solar space heating system works.
- [ ] Compare direct, indirect, and isolated passive solar gain systems.
- [ ] Identify the two most frequently used active solar systems.
- [ ] List the advantages and disadvantages of solar space heating.

■ DISPLAYS

1. Solar Energy Systems. Prepare a bulletin board display from materials secured from manufacturers of active solar energy systems. Warm air as well as warm water systems should be represented.
2. Collector Plates. Display a collection of solar collector elements from a variety of flat plate collectors. Contact manufacturers for samples.

■ INSTRUCTIONAL MATERIALS

Text: Pages 395-404
    Review Questions, Suggested Activities
Workbook: Pages 201-206
    Review Questions, Problems/Activities
Teacher's Resource Guide:
    Chapter 25—Teaching Strategy
    Chapter 25—Exam

■ TEACHING STRATEGY

- Prepare Display #1.
- Review chapter objectives.
- Introduce passive solar systems.

- Discuss direct gain systems.
- Present indirect gain systems.
- Discuss isolated gain systems.
- Assign workbook Problem 25-l.
- Introduce active solar systems.
- Prepare Display #2.
- Discuss warm air solar systems.
- Assign workbook Problem 25-2.
- Discuss warm water solar systems.
- Discuss advantages and disadvantages of solar heating.
- Assign one or more of the Suggested Activities in the text.
- Chapter Review
    - Assign Review Questions in the text. Discuss the correct answers.
    - Assign Review Questions in the workbook. Have students check their own answers.
    - Make transparencies of the solutions for Problems/Activities 25-1 and 25-2 and use for review.
- Evaluation
    - Administer the Chapter 25—Exam. Correct the exam and return.
    - Return graded problems with comments.

■ ANSWERS TO REVIEW QUESTIONS, TEXT Page 404

1. a. Passive.
   b. Active.
2. a. Convection.
   b. Conduction.
   c. Radiation.
3. a. Direct gain.
   b. Indirect gain.
   c. Isolated gain systems.
4. Sunlight passes through large areas of glazing into the interior of the dwelling and heats up the air inside.
5. To store heat for future use.

6. a. Concrete.
   b. Masonry.
   c. Stone.
7. False.
8. The indirect solar gain system has a large thermal mass between the glazing and the interior space.
9. True.
10. Trombe
11. Thermosiphoning is the result of a fluid expanding and rising.
12. True.
13. They change from solid to liquid as they heat up and are capable of storing large amounts of heat.
14. Solar heat is collected and stored in an area outside the living space.
15. a. Uses less interior space.
    b. Large interior space not exposed to the sun.
    c. Heat collection is easier to control.
16. True.
17. Active systems use pumps, fans, or other devices to distribute the heat to desired locations. Passive systems use convection, conduction, or radiation to distribute heat.
18. a. Warm air systems.
    b. Warm water systems.
19. 15-65 percent.
20. absorber
21. True.
22. Aluminum.
23. Black.
24. Stones or rock.
25. False.
26. False.
27. Water.
28. Freezing.
29. True.
30. A liquid-to-air heat exchanger or convector.

■ ANSWERS TO REVIEW QUESTIONS, WORKBOOK

PART I: COMPLETION

1. passive
2. direct
3. outside
4. isolated
5. active
6. warm air absorber plate
7. heat storage.
8. water
9. pump.

PART II: SHORT ANSWER/LISTING

1. A. Passive solar systems.
   B. Active solar systems.
2. Glass.
3. They are necessary to prevent the interior temperature from rising too high in the daytime and to keep it from falling too low at night.
4. The drum wall will store a large amount of heat. The appearance and noise created by expansion and contraction caused by heating and cooling may be offensive and problems may arise with evaporation, corrosion, and leaking.
5. A. South-facing orientation.
   B. Double glazing of glass, plastic, or fiberglass.
   C. Minimum air infiltration.
   D. Thick concrete floors which are isolated from the foundation and soil beneath.
   E. Large thermal mass.
6. A. The box should be airtight with highly transparent glazing.
   B. There should be adequate insulation to retain heat in cold weather.
7. The tilt is usually between 50 and 60 degrees and the best orientation is usually facing south.
8. A set of controls activates a blower which in turn moves the heated air into the living spaces.
9. A. The corrosive action of water and higher pressure than associated with an air-type system warrant greater concern in the design and construction of the water collectors.
   B. Freezing should be prevented by using a mixture of antifreeze and water, installing a draindown procedure, or using non-water fluids.

PART III: MULTIPLE CHOICE

1. C. Is a type of passive solar system.
2. B. Use a large thermal mass located between the sun and living space to store heat.
3. A. Reverse thermosiphoning.
4. D. All of the above.
5. B. Warm air solar system.
6. B. Aluminum.
7. A. Sufficiently large to store enough heat for three days of cloudy weather.
8. C. Large insulated tank usually located in the basement or crawl space.
9. B. Liquid-to-air heat exchangers such as baseboard convectors.

PART IV: MATCHING

1. F. Solar radiation.
2. B. Convection.
3. A. Conduction.
4. E. Radiation.
5. I. Trombe wall.
6. H. Thermosiphoning.
7. J. Water storage wall.
8. D. Glauber's salt.

9. G. Sun space.
10. C. Flat plate collectors.

PART V: PROBLEMS/ACTIVITIES

1. Solution on page 252.
2. Solution on page 253.

■ ANSWERS TO CHAPTER 25—EXAM

TRUE—FALSE
1. T
2. F
3. T
4. T
5. T

MULTIPLE CHOICE
1. B
2. A
3. C
4. D
5. B
6. A
7. B
8. C
9. A
10. B
11. C
12. D

SHORT ANSWER
1. A. Passive solar systems.
   B. Active solar systems.
2. A. Convection.
   B. Conduction.
   C. Radiation.
3. A. Direct gain systems.
   B. Indirect gain systems.
   C. Isolated gain or sun space systems.
4. A. Large amount of stone.
   B. Thick concrete walls and floors.
   C. Drums filled with water.
5. A. Trombe wall.
   B. Water storage wall.
6. A. It is inexpensive.
   B. It can store large amounts of heat .
7. The solar radiation is extracted using a solar collector outside the home. Heat is stored in a thermal mass beneath the structure. Thermosiphoning moves warm air up into the dwelling while cool air returns to the collector to be warmed again.
8. A. Warm air systems.
   B. Warm water systems.
9. A. Tilt.
   B. Orientation.
10. Rock or stone.
11. A. Bank of collectors.
    B. Warm water storage tank.
    C. Pump to circulate water.
    D. Heat exchange device.
    E. Controls for operating the system.
12. Threat of freezing.

1.

DIRECTIONS:
Complete each of the simplified structures below to illustrate the
type of Passive Solar system indicated.

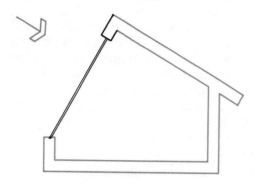

Direct Gain Sloped Wall

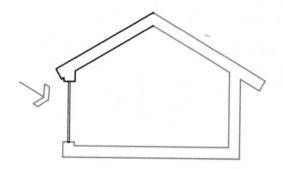

Direct Gain Vertical Wall

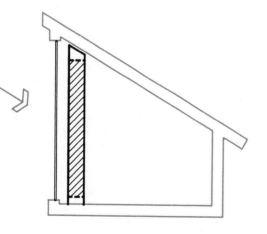

Indirect Gain Trombe Wall

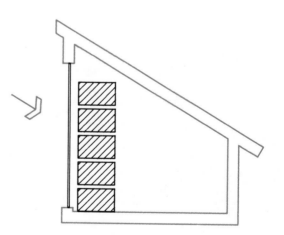

Indirect Gain Drum Wall

PASSIVE SOLAR HEATING

25-1

2.

DIRECTIONS:
Add solar collectors on the roof, thermal storage with blower in the basement, and connecting ducts to the simplified partial structure below. Show the collectors as 6" thick and 8 feet long, the ducts as 6" in diameter, and the storage as 4' x 8'. See Fig. 25–11 for design layout.

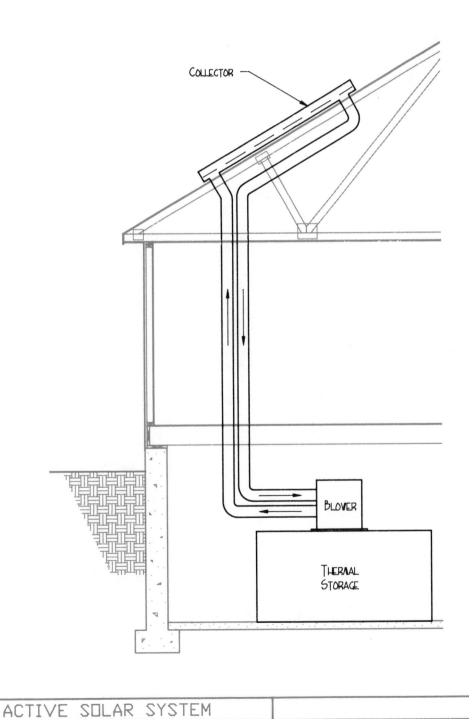

COLLECTOR

BLOWER

THERMAL
STORAGE

ACTIVE SOLAR SYSTEM

25-2

Chapter 25—Exam
SOLAR SPACE HEATING

Name _____

Period _____ **Date** _____ **Score** _____

TRUE—FALSE
Circle T if the statement is true or F if the statement is false.

T   F   1. Increased heating costs and dwindling fuel supplies are reasons to consider solar space heating.

T   F   2. Passive solar systems use pumps or fans to distribute heat.

T   F   3. The word "gain" refers to the way heat is extracted from solar radiation.

T   F   4. Direct gain systems are the most popular type of passive solar space heating systems.

T   F   5. Frame walls have little mass and, therefore, store small amounts of heat.

MULTIPLE CHOICE
Choose the answer that correctly completes the statement. Write the corresponding letter in the space provided.

_____ 1. The transfer of heat by a moving fluid is _____.
A. conduction
B. convection
C. radiation
D. saturation

_____ 2. The flow of heat through an object by transferring heat from one molecule to another is _____.
A. conduction
B. convection
C. radiation
D. osmosis

_____ 3. The flow of heat from a warm source through space in waves of infrared or visible light energy is _____.
A. conduction
B. convection
C. radiation
D. None of the above

_____ 4. Which of the following materials is capable of storing the most heat per cubic foot of volume?
A. Wood
B. Concrete
C. Steel
D. Water

_____ 5. In a(n) _____ system, a large thermal mass is placed between the sun and the living space.
A. direct gain
B. indirect gain
C. isolated gain
D. None of the above

_____ 6. The result of a fluid expanding and rising is called _____.
A. thermosiphoning
B. reverse thermosiphoning
C. conduction
D. transformation

_____ 7. A phase change material, such as _____, has some possible advantages as a thermal storage material.
A. sodium chloride
B. glauber's salt
C. mercury
D. water

_____ 8. Solar systems that collect and store solar energy in an area outside the living space are known as _____ systems.
A. direct gain
B. indirect gain
C. isolated gain
D. remote gain

_____ 9. A _____ is an example of an isolated gain system.
A. greenhouse or sun space
B. Trombe wall
C. drum wall
D. None of the above

_____ 10. A(n) _____ heating system utilizes pumps, fans, or other devices to distribute heat to desired locations.
A. passive solar
B. active solar
C. isolated gain
D. None of the above

_____ 11. Every solar collector has some type of _____ which is designed to absorb heat as the sun's rays strike it.
A. storage
B. glazing
C. absorber plate
D. heater element

_____ 12. The most efficient material commonly used for warm air absorber plates is _____.
A. aluminum
B. steel
C. ceramic
D. copper

Name _____

SHORT ANSWER
Answer the following questions using short answers.

1. Two basic systems have evolved for the utilization of solar energy for space heating. What are they?

   A. _____

   B. _____

2. What three means of distributing heat are used by purely passive solar heating systems?

   A. _____

   B. _____

   C. _____

3. Name the three most common types of passive solar designs.

   A. _____

   B. _____

   C. _____

4. What structural elements or additional items are generally used to form the large thermal mass required for direct gain systems?

   A. _____

   B. _____

   C. _____

5. Identify two types of walls that are used in indirect gain systems.

   A. _____

   B. _____

6. List two reasons why water is frequently used as a thermal mass.

   A. _____

   B. _____

7. Briefly explain how an isolated gain passive solar system works.

   _____

   _____

   _____

   _____

   _____

8. What are the two basic types of active solar heating systems?

   A. _____

   B. _____

9. In addition to the type of material used, two other factors are also important for maximum heat collection efficiency of an absorber plate. What are they?

   A. _____

   B. _____

10. What type of storage is generally used with a warm air active solar system?

    _____

11. What are the basic parts of a warm water solar system?

    A. _____

    B. _____

    C. _____

    D. _____

    E. _____

12. What one concern is present in warm water systems that is not present in warm air systems?

    _____

26 CHAPTER

Earth Sheltered Dwellings

■ OBJECTIVES

After studying this chapter, the student will be able to:
- ☐ Explain the purpose of a large thermal mass in earth sheltered dwellings.
- ☐ Review important site considerations for earth sheltered buildings.
- ☐ Explain why soil type is a major concern in the design of an earth sheltered structure.
- ☐ Summarize design variations of earth sheltered dwellings.

■ DISPLAYS

1. Soil Types. Create a display of typical soil types found in your local area. Identify those which are most suitable for earth sheltered dwellings. Use samples collected by students in Suggested Activity #2 in the text.
2. Earth Sheltered Dwellings. Create a bulletin board display composed of photos/pictures of earth sheltered dwellings. Identify each type of dwelling.

■ INSTRUCTIONAL MATERIALS

Text: Pages 405-412
   Review Questions, Suggested Activities
Workbook: Pages 207-211
   Review Questions, Problems/Activities
Teacher's Resource Guide:
   Chapter 26 — Teaching Strategy
   Chapter 26 — Exam

■ TEACHING STRATEGY

- Prepare Display #1.
- Review chapter objectives.
- Introduce site considerations.
- Discuss orientation on the site and topography as a design consideration.
- Discuss soil and groundwater considerations.
- Present energy conservation and structural systems.
- Discuss the cost of earth sheltered dwellings.
- Introduce design variations of earth sheltered dwellings.
- Assign workbook Problem 26-1.
- Discuss the slope design, atrium design, and penetrational design.
- Assign workbook Problem 26-2.
- Prepare Display #2.
- Cover the advantages and disadvantages of earth sheltered housing.
- Assign one or more of the Suggested Activities in the text.
- Chapter Review
   - Assign Review Questions in the text. Discuss the correct answers.
   - Assign Review Questions in the workbook. Have students check their own answers.
- Evaluation
   - Administer the Chapter 26 — Exam. Correct the exam and return.
   - Return graded problems with comments.

■ ANSWERS TO REVIEW QUESTIONS, TEXT
Pages 411-412

1. a. Orientation to sun and wind.
   b. Topography.
   c. Type of soil.
   d. Groundwater level.
   e. Heavy roof loads.
2. True. Assuming a location in the northern hemisphere, southern exposures will receive the most radiant energy.
3. a. Shutters.
   b. Vegetation.
   c. Overhangs.

4. Yes. Wind is an important consideration because a building exposed to cold winter winds will experience a dramatic heat loss. The building orientation should minimize the effect of the wind, thus reducing heat loss.
5. Northwest.
6. a. Contour of the land.
   b. Trees.
   c. Streams.
   d. Other natural features.
7. To reduce the use of energy.
8. Expansive clay.
9. 62.4 lbs./sq. ft. for each foot of depth.
10. surface area
11. Heat loss in a building is a function of the amount of surface area through which heat can escape. Therefore, a dwelling with very little exposed surface area will lose less heat.
12. a. Conventional flat roof systems.
    b. Vaults or domes.
13. a. Slope design.
    b. Atrium design.
    c. Penetrational design.
14. Penetrational design.
15. atrium

■ ANSWERS TO REVIEW QUESTIONS, WORKBOOK

PART I: SHORT ANSWER/LISTING

1. A. Orientation to the sun and wind.
   B. Topography.
   C. Type of soil.
   D. Groundwater level.
2. Southeast.
3. Earth sheltered houses are usually heavier and placed deeper into the earth than conventional houses. Excessive groundwater is a problem for this type of dwelling.
4. It expands when wet and the high pressure produced may cause structural damage.
5. A. Shape of the structure.
   B. Earth mass around the structure.
6. Cast-in-place concrete slabs, concrete planks, and wood or steel post and beam systems are the components of conventional systems. The dwelling is usually rectangular in shape with a flat or sloping roof.

   Concrete or steel culvert shapes and domes are used in unconventional systems because they can support heavy loads and permit unique designs. The earth mass may be utilized to a greater extent, but construction may be more difficult and costly.
7. The design is usually highly energy efficient due to the continuous earth mass, south-facing windows, and reduced wind on the structure.

PART II: MULTIPLE CHOICE

1. C. Solar energy may be used to heat the interior space.
2. A. Sloping.
3. B. Bearing capacity and tendency to expand when wet.
4. D. Compacted sand or gravel.
5. A. Has a small surface area exposed.
6. D. All of the above.
7. A. Probably better suited for warm climates.
8. B. Their high resistance to fire damage.

PART III: COMPLETION

1. south
2. deciduous
3. fine grained
4. good
5. large
6. slope
7. penetrational

PART IV: PROBLEMS/ACTIVITIES

1. Solution on page 261.
2. Solution on page 262.

■ ANSWERS TO CHAPTER 26—EXAM

TRUE—FALSE

1. T	4. F
2. F	5. T
3. T	

MULTIPLE CHOICE

1. C	3. B	5. A
2. B	4. B	6. B

SHORT ANSWER

1. A. Orientation to sun and wind.
   B. Topography.
   C. Type of soil.
   D. Groundwater level.
   E. Load-bearing elements of the structure.
2. A. Bearing capacity.
   B. Tendency to expand when wet.
3. A. Conventional flat roof systems (cast-in-place concrete slabs, concrete planks, post and beam systems).
   B. Vault and dome shapes.
4. A. Slope design.
   B. Atrium design.
   C. Penetrational design.
5. The penetrational design.
6. A. Long expected life span of the building.
   B. Low maintenance costs.
   C. Less cost for heating and cooling.
   D. High resistance to fire.

1.

DIRECTIONS:
Draw a simplified Section View of a single level residential structure
of the slope design for the site indicated below by the dotted line.
(See Fig. 26-10 in the text.)   The plan should incorporate the
following: 8 ft. ceiling, 24 ft. depth (front to back), 2 ft. of soil on
top of a 1 ft. thick ceiling, glass wall on south side, and 4 ft. bubble-
type skylight near the rear of the home.   Scale is 1/8"=1'-0".

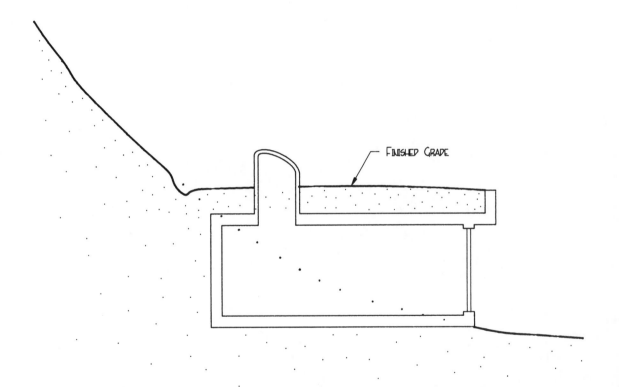

FINISHED GRADE

SCALE: 1/8"=1'-0"

| EARTH SHELTERED HOME | | 26-1 |

2.

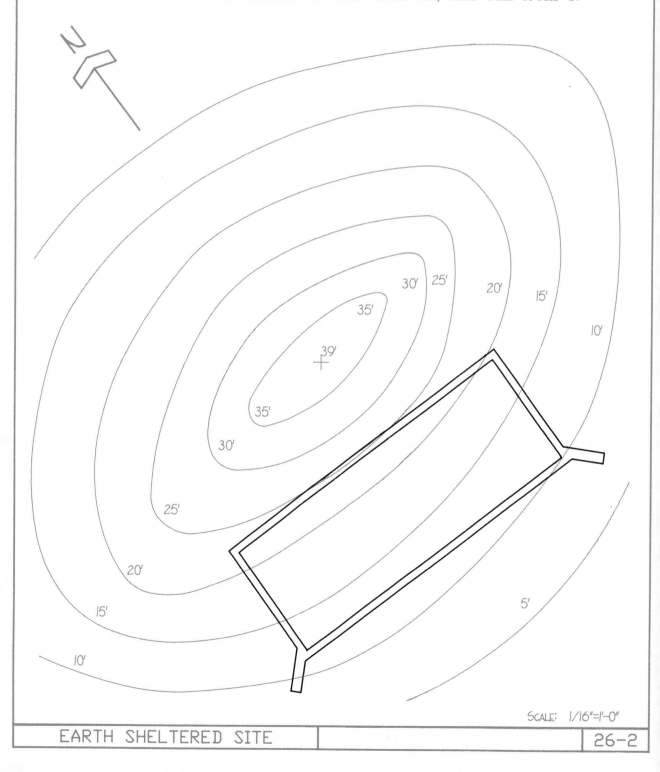

DIRECTIONS:
Study the Topographical Drawing of the site below and show the placement of a 24' x 60' earth sheltered home of the slope design. The location should take into consideration the direction of the sun for maximum heating, direction of winter winds and summer breezes, patterns of water runoff, and groundwater conditions. The scale of the drawing is 1/16"=1'-0".

Winter wind from NW, summer breezes from SE, and sun from S.

SCALE: 1/16"=1'-0"

EARTH SHELTERED SITE | | 26-2

Chapter 26—Exam
EARTH SHELTERED DWELLINGS

Name _____

Period _____ Date _____ Score _____

TRUE—FALSE
Circle T if the statement is true or F if the statement is false.

T   F   1. Earth is capable of providing a large thermal mass and may act as an insulator.

T   F   2. Winter winds in the northern hemisphere are primarily from the northeast.

T   F   3. The site should be selected first so that the building design and site complement each other.

T   F   4. Patterns of water runoff are independent of site contour.

T   F   5. Vegetation on the site is desirable for beautification as well as for erosion and noise reduction.

MULTIPLE CHOICE
Choose the answer that correctly completes the statement. Write the corresponding letter in the space provided.

_____ 1. One of the most important considerations in the design of energy-efficient earth sheltered dwellings is the _____.
A. soil bearing capacity
B. prevailing wind
C. orientation to the sun
D. landscape

_____ 2. Summer breezes in the northern hemisphere are generally from the _____.
A. northeast
B. southeast
C. northwest
D. southwest

_____ 3. Generally, _____ is recommended for backfill against the wall of an earth sheltered dwelling.
A. clay
B. sand and gravel
C. peat
D. inorganic silt

_____ 4. When soil is saturated with water, it presents a pressure of _____ lbs./sq. ft. for each foot of depth.
A. 50
B. 62.4
C. 74.6
D. 100

_____ 5. The earth sheltered structure known as the _____ maximizes earth cover around the dwelling by placing all windows and doors on one side of the structure.
A. slope design
B. atrium design
C. penetrational design
D. unidirectional design

_____ 6. The _____ places living areas around a central courtyard with all windows opening into the courtyard.
  A. slope design
  B. atrium design
  C. penetrational design
  D. unidirectional design

SHORT ANSWER
Answer the following questions using short answers.

1. Name several design aspects which are important for earth sheltered structures which may not be as important for conventional above-grade structures.

  A. _____

  B. _____

  C. _____

  D. _____

  E. _____

2. What are the two important soil characteristics that should be evaluated before deciding on a site for an earth sheltered dwelling?

  A. _____

  B. _____

3. What two basic systems are used in earth sheltered structures to support the roof load?

  A. _____

  _____

  B. _____

4. What are the three basic design variations of earth sheltered dwellings?

  A. _____

  B. _____

  C. _____

5. Which earth sheltered design provides window openings and access at various points around the structure?

  _____

6. List four advantages of earth sheltered housing.

  A. _____

  B. _____

  C. _____

  D. _____

27 CHAPTER

Dome Structures

■ OBJECTIVES

After studying this chapter, the student will be able to:
☐ Explain why a dome structure generally has less heat loss than a conventional structure of comparable size.
☐ Diagram how a typical dome provides free interior space.
☐ Describe how a typical dome is constructed.
☐ List several advantages and disadvantages of domes.

■ DISPLAYS

1. Dome Homes. Create a bulletin board display of photos of dome homes which are available from manufacturers. Show floor plans and finished products.
2. Dome Models. Display dome home models built by students as a part of Suggested Activity #2 in the text.

■ INSTRUCTIONAL MATERIALS

Text: Pages 413-420
   Review Questions, Suggested Activities
Workbook: Pages 213-216
   Review Questions, Problems/Activities
Teacher's Resource Guide:
   Chapter 27 — Teaching Strategy
   Chapter 27 — Exam

■ TEACHING STRATEGY

- Prepare Display #1.
- Review chapter objectives.
- Introduce dome structures.
- Discuss dome variations.

- Assign Suggested Activity #2 in the text.
- Discuss typical dome construction.
- Cover advantages and disadvantages of domes.
- Assign workbook Problems 27-1 and 27-2.
- Prepare Display #2.
- Assign one or more of the remaining Suggested Activities in the text.
- Chapter Review
  - Assign Review Questions in the text. Discuss the correct answers.
  - Assign Review Questions in the workbook. Have students check their own answers.
- Evaluation
  - Administer the Chapter 27 — Exam. Correct the exam and return.
  - Return graded problems with comments.

■ ANSWERS TO REVIEW QUESTIONS, TEXT Pages 418-419

1. R. Buckminster Fuller.
2. True.
3. a. Very strong structure.
   b. Unobstructed floor space.
   c. Low cost.
   d. Factory production.
   e. Reduced energy needs.
4. False. Domes have less heat loss per square foot of floor space due to reduced exterior exposure.
5. True.
6. triangle.
7. hexagons, pentagons
8. a. Construction lumber.   c. Insulation.
   b. Plywood.   d. Asphalt shingles.
                               e. Drywall.
9. A crane. Depending on the construction method used, it will be used to either place the shell of the dome on the foundation or to put the top hexagon in place.

10. a. Basement.
    b. Crawl space.
    Also: Slab foundation.
11. To add headroom.

■ ANSWERS TO REVIEW QUESTIONS, WORKBOOK

PART I: MULTIPLE CHOICE

1. A. Triangle.
2. B. The structure of the dome is self-supporting.
3. C. Hexagons, pentagons, and trapezoids.
4. B. Angles.
5. D. All of the above.
6. A. Wing.

PART II: COMPLETION

1. R. Buckminster Fuller.
2. asphalt
3. precut
4. 24 in.
5. three
6. less

PART III: SHORT ANSWER/LISTING

1. About 30 percent less than conventional housing.
2. A. Accuracy was difficult to obtain working with so many small triangles.
   B. Windows and doors were not easily incorporated into a plan which used small triangles.
3. 4 hexagons and 3 trapezoids.
4. Crane.
5. Yes, because they are the sole support for the structure.
6. The structure is generally stronger and requires less energy to heat than conventional type housing covering the same floor space.

■ PART IV: PROBLEMS/ACTIVITIES

1. Instructor will evaluate the solution based on the application of good design, accuracy, and quality of work.

■ ANSWERS TO CHAPTER 27—EXAM

TRUE—FALSE

1. T	4. T
2. T	5. F
3. T	

MULTIPLE CHOICE

1. C	4. A
2. B	5. C
3. D	6. B

SHORT ANSWER

1. A. Structural superiority.
   B. Unobstructed floor space.
   C. Low cost.
   D. Factory production.
   E. Reduced energy needs.
2. A. Asphalt shingles.
   B. Cedar shakes.
3. Any one of the standard foundation types used for conventional construction.
4. A. Very efficient system which is strong and versatile.
   B. Provides an open, obstruction-free floor space.
   C. Factory production speeds erection.
   D. Requires less energy for heating or cooling for the same area.
   E. Economical to build.
   F. Interior is exciting and fun to decorate.

Chapter 27—Exam
DOME STRUCTURES

Name _____

Period _____ **Date** _____ **Score** _____

TRUE—FALSE
Circle T if the statement is true or F if the statement is false.

T   F   1. Dome structures are not new to architecture.

T   F   2. Heat loss in a dome is reduced about 30% over a rectangular structure with the same amount of area.

T   F   3. No additional interior or exterior support system is required for a dome.

T   F   4. A dome home can be placed on almost any site.

T   F   5. Most manufactured dome homes are true geodesic domes.

MULTIPLE CHOICE
Choose the answer that correctly completes the statement. Write the corresponding letter in the space provided.

_____ 1. The dome reduces the quantity of building materials needed per square foot of usable area by about _____ percent over conventional construction.
A. 10
B. 20
C. 30
D. 40

_____ 2. Manufactured dome homes are generally available in diameter ranging from 26 to _____ feet.
A. 50
B. 60
C. 70
D. 80

_____ 3. A true geodesic dome is composed of identical triangles, but most manufactured models use _____.
A. isosceles triangles
B. trapezoids
C. raised pentagons and hexagons
D. All of the above

_____ 4. The construction of individual panels used in residential dome structures is _____.
A. similar to conventional construction
B. similar to aircraft construction
C. only performed in a factory
D. None of the above

_____ 5. Individual panels in a dome structure are usually _____ together.
A. nailed
B. glued
C. bolted
D. clamped

_____ 6. Some dome models require _____ walls to support the entire structure while providing additional headroom on the second floor.
  A. wing
  B. riser
  C. dwarf
  D. flying

SHORT ANSWER
Answer the following questions using short answers.

1. List five attributes of residential dome structures.

  A. _____

  B. _____

  C. _____

  D. _____

  E. _____

2. What two popular materials are generally used to weatherproof the exterior of a dome home?

  A. _____

  B. _____

3. What type of foundation may be used for a dome structure?

  _____

  _____

4. List six advantages of the dome structure

  A. _____

  B. _____

  C. _____

  D. _____

  E. _____

  F. _____

28 CHAPTER

Modular Applications

■ OBJECTIVES

After studying this chapter, the student will be able to:
□ List the advantages of modular applications in the construction industry.
□ Apply modular concepts to the design of a simple residence.
□ Explain the term "industrialized housing."
□ Describe the primary differences between panelized construction, precuts, and modular components.

■ DISPLAYS

1. Modular Applications. Prepare a bulletin board which shows a variety of modular applications such as modular components, preassembled panels, room modules, etc.
2. Student Designs. Display student modular garage designs generated in Suggested Activity #4 in the text.
3. Manufacturer's Literature. Show literature from manufacturers of standard roof and wall panels. See Suggested Activity #3 in text for sources.

■ INSTRUCTIONAL MATERIALS

Text: Pages 421-428
　Review Questions, Suggested Activities
Workbook: Pages 217-219
　Review Questions, Problems/Activities
Teacher's Resource Guide:
　Chapter 28 — Teaching Strategy
　Chapter 28 — Exam

■ TEACHING STRATEGY

- Prepare Display #1.
- Review chapter objectives.
- Introduce modular construction.
- Cover standardization and modular components.
- Assign Suggested Activity #4 in the text.
- Discuss industrialized housing.
- Prepare Display #2 and/or #3.
- Assign workbook Problem 28-1.
- Assign one or more of the remaining Suggested Activities in the text.
- Chapter Review
　— Assign Review Questions in the text. Discuss the correct answers.
　— Assign Review Questions in the workbook. Have students check their own answers.
　— Make a transparency of the solution to Problem/Activity 28-1 and use for review.
- Evaluation
　— Administer the Chapter 28 — Exam. Correct the exam and return.
　— Return graded problems with comments.

■ ANSWERS TO REVIEW QUESTIONS, TEXT Page 428

1. Precut lumber, factory wall assemblies, modular coordination, and industrialized housing.
2. modular size
3. components.
4. a. Design freedom and appeal.
　b. High strength-to-weight ratio.
　c. Uniform quality.
　d. Efficient use of materials.
　Also: Lower cost and reduced time.
5. a. Standard module is a 4 in. cube.
　b. Major module is a 48 in. cube.
　c. Minor modules are 16 in. cube and 24 in. cube.
6. 4
7. 16
8. dot, arrowhead.

9. on the top of the subfloor.
10. houses built in a factory.
11. a. Shipping regulations.
    b. Fair size home.
12. a. Jigs and fixtures produce greater accuracy.
    b. Better lumber is used.

■ ANSWERS TO REVIEW QUESTIONS, WORKBOOK

PART I: COMPLETION

1. "stick-built."
2. modular
3. 16
4. dot
5. assembly
6. house

PART II: SHORT ANSWER/LISTING

1. Less time and cost in house construction.
2. Minor module—16 x 16 x 16 or 24 x 24 x 24.
   Major module—48 x 48 x 48.
3. Modular grid.
4. Building parts which have been preassembled in the plant or on the site.
5. A. Design freedom and esthetic appeal.
   B. High strength-to-weight ratios.
   C. Uniform quality.
   Also: More efficient use of materials, lower cost, and less time required for installation.
6. Heavy steel.

PART III: MULTIPLE CHOICE

1. C. Factory-built homes.
2. B. Minor.
3. A. On the grid line.
4. B. Modular components.
5. C. Jigs and fixtures are used to cut and fit parts together.

6. A. The modules are usually complete with plumbing, wiring, finished floors, and doors.

PART IV: PROBLEMS/ACTIVITIES

1. Solution on page 271.

■ ANSWERS TO CHAPTER 28—EXAM

TRUE—FALSE

1. F	4. T
2. T	5. T
3. T	

MULTIPLE CHOICE

1. B	7. D
2. B	8. D
3. C	9. A
4. D	10. C
5. A	11. B
6. B	

SHORT ANSWER

1. A. Design freedom and aesthetic appeal.
   B. High strength-to-weight ratio.
   C. Uniform quality.
   D. More efficient use of materials.
   E. Lower cost and time required for installation.
2. A. Plumbing.
   B. Wiring.
   C. Finished floors.
   D. Doors and windows.
3. A. Kitchen.
   B. Bath.
   C. Living room.

1.

DIRECTIONS:
Using the modular grid below, draw the plan view wall framing plan for a 10'-0" x 12'-0" frame Storage Building with siding. (Be sure to apply the modular concepts presented in the text.) Provide an access door at least 36" wide and two windows in your design. The scale is 1/2"=1'-0".

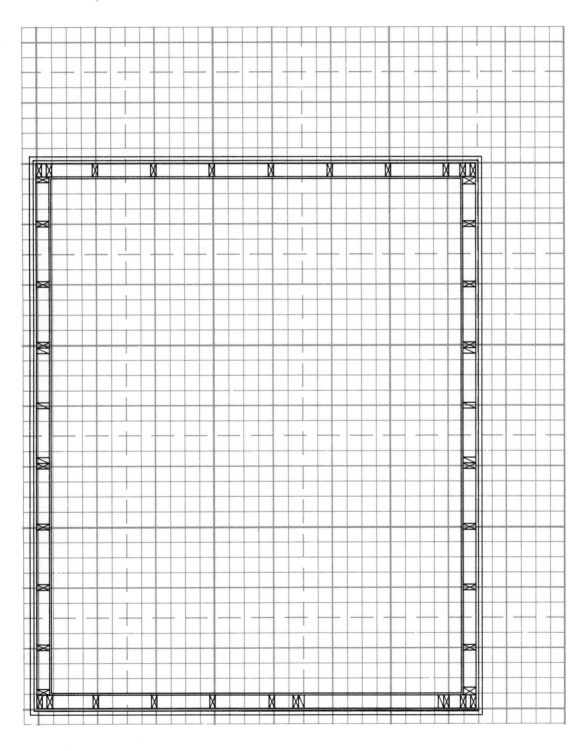

MODULAR CONSTRUCTION   28-1

Chapter 28—Exam
MODULAR APPLICATIONS

Name _____

Period _____ **Date** _____ **Score** _____

TRUE—FALSE
Circle T if the statement is true or F if the statement is false.

T   F   1. "Stick-built" homes are constructed in a factory.

T   F   2. The modular concept can be applied to any style of house design.

T   F   3. Material which is 16" x 32" is modular.

T   F   4. A modular plan includes length, width, and height using the standard module.

T   F   5. The major module is 4'-0" or 12 standard modules.

MULTIPLE CHOICE
Choose the answer that correctly completes the statement. Write the corresponding letter in the space provided.

_____ 1. Application of the modular concept to on-site construction or factory-built homes must involve _____.
A. more costly homes
B. standardization
C. fewer design possibilities
D. increased construction time

_____ 2. All modules are multiples of _____ inches.
A. 2
B. 4
C. 8
D. 12

_____ 3. Minor modules are _____ inches.
A. 8 and 12
B. 12 and 16
C. 16 and 24
D. 24 and 36

_____ 4. Exterior walls are generally multiples of _____ inches if feasible in the modular system.
A. 12
B. 24
C. 36
D. 48

_____ 5. Details of a modular structure should begin and terminate _____.
A. on a grid line
B. wherever it is convenient
C. where the room layout dictates
D. None of the above

_____ 6. Dimensions terminating on a grid line are shown with _____.
A. a dot
B. an arrow
C. a slash
D. any symbol desired

_____ 7. Partitions are usually _____ grid lines.
　　　　　　　　　A. not related to
　　　　　　　　　B. between
　　　　　　　　　C. beside one or more
　　　　　　　　　D. centered on

_____ 8. Which of the following are examples of typical modular components?
　　　　　　　　　A. floor panels
　　　　　　　　　B. roof panels
　　　　　　　　　C. wall sections
　　　　　　　　　D. All of the above

_____ 9. The term _____ refers to houses built in a factory.
　　　　　　　　　A. industrialized housing
　　　　　　　　　B. stick-built
　　　　　　　　　C. modular components
　　　　　　　　　D. precut lumber

_____ 10. The ideal width of a factory-built housing module is generally _____ feet because it is large enough for a room and it is the maximum width most states allow to be transported on the highway.
　　　　　　　　　A. 10
　　　　　　　　　B. 12
　　　　　　　　　C. 14
　　　　　　　　　D. 16

_____ 11. The accuracy and quality of factory-built homes is better than traditional construction because of the use of better quality lumber and _____ are used to cut and fit parts.
　　　　　　　　　A. gang saws
　　　　　　　　　B. jigs and fixtures
　　　　　　　　　C. trained workers
　　　　　　　　　D. None of the above

SHORT ANSWER
Answer the following questions using short answers.

1. List the advantages of prefabricated panels.

　A. _____

　B. _____

　C. _____

　D. _____

　E. _____

2. Most factory-built modules are more than an empty shell. What is included in a typical module?

　A. _____

　B. _____

　C. _____

　D. _____

3. What are two examples of a module within a module?

　A. _____

　B. _____

　C. _____

29 CHAPTER

Perspective Drawings

■ OBJECTIVES

After studying this chapter, the student will be able to:
- ☐ Explain the purpose of using a perspective drawing.
- ☐ Explain the difference between one-, two-, and three-point perspectives.
- ☐ Prepare a one- or two-point perspective drawing using the office method.
- ☐ Explain how changing the viewing position, angle, and height changes the perspective.
- ☐ Make a simple perspective using a grid.

■ DISPLAYS

1. Perspective Drawings. Create a display using one and two- point perspective drawings from previous classes or your own work. Label each drawing as to type of perspective and rendering technique used.
2. Perspectives of Homes. Use perspective drawings of homes cut from magazines to create a bulletin board display. Use samples submitted by students as a part of Suggested Activity #3 in the text.

■ INSTRUCTIONAL MATERIALS

Text: Pages 429-452
   Review Questions, Suggested Activities
Workbook: Pages 221-231
   Review Questions, Problems/Activities
Teacher's Resource Guide:
   Chapter 29 — Teaching Strategy
   Chapter 29 — Exam

■ TEACHING STRATEGY

- Prepare Display #1.
- Review chapter objectives.
- Introduce pictorial drawings.
- Introduce perspectives.
- Discuss two-point perspective.
- Draw several objects on the chalkboard using the step-by-step procedure discussed in the text.
- Assign workbook Problems 29-1, 29-2, 29-3, and 29-4.
- Discuss one-point perspectives.
- Prepare Display #2.
- Draw several objects on the chalkboard using the step-by-step procedure discussed in the text.
- Assign workbook Problems 29-5, 29-6, 29-7, and 29-8.
- Discuss perspective grids.
- Discuss and demonstrate drawing complex features in perspective.
- Assign one or more of the Suggested Activities in the text.
- Chapter Review
  - Assign Review Questions in the text. Discuss the correct answers.
  - Assign Review Questions in the workbook. Have students check their own answers.
  - Make transparencies of the solutions to Problems/Activities 29-1 and 29-5 and use for review.
- Evaluation
  - Administer the Chapter 29 — Exam. Correct the exam and return.
  - Return graded problems with comments.

■ ANSWERS TO REVIEW QUESTIONS, TEXT Page 452

1. a. Isometric.
   b. Oblique.
   c. Perspective.
2. a. One-point.
   b. Two-point.
   c. Three-point.

3. two-point.
4. elevation
5. height of the observer's eye.
6. the corner touches the picture plane.
7. larger
8. station point.
9. Position of the station point.
10. true height line.
11. horizon
12. two
13. increase
14. 30-60 degrees.
15. using the cone of vision rule.
16. distortion.
17. a. Bird's eye view (20 to 30 ft.).
    b. Observer's eye view (5 to 6 ft.).
    c. Worm's eye view (ground level or below).
18. They will move closer together.
19. interior
20. projecting site lines from the station point (elevation) to the object.
21. limited choice.
22. grid lines.

■ ANSWERS TO REVIEW QUESTIONS, WORKBOOK

PART I: MATCHING

1. C. Perspective.
2. H. Three-point perspective.
3. A. Ground line.
4. B. Horizon line.
5. E. Picture plane.
6. G. Station point.
7. I. True length line.
8. J. Vanishing points.
9. F. Plan view.
10. D. Perspective grid.

PART II: SHORT ANSWER/LISTING

1. A. One-point perspectives—usually interior drawings, for example, furniture layouts.
   B. Two-point perspectives—usually exterior views of residential structures.
   C. Three-point perspectives—usually exterior views of tall commercial structures.
2. A. Elevation.
   B. Plan.
   C. Perspective drawing.
3. Two.
4. 30 degrees on one side and 60 degrees on the other side.
5. A. The specific object to be drawn.
   B. The features of the object to be emphasized.
6. Parallel.
7. Draw two construction lines from the station point parallel to the sides of the object in the plan view to the picture plane line. Drop vertical lines from the point where the construction lines cross the picture plane line to the horizon line. These points are the left and right vanishing points.
8. First draw the object as though it had sharp lines and soften them later.

PART III: MULTIPLE CHOICE

1. C. Parallel.
2. B. The perspective of the object will be above the ground line.
3. A. They generate a photo-like drawing that is very accurate in detail.
4. C. 30 and 45 degrees.
5. C. All of the above.
6. B. Ground line.

PART IV: COMPLETION

1. station point
2. larger
3. station point
4. 20 to 30 ft.
5. plan view
6. true length
7. may not be
8. points

PART V: PROBLEMS/ACTIVITIES

1. A. Plan view.
   B. Picture plane.
   C. Cone of vision.
   D. Station point.
   E. Horizon line.
   F. Right vanishing point.
   G. Elevation view.
   H. Ground line.
   I. Perspective.
   J. Left vanishing point.
2. Solution on page 278.
3. Solution on page 279.
4. Instructor will evaluate solution based on accuracy and quality of view.
5. Solution on page 280.
6. Solution on page 281.
7. Solution on page 282.
8. Instructor will evaluate the solution based on how well it communicates the idea and accuracy of the construction.

■ ANSWERS TO CHAPTER 29—EXAM

TRUE—FALSE

1. T
2. T
3. F
4. T
5. T

MULTIPLE CHOICE

1. B	7. D
2. D	8. B
3. A	9. B
4. B	10. D
5. C	11. A
6. D	

SHORT ANSWER

1. A. One-point or parallel perspective.
   B. Two-point or angular perspective.
   C. Three-point or oblique perspective.
2. Tall, commercial-type buildings.
3. A. Elevation.
   B. Plan view.
   C. Perspective drawing.
4. At the station point.
5. Two.
6. Exterior views.
7. The drawing will be distorted and unrealistic.
8. Superimpose a grid over the object.

2.

DIRECTIONS:
Draw a two–point perspective of the object using the setup provided.
Show all construction lines, but darken in visible object lines. Omit
hidden lines from the pictorial.

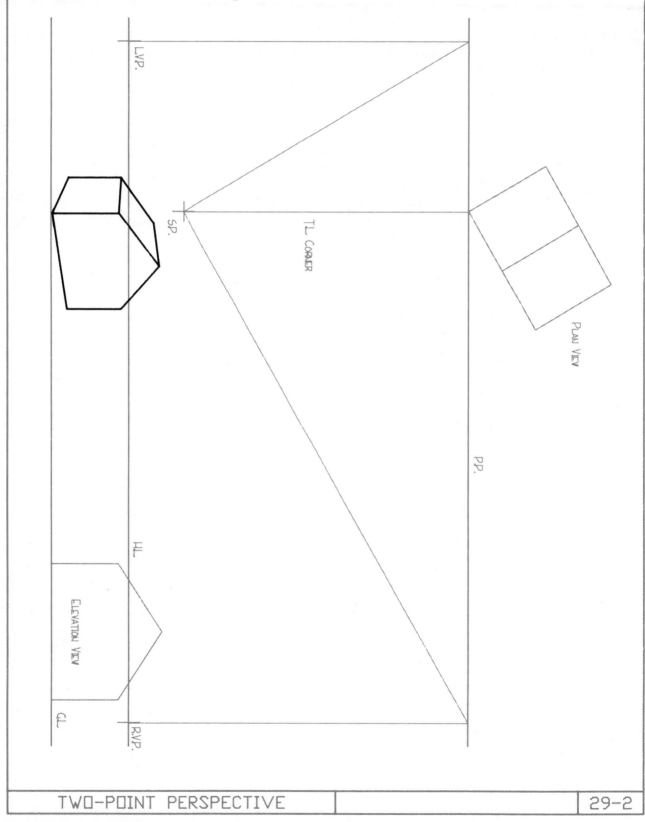

LVP.

S.P.

T.L. CORNER

PLAN VIEW

P.P.

H.L.

ELEVATION VIEW

G.L.

R.VP.

TWO-POINT PERSPECTIVE

29-2

3.

DIRECTIONS:
Draw a two-point perspective of the object as indicated. Show all construction lines, but darken in the visible lines of the object.

LVP.

SP.

H.L.

RVP.

G.L.

PP.

TWO-POINT PERSPECTIVE

29-3

5.

DIRECTIONS:
Complete the One-Point Perspective drawing below using the
procedure described in the text.   Show your construction using
light construction lines.   Darken the visible object lines.

Left Side

P.P.

P.P.

SP e

SP p

Floor Line

Plan View

ONE-POINT PERSPECTIVE   29-5

DIRECTIONS:
Draw a One-Point Perspective of the room, table, and rug indicated below. Show construction lines as very light lines, darken in visible object lines, and omit hidden lines.

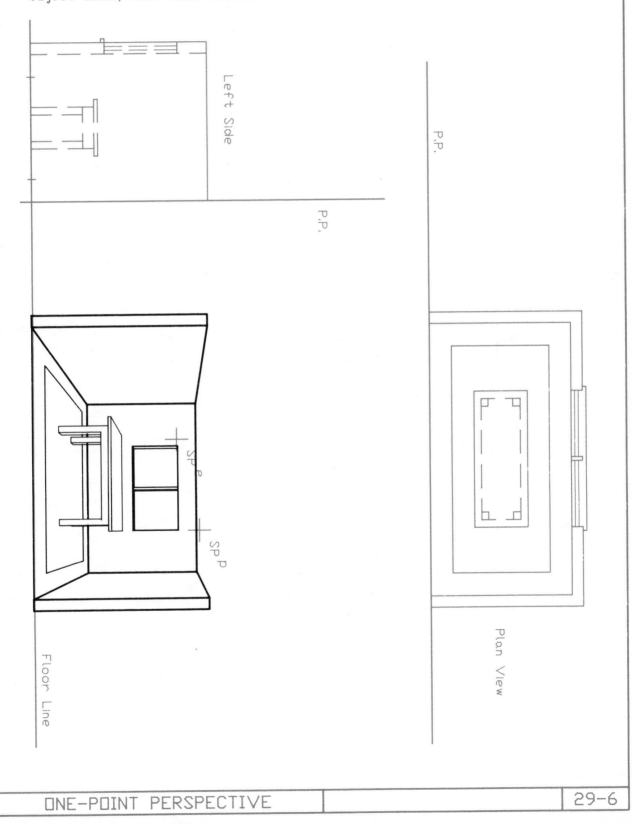

Left Side

P.P.

P.P.

SP P

SP P

Floor Line

Plan View

ONE-POINT PERSPECTIVE

29-6

7.

DIRECTIONS:
Draw a One—Point Perspective of the room and contents (simplified furniture pieces) below. Show construction lines as very light lines, darken in visible object lines, and omit hidden lines.

Left Side

P.P.

P.P.

Floor Line

SP p

SP e

Plan View

| ONE—POINT PERSPECTIVE | | 29-7 |

Chapter 29—Exam
PERSPECTIVE DRAWINGS

Name _____

Period _____ **Date** _____ **Score** _____

TRUE—FALSE
Circle T if the statement is true or F if the statement is false.

T   F   1. A type of pictorial drawing commonly used for communication purposes is the perspective.

T   F   2. Isometric and oblique drawings are types of pictorial drawings.

T   F   3. In perspectives, the station point is infinitely far from the object.

T   F   4. The picture plane could be in front of, behind, or pass through the object.

T   F   5. The picture plane is a transparent plane on which the perspective is drawn.

MULTIPLE CHOICE
Choose the answer that correctly completes the statement. Write the corresponding letter in the space provided.

_____ 1. A two-point perspective has _____ vanishing points.
    A. one
    B. two
    C. three
    D. zero

_____ 2. In perspective drawings, the _____ is the location of the observer's eye.
    A. vanishing point
    B. horizon line
    C. picture plane
    D. station point

_____ 3. The _____ represents a horizontal plane that is called the ground plane.
    A. ground line
    B. elevation line
    C. height line
    D. picture plane

_____ 4. The distance between the ground line and horizon line represents the _____.
    A. height of the object
    B. height of the observer's eye above the ground
    C. distance the observer is away from the object
    D. None of the above

_____ 5. The picture plane is normally located between the object and _____.
    A. horizon line
    B. ground line
    C. station point
    D. right side view

_____ 6. Any portion of the object which touches the picture plane will be _____ in the perspective drawing.
    A. hidden from view
    B. larger than scale
    C. smaller than scale
    D. true size

_____ 7. It is always necessary to locate at least one _____ in a two-point perspective drawing so that height measurements can be made.
   A. side of the object
   B. full-size view
   C. angular view
   D. true-length line

_____ 8. In most instances, the station point is positioned so that it forms a cone of vision of _____ degrees with respect to the object.
   A. 15-30
   B. 30-45
   C. 45-60
   D. over 60

_____ 9. The height of the observer's eye is represented by the distance between the _____ and _____.
   A. horizon line; picture plane
   B. horizon line; ground line
   C. ground line; picture plane
   D. station point; picture plane

_____ 10. One-point perspectives are commonly used for _____.
   A. room and furniture layouts
   B. kitchen cabinet pictorial details
   C. interior space studies
   D. All of the above

_____ 11. In a one-point perspective, both views of the station point must be the same distance from the _____.
   A. picture plane
   B. horizon line
   C. ground line
   D. edge of the paper

SHORT ANSWER
Answer the following questions using short answers.

1. List the three basic types of perspectives.

   A. _____

   B. _____

   C. _____

2. What type of structures are three-point perspectives used for?

   _____

3. What are the three parts of a perspective layout?

   A. _____

   B. _____

   C. _____

4. Where do the visual rays or sight lines begin?

   _____

5. How many views of the station point are usually shown in a one-point perspective?

_____

6. What type of view is the two-point perspective especially suited for?

_____

7. What will the result be if the station point is too close to the object?

_____

8. What general approach may be used to draw circular or other irregular objects in perspective since few, if any, of the object elements are parallel to the principle reference planes?

_____

Presentation Drawings

■ **OBJECTIVES**

After studying this chapter, the student will be able to:
☐ List methods commonly used to increase the degree of realism in a presentation plan.
☐ Render common materials using a variety of techniques.
☐ Demonstrate ability to ink a rendering.
☐ Devise a typical presentation floor plan.
☐ Demonstrate the ability to represent typical entouragé symbols.

■ **DISPLAYS**

1. Architectural Renderings. Collect renderings of architectural structures and display them in the classroom to provide examples of style and inspiration. Use samples submitted by students as a part of Suggested Activity #2 in text.
2. Student Renderings. Use student work to create a bulletin board display of renderings as detailed in Suggested Activity #6 in the text.

■ **INSTRUCTIONAL MATERIALS**

Text: Pages 453-470
    Review Questions, Suggested Activities
Workbook: Pages 233-237
    Review Questions, Problems/Activities
Teacher's Resource Guide:
    Chapter 30—Teaching Strategy
    Chapter 30—Exam

■ **TEACHING STRATEGY**

- Prepare Display #1.
- Review chapter objectives.
- Introduce presentation drawings.
- Introduce rendering.

- Discuss pencil rendering and ink rendering.
- Design workbook Problems 30-1 and 30-2.
- Discuss watercolor rendering.
- Assign Suggested Activity #6 in the text.
- Discuss tempera, colored pencil, magic marker, and scratch board rendering.
- Prepare Display #2.
- Discuss appliqué and airbrush rendering.
- Discuss entouragé and types of presentation plans—exterior perspectives, rendered elevations, plot plans, floor plans, and sections.
- Assign workbook Problem 30-3.
- Assign one or more of the remaining Suggested Activities in the text.
- Chapter Review
    —Assign Review Questions in the text. Discuss the correct answers.
    —Assign Review Questions in the workbook. Have students check their own answers.
- Evaluation
    —Administer the Chapter 30—Exam. Correct the exam and return.
    —Return graded problems with comments.

■ **ANSWERS TO REVIEW QUESTIONS, TEXT Page 468**

1. to add realism.
2. a. Pencil.   d. Colored pencils.
   b. Ink.   e. Scratch board.
   c. Tempera.   f. Magic marker.
   Also: Appliqué, air brush, combination of techniques.
3. pencil rendering.
4. ink.
5. appliqué
6. air brush
7. The surroundings such as trees, cars, and people.
8. To add realism to the drawing and show the structure in its proper setting.

9. a. Perspective.
    b. Floor plan.
    c. Plot plan.
    d. Section.
    e. Elevation.
10. orthographic
11. a. Furniture arrangement.
    b. Area utilization.
    c. Conveniences.

■ ANSWERS TO REVIEW QUESTIONS, WORKBOOK

PART I: SHORT ANSWER/LISTING

1. They are more realistic in appearance than construction drawings.
2. A. Pencil.   E. Water color.
   B. Ink.   F. Scratch board.
   C. Tempera.   G. Appliqué.
   D. Colored pencil. H. Air brush.
   Also: Magic markers and a combination of techniques.
3. Colored pencil.
4. Appliqué rendering is created by using a pressure-sensitive transparent film over a drawing to create texture, color, or add detail. It may be used on a presentation drawing of a living room to show color and texture of the furnishings.
5. A. To give prospective clients a better idea of the appearance of a dwelling in its surroundings.
   B. To advertise their product to the public.
6. So that the product is represented exactly as it will appear in real life.

PART II: MULTIPLE CHOICE

1. B. Pencil.
2. A. Water color.
3. C. Magic markers.
4. D. Air brush.
5. B. Presentation elevation.
6. C. Presentation floor plan.

PART III: COMPLETION

1. Ink

2. tempera.
3. scratch board
4. entourage.
5. presentation plot
6. sections

■ PART IV: PROBLEMS/ACTIVITIES

1. Display student work which best demonstrates the art of pencil rendering.
2. Display student work which best illustrates the art of ink rendering.
3. Evaluate the solution based on realism and the accuracy of the rendering.

■ ANSWERS TO CHAPTER 30—EXAM

TRUE—FALSE

1. T   4. T
2. T   5. F
3. T

MULTIPLE CHOICE

1. B   5. B
2. C   6. A
3. A   7. D
4. C

SHORT ANSWER

1. A. Pencil.
   B. Ink.
   C. Tempera.
   D. Colored pencils.
   E. Magic markers.
   F. Watercolor.
   G. Scratch board.
   H. Appliqué.
   I. Air brush.
   J. Combination of techniques.
2. Lines are scratched through a special black coated illustration board type material.
3. Appliqué rendering.
4. A. To help "sell" the plan to a prospective client.
   B. For advertising.
5. A. Furniture arrangement.
   B. Area utilization.
   C. Conveniences.

Chapter 30—Exam
PRESENTATION DRAWINGS

Name _____

Period _____ **Date** _____ **Score** _____

TRUE—FALSE
Circle T if the statement is true or F if the statement is false.

T   F   1. Presentation drawings are usually rendered to enhance their appearance.

T   F   2. One of the problems encountered in pencil rendering is keeping the drawing clean.

T   F   3. Various techniques and materials are often combined in a single rendering.

T   F   4. Even the beginning student can gain success with colored pencil rendering.

T   F   5. Tempera paint is a type of oil paint.

MULTIPLE CHOICE
Choose the answer that correctly completes the statement. Write the corresponding letter in the space provided.

_____ 1. Renderings to be used for reproduction are best done in _____.
   A. pencil
   B. ink
   C. magic marker
   D. water color

_____ 2. Water color rendering is one of the _____.
   A. least effective rendering techniques
   B. easiest methods to master
   C. most difficult methods to execute
   D. methods most often chosen by beginners

_____ 3. Presentation plot plans are frequently rendered using the _____ rendering technique.
   A. magic marker
   B. tempera
   C. scratch board
   D. pencil

_____ 4. What type of rendering produces white lines on a black background?
   A. Ink rendering
   B. Magic marker rendering
   C. Scratch board rendering
   D. Appliqué rendering

_____ 5. Professional illustrators frequently choose _____ rendering for their presentations.
   A. pencil
   B. air brush
   C. tempera
   D. magic marker

_____ 6. Surroundings such as trees, shrubs, cars, people, and terrain are referred to as _____.
   A. entouragé
   B. topographical features
   C. details
   D. nonessential items

_____ 7. A rendered elevation _____.
    A. is an orthographic-type drawing
    B. uses material symbols, trees, and other features to give the appearance of depth
    C. is sometimes used instead of an exterior perspective
    D. All of the above

SHORT ANSWER
Answer the following questions using short answers.

1. Identify ten methods of rendering that are popular.

    A. _____

    B. _____

    C. _____

    D. _____

    E. _____

    F. _____

    G. _____

    H. _____

    I. _____

    J. _____

2. How are scratch board renderings produced?

_____

_____

3. What type of rendering is accomplished by attaching a pressure-sensitive transparent film over a drawing?

_____

4. What are the primary uses of a rendering?

    A. _____

    B. _____

5. Presentation floor plans may be used to emphasize features such as:

    A. _____

    B. _____

    C. _____

Architectural Models

■ **OBJECTIVES**

After studying this chapter, the student will be able to:
☐ Explain the various types of archtiectural models used to represent residential structures.
☐ List the features commonly included in a presentation model.
☐ Summarize the steps for constructing a balsa wood model.

■ **DISPLAYS**

1. Architectural Models. Display several architectural models in the classroom for examination.
2. Model Materials. Collect typical architectural model materials and display them on the bulletin board. Label each material.
3. Model Fixtures. Display model fixtures carved by students as required in Suggested Activity #4 in the text.

■ **INSTRUCTIONAL MATERIALS**

Text: Pages 471-480
    Review Questions, Suggested Activities
Workbook: Pages 239-241
    Review Questions, Problems/Activities
Teacher's Resource Guide:
    Chapter 31 — Teaching Strategy
    Chapter 31 — Exam

■ **TEACHING STRATEGY**

• Prepare Display #1.
• Review chapter objectives.
• Discuss types of models — structural models and presentation models.
• Present materials used in model construction.
• Prepare Display #2.
• Cover the procedure for constructing a balsa model.
• Assign workbook Problems 31-1, 31-2, and 31-3.
• Prepare Display #3.
• Assign one or more of the Suggested Activities in the text.
• Chapter Review
  — Assign Review Questions in the text. Discuss the correct answers.
  — Assign Review Questions in the workbook. Have students check their own answers.
• Evaluation
  — Administer the Chapter 31 — Exam. Correct the exam and return.
  — Return graded problems with comments.

■ **ANSWERS TO REVIEW QUESTIONS, TEXT Pages 479-480**

1. a. Small-scale solid models.
   b. Structural models.
   c. Presentation models.
2. 1/4" = 1'-0".
3. a. Styrofoam®.
   b. Cardboard.
   c. Balsa.
4. to obtain a set of plans.
5. the site is rolling.
6. 30" x 30" or 30" x 36".
7. 3/4
8. 3/16" or 1/4".
9. 1/8
10. tempera.
11. furniture

■ ANSWERS TO REVIEW QUESTIONS, WORKBOOK

PART I: MULTIPLE CHOICE

1. A. Small scale solid.
2. C. 1/2" = 1'-0" or 1" = 1'-0".
3. B. They can be finished to resemble various exterior building materials.
4. A. Floor plan.
5. B. 1/8.
6. C. Tempera.

PART II: COMPLETION

1. 1/8" = 1'-0".
2. presentation
3. balsa.
4. flat
5. miter
6. Plexiglas™.
7. plan
8. sheathing
9. shrubbery.

PART III: SHORT ANSWER/LISTING

1. A. Small scale solid models.
   B. Structural models.
   C. Presentation models.
2. Structural model.
3. 1/4" = 1'-0".
4. Plaster of paris.
   Styrofoam®.
   Cardboard.
5. A. Floor plan.
   B. Elevations.
6. 3/16 or 1/4 in. thick.
7. A. X-acto knife.
   B. Scale.

C. Square.
D. Metal straightedge.
8. Scoring the wood, gluing on thin strips, or applying printed or embossed sheets.
9. Paint with a water-base paint and then wipe.
10. Sandpaper or fine gravel.

■ ANSWERS TO PROBLEMS/ACTIVITIES, WORKBOOK

PART IV: PROBLEMS/ACTIVITIES

1. Instructor will evaluate the model according to the construction techniques suggested in the text.
2. Instructor will evaluate model according to techniques discussed in the text and actual construction procedures which were followed.
3. Instructor will evaluate model according to construction techniques suggested in the text.

■ ANSWERS TO CHAPTER 31—EXAM

TRUE—FALSE

1. T
2. T
3. T
4. T
5. T

MULTIPLE CHOICE

1. C
2. D
3. D
4. B
5. A
6. C
7. A

SHORT ANSWER

1. Small scale solid model.
2. 1/4" = 1'-0".
3. Flock.
4. Sandpaper strips.

Chapter 31—Exam
ARCHITECTURAL MODELS

Name _____

Period _____ **Date** _____ **Score** _____

TRUE—FALSE
Circle T if the statement is true or F if the statement is false.

T   F   1. Models are useful in checking the final appearance of an architectural design.

T   F   2. Very little detail is shown on small scale solid models.

T   F   3. Part of the siding and roofing is left off a structural model.

T   F   4. Most residential models are presentation models.

T   F   5. Plants may be purchased or fabricated from sponge and/or twigs.

MULTIPLE CHOICE
Choose the answer that correctly completes the statement. Write the corresponding letter in the space provided.

_____ 1. A _____ model is usually built at 1/2" = 1'-0" or 1" = 1'-0" scale to show the basic construction.
A. small-scale solid
B. large-scale solid
C. structural
D. presentation

_____ 2. The purpose of a _____ model is to show appearance of the finished building as realistically as possible.
A. small-scale solid
B. structural
C. large-scale solid
D. presentation

_____ 3. What materials are commonly used for architectural model construction?
A. Styrofoam® sheets.
B. Balsa wood.
C. Cardboard or illustration board.
D. All of the above

_____ 4. The preferred material for a presentation architectural model is _____ because it is easy to cut, sands well, does not warp, and does not show pin holes.
A. Styrofoam® sheets
B. balsa wood
C. cardboard or illustration board
D. plaster of paris

_____ 5. The two drawings that are generally sufficient to build an architectural model are the _____ and _____.
A. floor plan; elevations
B. floor plan; foundation plan
C. floor plan; plot plan
D. plot plan; elevations

_____ 6. On a presentation model, wall corners should be _____.
    A. butt jointed
    B. dovetailed
    C. mitered
    D. pinned together

_____ 7. Furniture and major fixtures can be carved from _____.
    A. soap or wood
    B. plaster of paris
    C. clay
    D. foam blocks

SHORT ANSWER

Answer each of the questions using short answers.

1. What type of architectural model is used to show how a building relates to surrounding buildings?

2. At which scale are presentation models usually built?

3. What material is used on a model to represent grass?

4. What material may be used to represent a shingle roof?

Material and Tradework Specifications

■ OBJECTIVES

After studying this chapter, the student will be able to:
□ Explain the purpose of material and tradework specifications.
□ List the sources of specification guides.
□ Recognize the format followed by typical contract specification sheets.
□ Use a "description of materials" form.

■ DISPLAYS

1. Contract Specifications. Secure a set of contract specifications from a local builder or loan officer. Display it on the bulletin board for student examination.
2. Description of Materials. Display a set of Description of Materials for a structure to be built in your area. Check with a builder or local lumber company for a sample.

■ INSTRUCTIONAL MATERIALS

Text: Pages 481-488
    Review Questions, Suggested Activities
Workbook: Pages 243-244
    Review Questions, Problems/Activities
Teacher's Resource Guide:
    Chapter 32—Teaching Strategy
    Chapter 32—Exam

■ TEACHING STRATEGY

- Prepare Display #1.
- Review chapter objectives.
- Introduce material and tradework specifications.
- Present specification formats.
- Review examples of specifications.
- Prepare Display #2.
- Present Description of Materials.
- Assign workbook Problem 32-1.
- Assign one or more of the Suggested Activities in the text.
- Chapter Review
  - Assign Review Questions in the text. Discuss the correct answers.
  - Assign Review Questions in the workbook. Have students check their own answers.
- Evaluation
  - Administer the Chapter 32—Exam. Correct the exam and return.
  - Return graded problems with comments.

■ ANSWERS TO REVIEW QUESTIONS, TEXT Page 488

1. a. Description of the materials to be used.
   b. Description of all required building operations.
   c. A cash allowance for fixtures, hardware, etc.
   d. Specifications must refer directly to working drawings.
   e. A statement of quality of tradework.
   f. Stated liability coverage by the contractor.
2. It gives the customer an opportunity to express individual tastes and mode of living.
3. The house is being constructed for sale.
4. contract
5. a. Lighting fixtures.
   b. Hardware.
   c. Floor coverings.
   d. Bricks or other similar materials.
6. It insures that there will be no misunderstanding on quality or disappointment on the part of the owner.
7. Because these construction details are on the working drawings and it is not necessary to repeat them.

■ ANSWERS TO REVIEW QUESTIONS, WORKBOOK

PART I: SHORT ANSWER/LISTING

1. Material and tradework specifications.
2. Specification sheets and set of construction drawings.
3. The client should discuss the quality of work with the architect so that the two can agree on the level to be used.
4. From an architect, American Institute of Architects, Veterans Administration, or Federal Housing Administration.
5. Brand name, model number, and color.
6. Building contractor.

PART II: COMPLETION

1. architect
2. architect, client
3. building
4. client
5. size

PART III: PROBLEMS/ACTIVITIES

1. Instructor will evaluate the form according to its completeness and thoroughness.

■ ANSWERS TO CHAPTER 32—EXAM

TRUE—FALSE

1. T
2. T
3. T
4. T
5. T

MULTIPLE CHOICE

1. C
2. B
3. D
4. B
5. A

Chapter 32—Exam
MATERIAL AND TRADEWORK SPECIFICATIONS

Name _____

Period _____ **Date** _____ **Score** _____

TRUE—FALSE
Circle T if the statement is true or F if the statement is false.

T   F   1. The architect is generally responsible for the preparation of material and trade specifications.

T   F   2. Working drawings and specifications are binding on the builder and owner.

T   F   3. Specification forms are available which reduce the time required to prepare specifications.

T   F   4. Tradework and quality of construction is more difficult to define than material specifications.

T   F   5. Liability covered by the contractor during construction is covered in the specifications.

MULTIPLE CHOICE
Choose the answer that correctly completes the statement. Write the corresponding letter in the space provided.

_____ 1. The specifications provide written information on _____ which supplement the drawings and become part of the complete set of building plans.
    A. building procedure
    B. subcontractors to be used
    C. details and products
    D. None of the above

_____ 2. The _____ form has become one of the leading guides for writing specifications.
    A. Lumberman's Association
    B. Veteran's Administration
    C. American Plywood Association
    D. Builders of America

_____ 3. Specification forms generally include _____.
    A. a description of the materials to be used
    B. a list of required building operations
    C. notes relative to cash allowances for such items as lighting fixtures
    D. All of the above

_____ 4. Which of the following are usually major headings under building operations in the specifications?
    A. Countertops.
    B. Millwork.
    C. Drywall.
    D. Glazing.

_____ 5. The architect generally writes the complete specifications for a house when it is being constructed for _____.
    A. a private owner
    B. sale
    C. All of the above
    D. None of the above

Estimating Building Cost

■ OBJECTIVES

After studying this chapter, the student will be able to:
☐ Explain what is involved in developing an estimate of building costs.
☐ Generate a typical materials list for a simple structure.
☐ Estimate the cost of a residential structure using the square foot or cubic foot method.

■ DISPLAYS

1. Plan and Estimated Building Cost. Select a simple house plan and calculate an estimated building cost. Put the plan and cost estimate on the bulletin board for inspection by students.
2. Pay Rates for Skilled Trades. Create a display using current rates charged by skilled tradespersons. See Suggested Activity #3 in the text.

■ INSTRUCTIONAL MATERIALS

Text: Pages 489-496
   Review Questions, Suggested Activities
Workbook: Pages 245-250
   Review Questions, Problems/Activities
Teacher's Resource Guide:
   Chapter 33 — Teaching Strategy
   Chapter 33 — Exam

■ TEACHING STRATEGY

- Prepare Display #1.
- Review chapter objectives.
- Discuss preliminary estimates.
- Discuss estimates which are more accurate.
- Prepare Display #2.
- Assign workbook Problem 33-1.

- Assign one or more of the Suggested Activities in the text.
- Chapter Review
   — Assign Review Questions in the text. Discuss the correct answers.
   — Assign Review Questions in the workbook. Have students check their own answers.
- Evaluation
   — Administer the Chapter 33 — Exam. Correct the exam and return.
   — Return graded problems with comments.

■ ANSWERS TO REVIEW QUESTIONS, TEXT Page 495

1. a. Square foot method.
   b. Cubic foot method.
2. $50 per sq. ft.
3. Determine the exact quantity and cost of materials, labor, permits, etc.
4. a. Building.
   b. Electrical.
   c. Plumbing.
   d. Health.
5. consulting local contractors and builders.
6. sources where the materials will be purchased.

■ ANSWERS TO REVIEW QUESTIONS, WORKBOOK

PART I: COMPLETION

1. estimating.
2. builders
3. area
4. specifications.
5. height.
6. 60
7. sewer

PART II: SHORT ANSWER/LISTING

1. Square foot method and cubic foot method.
2. Yes.
3. Add to the cost.
4. Determine the quantity, quality, and cost of materials required, and the cost of labor. Also, include an allowance for material waste, supervision, and overhead.
5. The order of the headings usually follows the construction sequence.
6. A. Building permit.
   B. Plumbing permit.
   C. Electrical permit.
   D. Health permit.

PART III: MULTIPLE CHOICE

1. B. One-half.
2. A. More expensive to build than two-story homes.
3. C. Materials list.
4. A. The supplier to be used in the construction of the house.
5. C. All of the above.
6. A. Workers in the event of injury and materials against theft.

PART IV: PROBLEMS/ACTIVITIES

1. Instructor will evaluate the materials list according to its completeness and thoroughness.

■ ANSWERS TO CHAPTER 33—EXAM

TRUE—FALSE
1. T	4. T
2. F	5. T
3. T	

MULTIPLE CHOICE
1. C	4. C	7. B
2. A	5. B	8. D
3. B	6. C	9. C

Chapter 33—Exam
ESTIMATING BUILDING COST

Name _____

Period _____ **Date** _____ **Score** _____

TRUE—FALSE
Circle T if the statement is true or F if the statement is false.

T   F   1. A cost estimate should be made after the construction drawings and specifications are completed.

T   F   2. The cost to build living space and garage space are figured at the same rate.

T   F   3. The cost for land is not included in any preliminary estimates.

T   F   4. Accurate cost estimates should be based on cost of materials and labor, overhead, permits, etc.

T   F   5. Preparing a materials list is time consuming, but very useful.

MULTIPLE CHOICE
Choose the answer that correctly completes the statement. Write the corresponding letter in the space provided.

_____ 1. Two methods of providing a rough estimate of building a home are the _____ and _____.
A. past practices method; actual cost method
B. square foot method; past practices method
C. cubic foot method; square foot method
D. cubic foot method; actual cost method

_____ 2. What is the first step for either of the rough estimate methods used for residential cost determination?
A. Calculate the area of the house.
B. Count the number of rooms.
C. Determine the volume of the house.
D. List all of the materials to be used.

_____ 3. A house that is 24' x 60' and has a detached garage of 20' x 20' has _____ square feet of living space.
A. 1840
B. 1440
C. 400
D. None of the above

_____ 4. The cost of the living area of a house is calculated at _____ the rate of garage space using the square foot method.
A. one-half
B. the same rate as
C. twice
D. None of the above

_____ 5. How much would a garage cost if the rate were $25/square foot and the garage were 20' x 20' in size? Use the square foot method.
A. $1,000.
B. $10,000.
C. $100,000.
D. None of the above

_____ 6. The volume of the living space of a 24' x 60' ranch home with standard ceiling heights is _____.
   A. 1440 sq. ft.
   B. 14,400 cu. ft.
   C. 11,520 cu. ft.
   D. None of the above

_____ 7. How much would the house and garage in Question #3 cost to build if the cost per square foot were $50 for the living space?
   A. $72,000.
   B. $82,000.
   C. $92,000.
   D. None of the above

_____ 8. It is reasonable to expect the labor cost to build a new home to be _____ percent of the total cost.
   A. 20-40
   B. 30-50
   C. 40-60
   D. 60-80

_____ 9. In addition to materials and labor, what other items should be included in the cost of building a house?
   A. Fee for permits and hookups.
   B. Cost of insurance to protect materials and workers.
   C. Both A and B
   D. None of the above

34 CHAPTER

Computer Applications

■ OBJECTIVES

After studying this chapter, the student will be able to:
- ☐ Discuss a variety of broad areas where computers are being used in architecture and construction.
- ☐ Recognize the advantages of computer analysis for the constructor or designer.
- ☐ Define terms related to computer applications in architecture.
- ☐ Discuss the type of information generally shown on a PERT chart.

■ DISPLAYS

1. Computer Applications. Create a bulletin board display which shows several typical computer applications which are related to architecture and/or construction.
2. Software Programs. Display one or more software programs for architecture or construction applications.
3. Tutorial Program. Install a tutorial program in your microcomputer which demonstrates a software program related to architecture or construction. Encourage the class to use the tutorial.

■ INSTRUCTIONAL MATERIALS

Text: Pages 497-508
    Review Questions, Suggested Activities
Workbook: Pages 251-253
    Review Questions, Problems/Activities
Teacher's Resource Guide:
    Chapter 34—Teaching Strategy
    Chapter 34—Exam

■ TEACHING STRATEGY

- Prepare Display #1.
- Review chapter objectives.
- Introduce computer applications.
- Discuss site planning and mapping.
- Present structural analysis using the computer.
- Present computer-aided drafting and design (CADD).
- Assign workbook Problem 34-1.
- Prepare Display #2.
- Discuss computer graphics representation.
- Discuss energy analysis.
- Cover project management with the computer.
- Prepare Display #3.
- Discuss computer simulation.
- Assign one or more of the Suggested Activities in the text.
- Chapter Review
  - Assign Review Questions in the text. Discuss the correct answers.
  - Assign Review Questions in the workbook. Have students check their own answers.
- Evaluation
  - Administer the Chapter 34—Exam. Correct the exam and return.
  - Return graded problems with comments.

■ ANSWERS TO REVIEW QUESTIONS, TEXT
Pages 506-507

1. a. Structural analysis.
   b. Site planning and mapping.
   c. Computer-aided drafting and design.
   d. Project management.
   e. Energy analysis.
   f. Computer graphic presentations.
   g. Computer simulation.

2. Large scale projects such as subdivisions. Also: Multifamily complexes and nonconventional structures.
3. Structural analysis allows the architect to design building components able to withstand stress and weight from the building and from any use the structure experiences. This is important in earth sheltered dwellings as they must withstand great stress from their earth covering. An architect can use the computer to calculate stress forces in such structures.
4. Saves time by using a menu of standard components and symbols. Increases accuracy.
5. communication.
6. Refer to Fig. 34-16 in text.
7. project management.

■ ANSWERS TO REVIEW QUESTIONS, WORKBOOK

PART I: SHORT ANSWER/LISTING

1. The availability of software.
2. A. Estimating.
   B. Site planning and mapping.
   C. Structural analysis.
   D. Computer-aided drafting and design (CADD).
   E. Computer graphic presentations.
   Also: Energy analysis, project management, and computer simulations.
3. In the area of site planning and mapping, the computer can generate pictorial representations of contours derived from XYZ coordinate data.
4. Earth sheltered homes and dome structures.
5. The architect or designer can call up drawings and make additions or corrections in a matter of minutes compared to having to completely redraw a project by hand which could take hours. The system is cost effective and it improves accuracy.
6. A. Exact representations may be produced quickly.
   B. The structure may be viewed from any position.
   C. Corrections or alterations are quickly and easily performed.
7. A. Isometric.
   B. Oblique.
   C. Perspective.
8. The architect can design an energy-efficient structure by using suitable insulation and the proper heating system.

9. It helps the contractor to improve productivity and efficiency to make a profit.
10. Project Evaluation and Review Technique.

PART II: COMPLETION

1. computer
2. site planning and mapping
3. building
4. structural
5. menu
6. plotters
7. energy analysis.
8. owner
9. project management
10. simulation.

PART III: MATCHING

1. F. Site planning and mapping.
2. G. Structural analysis.
3. A. CADD.
4. B. Computer graphics.
5. D. Energy analysis.
6. E. Project management.
7. C. Computer simulations.

■ ANSWERS TO CHAPTER 34—EXAM

TRUE—FALSE

1. F	4. T
2. T	5. T
3. T	

MULTIPLE CHOICE

1. D	4. B
2. B	5. C
3. D	6. B

SHORT ANSWER

1. A. Estimating
   B. Site planning and mapping
   C. Structural analysis
   D. CADD
   E. Computer graphic presentations
   F. Energy analysis
   Others: Project management and computer simulations
2. A. Saves time
   B. Improves accuracy
3. A. Planning the management
   B. Performing cost estimates
   C. Producing financial models
   D. Scheduling for the building operations

Chapter 34—Exam
COMPUTER APPLICATIONS

Name _____

Period _____ **Date** _____ **Score** _____

TRUE—FALSE
Circle T if the statement is true or F if the statement is false.

T   F   1. Computers have had very little impact on designing and building structures.

T   F   2. Site planning and mapping are required for most large-scale projects.

T   F   3. Elastic stability analysis is an example of structural analysis.

T   F   4. CADD is the largest and most familiar area of computer application in architecture.

T   F   5. Graphic presentations are communication tools.

MULTIPLE CHOICE
Choose the answer that correctly completes the statement. Write the corresponding letter in the space provided.

_____ 1. Which of the following is a part of site planning and mapping?
A. Water surface profile analysis.
B. Automated contour mapping.
C. Heat transfer and analysis.
D. Both A and B

_____ 2. An architect can design building components that are able to withstand stress and weight from the building and from any use the structure experiences by using _____.
A. energy analysis
B. structural analysis
C. computer-aided drafting
D. project management

_____ 3. Which of the following applications are generally a part of CADD software programs?
A. Creation and storage of drawings with easy modifications.
B. Area calculation.
C. Automatic dimensioning.
D. All of the above

_____ 4. Designers can plan energy-efficient buildings using _____ programs.
A. computer graphic representations
B. energy analysis
C. structural analysis
D. project management

_____ 5. What do the letters "PERT" represent?
A. Probability Effort Requirement Testing
B. Pertinent Energy Reporting Technique
C. Project Evaluation and Review Technique
D. Potential-Essential-Required Tactics

_____ 6. Which of the following areas are a part of computer simulation?
   A. Generation of standard symbols and shading.
   B. Modeling behavior of continuous systems.
   C. Producing ruled line drawings.
   D. None of the above

SHORT ANSWER

Answer the following questions using short answers.

1. List six areas where software can be utilized to aid the architect, drafter, or builder.

   A. _____

   B. _____

   C. _____

   D. _____

   E. _____

   F. _____

2. What are two advantages of using CADD over traditional methods of drafting?

   A. _____

   B. _____

3. What areas of project management can be enhanced using a computer?

   A. _____

   B. _____

   C. _____

   D. _____

35 CHAPTER

Introduction to Computer-Aided Drafting and Design

■ OBJECTIVES

After studying this chapter, the student will be able to:
□ Explain why CADD is important to the fields of architecture and construction.
□ List the components of modern microcomputers and explain their basic functions.
□ Specify the characteristics of monitors that are important for a CADD system.
□ Recognize common input and pointing devices used with a CADD system.
□ Discuss several graphics output devices that are installed for CADD applications.

■ DISPLAYS

1. CADD Systems. Use the specification sheets, descriptive literature, and price lists collected by your students in Suggested Activity #2 to create a bulletin board display.
2. CADD Drawings. Display several examples of drawings that were created on a typical CADD system.

■ INSTRUCTIONAL MATERIALS

Text: Pages 509-522
Review Questions, Suggested Activities
Workbook: Pages 255-260
Review Questions, Problems/Activities
Teacher's Resource Guide:
Chapter 35—Teaching Strategy
Chapter 35—Exam

■ TEACHING STRATEGY

• Prepare Display #1.
• Review chapter objectives.
• Introduce computer-aided drafting and design.

• Discuss the various components of the computer—CPU, RAM, math coprocessors, permanent storage devices, and standard ports.
• Discuss monitors and graphics adaptors.
• Discuss input and pointing devices—keyboard, mouse, digitizing tablet, and miscellaneous input devices.
• Prepare Display #2.
• Discuss graphics output devices—pen plotters, laser printers, electrostatic plotters, color impact printers, daisy wheel printers, and film recorders.
• Assign workbook Problem 35-1.
• Assign one or more of the Suggested Activities in the text.
• Chapter Review
—Assign Review Questions in the text. Discuss the correct answers.
—Assign Review Questions in the workbook. Have students check their own answers.
• Evaluation
—Administer the Chapter 35—Exam. Correct the exam and return.
—Return graded problems with comments.

■ ANSWERS TO REVIEW QUESTIONS, TEXT
Pages 521-522

1. CAD.
2. a. Mainframe computer.
   b. Super-minicomputer.
   c. Minicomputer.
   d. Microcomputer.
3. Symbols can be developed, stored, and recalled when needed, eliminating the need to redraw them each time.
4. a. Computer or processor.
   b. Monitor.
   c. Graphics adapter.
   d. Input and pointing device.
   e. Graphics output device.

5. Microcomputer.
6. K.
7. Central processing unit.
8. 32
9. floppy disks, hard disks.
10. To speed up calculations.
11. serial
12. monitor or display
13. a. Monochrome.
    b. Color.
14. c. 640 x 480 pixels.
15. keyboard
16. b. Pen ball.
17. a. Pick items from a menu overlay.
    b. Input (digitize) drawings.
    c. Move the cursor on the screen.
18. soft, hard
19. pen plotter
20. electrostatic

■ ANSWERS TO REVIEW QUESTIONS, WORKBOOK

PART I: COMPLETION

1. CADD
2. engineering
3. processing
4. CPU.
5. math coprocessor
6. parallel
7. Resolution
8. membrane
9. digitizing
10. pen
11. speed
12. electrostatic
13. film
14. printed circuit boards

PART II: SHORT ANSWER/LISTING

1. A. It enables the designer to plan a structure or part of a structure.
   B. It enables the designer to make modifications without having to draw the whole plan.
   Also: It can call up symbols or base drawings from computer storage. It automatically duplicates forms and shapes commonly used. It produces schedules or analyses. It produces Hardcopies of complete drawings or drawing elements in a few minutes.
2. The revision of CADD drawings.
3. A. Computer or processor.
   B. Monitor.
   C. Graphics adapter.
   D. Input and pointing device.
   E. Graphics output device.
4. Microcomputers.
5. A math coprocessor speeds up the calculations required for the generation of graphics.
6. The information is stored on the hard disk with the floppies used as a backup.
7. Color is better suited for CADD graphics.
8. A graphics adapter.
9. A. Keyboard.
   B. Mouse.
   C. Digitizing tablet.
   D. Puck.
   E. Light pen.
   Also: Joystick, stylus pen, thumbwheels, and track ball.
10. One type has a small ball that moves to indicate position. The movements are picked up by the screen cursor. Another type has a small light source which shines on a metal pad containing a metal grid. The cursor on the screen is controlled by the light and grid.
11. Stylus or puck.
12. A. Pen plotters.
    B. Laser printers.
    C. Thermal and electrostatic plotters.
    Also: Color impact printers, daisy wheel printers, and film recorders.
13. The drawing moves from front to back while the pen moves from side to side.

PART III: MULTIPLE CHOICE

1. C. Easy to use and fast.
2. A. Symbols library.
3. B. Mainframe.
4. C. 640K.
5. A. 5 1/4 in.
6. B. Straighter lines.
7. C. Calculator style.
8. D. 1,000.
9. A. Softcopy.
10. A. That it is easy to monitor the drawing while it is being drawn.
11. C. They are efficient for desktop publishing.
12. B. Color impact printer.

PART IV: MATCHING

1. A. CADD.
2. C. Computer.
3. F. Minicomputer.
4. J. RAM.
5. B. CPU.
6. G. Monitor.
7. I. Pixel.
8. E. Keyboard.
9. H. Mouse.
10. D. Digitizing tablet.

PART V: PROBLEMS/ACTIVITIES

1. A. Graphics output device.
   B. Monitor.
   C. Printer.
   D. Digitizer.
   E. Pointing Device.
   F. Keyboard.

■ ANSWERS TO CHAPTER 35—EXAM

TRUE—FALSE

1. T   4. T
2. T   5. T
3. F

MULTIPLE CHOICE

1. B   10. D
2. A   11. B
3. D   12. A
4. C   13. D
5. A   14. B
6. D   15. A
7. B   16. B
8. C   17. D
9. D

SHORT ANSWER

1. A. Three-dimensional design functions.
   B. Analysis capabilities.
   C. Schedule production.
   D. Reporting.
2. A. Computer or processor.
   B. Monitor.
   C. Input and pointing device.
   D. Hardcopy device.
3. A. Mainframe computers.
   B. Super-minicomputers.
   C. Minicomputers.
   D. Microcomputers.
4. A. Parallel.
   B. Serial.
5. A. Monochrome.
   B. Color.
6. A. Membrane.
   B. Calculator-style.
   C. Typewriter-style.

MATCHING

1. H   6. I
2. D   7. B
3. J   8. C
4. A   9. E
5. F   10. G

Chapter 35—Exam
INTRODUCTION TO COMPUTER-AIDED DRAFTING AND DESIGN

Name _____

Period _____ **Date** _____ **Score** _____

TRUE—FALSE
Circle T if the statement is true or F if the statement is false.

T   F   1. CADD is an acronym for computer-aided drafting and design.

T   F   2. CADD allows the designer to modify a design without having to redraw the entire plan.

T   F   3. The heart of a CADD system is the plotter.

T   F   4. A mainframe computer is usually able to handle many users at the same time without sacrificing speed.

T   F   5. CPUs are classified according to the number of program instructions they can process at one time.

MULTIPLE CHOICE
Choose the answer that correctly completes the statement. Write the corresponding letter in the space provided.

_____ 1. CADD saves time in what specific area?
A. Making original drawings.
B. Revising drawings.
C. Working with a client.
D. None of the above

_____ 2. Equipment such a plotters, digitizing tablets, and monitors are _____ devices.
A. peripheral
B. dedicated
C. serial
D. optional

_____ 3. The smallest computers that support CADD programs are _____.
A. personal computers
B. PCs
C. microcomputers
D. All of the above

_____ 4. Microcomputers used for CADD software programs should generally have a minimum of _____ RAM.
A. 120
B. 240
C. 640
D. 880

_____ 5. Each input and output device requires its own _____.
A. port
B. CPU
C. drive
D. expansion slot

_____ 6. The monitor allows the computer to communicate with the _____.
   A. plotter
   B. software
   C. digitizing tablet
   D. operator

_____ 7. In monitors, _____ is usually more important than size.
   A. curvature
   B. resolution
   C. diagonal measure
   D. weight

_____ 8. A CADD monitor should have a resolution of at least _____ pixels.
   A. 120 x 240
   B. 240 x 480
   C. 640 x 480
   D. 1000 x 1000

_____ 9. Typical graphics adapters include _____ and _____.
   A. EGA; VGA
   B. EGA; MDA
   C. MDA; CGA
   D. All of the above

_____ 10. Which of the following is not an input device?
   A. Keyboard.
   B. Digitizing tablet.
   C. Track ball.
   D. Stylus wheel.

_____ 11. Menu overlays are generally used with a _____.
   A. graphics adaptor
   B. digitizing tablet
   C. mouse
   D. None of the above

_____ 12. Softcopy information is output to the _____.
   A. monitor
   B. plotter
   C. printer
   D. digitizing tablet

_____ 13. The _____ is the most popular device for producing high-quality CADD line drawings.
   A. laser printer
   B. thermal plotter
   C. color impact printer
   D. pen plotter

_____ 14. Some pen plotters draw lines from 15 to _____ in./sec. while maintaining an accuracy of 0.001 in. repeatability.
   A. 20
   B. 25
   C. 50
   D. 100

_____ 15. The _____ is a popular output device where line drawings and text material are integrated.
  A. laser printer
  B. pen plotter
  C. film recorder
  D. daisy wheel printer

_____ 16. The _____ is generally considered the most versatile type of plotter. Its speed is over 75 times as fast as a pen plotter, but is much less accurate.
  A. color impact printer
  B. electrostatic plotter
  C. laser printer
  D. daisy wheel printer

_____ 17. Film recorders produce _____.
  A. 35mm slides
  B. color prints
  C. transparencies
  D. All of the above

SHORT ANSWER
Answer each of the questions using short answers.

1. In addition to two-dimensional drafting, many CADD software packages contain other capabilities. Name four of the most common capabilities.

  A. _____

  B. _____

  C. _____

  D. _____

2. List the four basic components of a typical CADD system.

  A. _____

  B. _____

  C. _____

  D. _____

3. What are the four main classifications of computers?

  A. _____

  B. _____

  C. _____

  D. _____

4. What are the two types of ports generally used with microcomputers?

  A. _____

  B. _____

5. What are the two main categories of monitors?

  A. _____

  B. _____

6. Name the three common types of keyboards.

A. _____

B. _____

C. _____

MATCHING

Select the answer that correctly matches each term. Place your answer in the space provided.

_____ 1. Turnkey system

_____ 2. RAM

_____ 3. K

_____ 4. CPU

_____ 5. Math coprocessor

_____ 6. 3 1/2", 5 1/4", 8"

_____ 7. Parallel

_____ 8. Pixel

_____ 9. Mouse

_____ 10. Puck

A. Central processing unit.
B. Microcomputer port.
C. Picture element.
D. Random access memory.
E. Input device to identify points on the screen.
F. Takes some of the load off the CPU.
G. Used with a digitizing tablet.
H. Self-contained.
I. Floppy disk sizes.
J. Kilobyte.

36
CHAPTER

CADD Software

■ OBJECTIVES

After studying this chapter, the student will be able to:
- ☐ Explain the benefits of using CADD in generating architectural designs.
- ☐ Identify several factors that should be considered when purchasing a CADD system.
- ☐ Describe the characteristics of a general-purpose CADD program.
- ☐ Describe the features of an AEC architectural CADD program.
- ☐ Select a CADD package to perform certain tasks based on characteristics of software presented in the chapter.

■ DISPLAYS

1. Architecture/Construction Software. Prepare a bulletin board display using specification sheets from an AEC software package. Highlight outstanding features. Include drawings, schedules, etc. produced with the package.
2. How To Use This CADD Package. Assemble the step-by-step procedure for using an AEC software package which you have available in your classroom. Display the procedure on the bulletin board for students to study.

■ INSTRUCTIONAL MATERIALS

Text: Pages 523-538
   Review Questions, Suggested Activities
Workbook: Pages 261-266
   Review Questions, Problems/Activities
Teacher's Resource Guide:
   Chapter 36 — Teaching Strategy
   Chapter 36 — Exam

■ TEACHING STRATEGY

- Prepare Display #1.
- Review chapter objectives.
- Introduce CADD software. Define software.
- Discuss the benefits of CADD in architecture.
- Discuss selecting a CADD package.
- Present general-purpose CADD packages.
- Review general-purpose CADD package characteristics.
- Prepare Display #2.
- Assign workbook Problem 36-1.
- Introduce AEC CADD packages.
- Assign workbook Problem 36-2.
- Assign one or more of the Suggested Activities in the text.
- Chapter Review
  - Assign Review Questions in the text. Discuss the correct answers.
  - Assign Review Questions in the workbook. Have students check their own answers.
- Evaluation
  - Administer the Chapter 36 — Exam. Correct the exam and return.
  - Return graded problems with comments.

■ ANSWERS TO REVIEW QUESTIONS, TEXT
Pages 536-537

1. Selecting the software.
2. All types.
3. a. Provides a flexible way to generate drawings.
   b. Automatic generation of schedules.
   c. Making changes and corrections is fast and easy.
   d. CADD drawings are uniform and aid in communication.
   e. Poor-quality line work and sloppy drawings not a factor.

f. Time saved in making repetitive features.
g. Complex details can be saved and used over and over again.
h. The cost is affordable.
4. a. How easy is the program to use?
   b. Does the program require special hardware?
   c. How well does the package meet your needs?
   d. What kind of support does the company provide?
   e. What are the hardware requirements?
   f. What does the warranty cover?
   g. What specific features does the software have?
   h. How much does it cost?
5. General-purpose CADD package.
6. architectural, engineering, and construction.
7. a. Math coprocessor.
   b. Digitizing tablet.
   Also: Mouse, plotter, and EMS memory.
8. 2.5D.
9. a. Lines.
   b. Points.
   c. Circles.
   d. Arcs.
   Also: Boxes, polylines, fillets, chamfers, and freehand sketching.
10. d. All of the above.
11. a. 0 to unlimited.
12. a. Continuous.   d. Center line.
    b. Dashed line.   e. Phantom.
    c. Hidden line.   f. Border.
13. b. 12'-6".
14. display or monitor.
15. c. Redraw.
16. Sections.
17. Three-dimensional shading
18. c. Cone.
19. a. From space diagram.
    b. Continuous walls.
    c. From dimensions.
20. a. Windows and doors.
    b. Plumbing symbols.
    c. HVAC.
    d. Construction details.
    e. Plant symbols.
    Also: Site Symbols.
21. background

■ ANSWERS TO REVIEW QUESTIONS, WORKBOOK

PART I: SHORT ANSWER/LISTING

1. It instructs the hardware to carry out certain tasks.
2. Much time can be saved in the initial execution of the schedules and in correcting or making additions to the schedules.
3. Symbols from the CADD library can be called up and put into place in a short time. The sym-

bols are used frequently and are standard.
4. A. Brick, stone, blocks, and other building materials.
   B. Window details.
   C. Typical wall sections.
   D. Stair designs.
   E. cabinet details.
   Also: Paving and gutter sections; culverts and roof and floor truss details.
5. A. 2D.
   B. 2.5D.
   C. 3D.
6. A. Tablet.
   B. Pointing device.
   C. Keyboard.
7. Shaded drawings are useful for communicating designs to a client, producing materials for advertising purposes, and creating presentation models.
8. They are designed for architecture, engineering, and construction applications.
9. A. Top.
   B. Front.
   C. Rear.
   D. Right and left sides.
   E. From each principal corner.
   F. Global viewpoint.
   G. Solid modeling.
   H. Isometric.
   I. Perspective.
10. A. Tub.
    B. Lavatory.
    C. Shower stall.
    D. Toilet.
    E. Bidet.
    F. Plumbing lines.
    G. Valves.
11. They are used as underlays to compare features or to construct new drawings.

PART II: COMPLETION

1. CADD
2. easy
3. uniformity
4. general-purpose
5. support
6. linetypes
7. DXF
8. CPL.
9. wall
10. will

PART III: MULTIPLE CHOICE

1. B. CADD systems.
2. D. All of the above.
3. C. The lettering and lines on CADD drawings are always clear and concise.

4. D. Will the CADD system function in a high dust environment?
5. A. Copy, erase, move, scale, rotate, trim, break, explode.
6. B. Architectural, engineering, scientific, decimal, and fractional.
7. C. Area, distance, and angles.
8. A. About the same as.
9. B. AEC CADD packages.

PART IV: MATCHING

1. C. Entities.
2. E. Layers.
3. A. Display controls.
4. B. Drawing aids.
5. G. 2D drawing.
6. I. 3D primitives.
7. D. HVAC.
8. H. Title symbols.
9. F. Schedule generation.

PART V: PROBLEMS/ACTIVITIES

1. Solution on page 318.
2. Solution on page 319.

■ ANSWERS TO CHAPTER 36—EXAM

TRUE—FALSE

1. T
2. T
3. F
4. F
5. T

MULTIPLE CHOICE

1. C
2. B
3. B
4. C
5. D

SHORT ANSWER

1. A. 2D.
   B. 2.5D.
   C. 3D.
2. A group of entities that may be manipulated as a group.
3. A. Architectural.
   B. Engineering.
   C. Scientific.
   D. Decimal.
   E. Fractional.
4. By digitizing the drawing.
5. A. From space diagrams.
   B. From continuous walls.
   C. From dimensions.

MATCHING

1. H
2. E
3. A
4. J
5. B
6. F
7. C
8. D
9. L
10. I
11. K
12. G
13. M
14. C
15. G
16. A
17. I
18. B
19. D
20. H
21. E
22. F
23. K
24. J

1.

DIRECTIONS:
Connect each of the general purpose CADD characteristics on the left
with the appropriate example on the right.

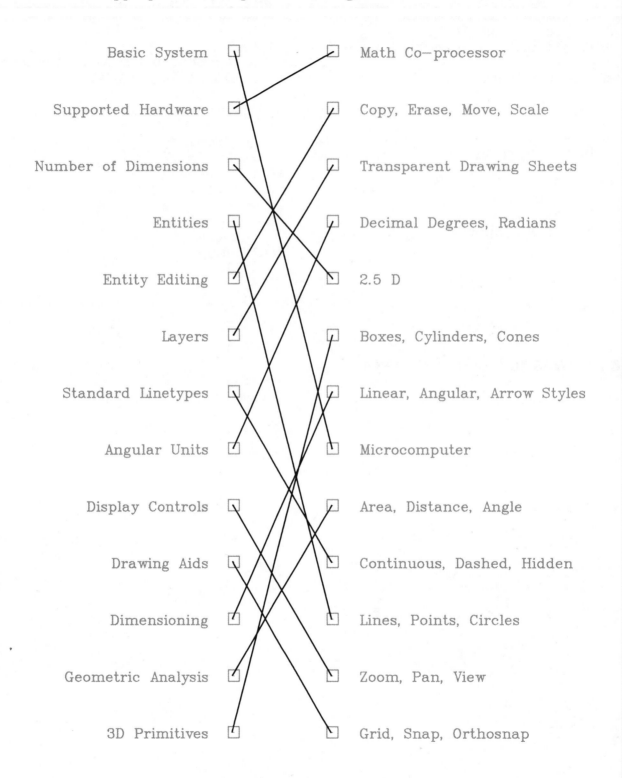

Basic System ☐	☐ Math Co—processor
Supported Hardware ☐	☐ Copy, Erase, Move, Scale
Number of Dimensions ☐	☐ Transparent Drawing Sheets
Entities ☐	☐ Decimal Degrees, Radians
Entity Editing ☐	☐ 2.5 D
Layers ☐	☐ Boxes, Cylinders, Cones
Standard Linetypes ☐	☐ Linear, Angular, Arrow Styles
Angular Units ☐	☐ Microcomputer
Display Controls ☐	☐ Area, Distance, Angle
Drawing Aids ☐	☐ Continuous, Dashed, Hidden
Dimensioning ☐	☐ Lines, Points, Circles
Geometric Analysis ☐	☐ Zoom, Pan, View
3D Primitives ☐	☐ Grid, Snap, Orthosnap

GENERAL PURPOSE CADD		36—1

2.

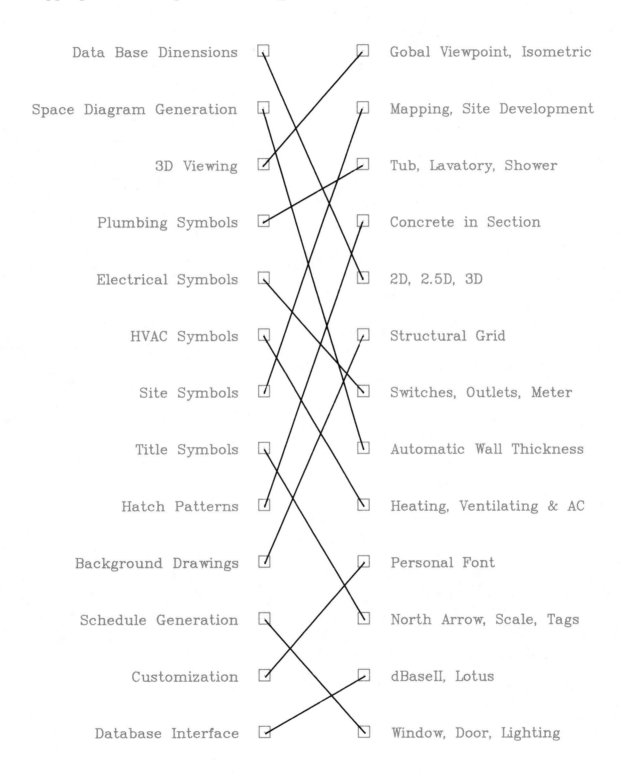

DIRECTIONS:
Connect each of the AEC CADD characteristics on the left with the appropriate example on the right.

Data Base Dinensions ☐	☐ Gobal Viewpoint, Isometric
Space Diagram Generation ☐	☐ Mapping, Site Development
3D Viewing ☐	☐ Tub, Lavatory, Shower
Plumbing Symbols ☐	☐ Concrete in Section
Electrical Symbols ☐	☐ 2D, 2.5D, 3D
HVAC Symbols ☐	☐ Structural Grid
Site Symbols ☐	☐ Switches, Outlets, Meter
Title Symbols ☐	☐ Automatic Wall Thickness
Hatch Patterns ☐	☐ Heating, Ventilating & AC
Background Drawings ☐	☐ Personal Font
Schedule Generation ☐	☐ North Arrow, Scale, Tags
Customization ☐	☐ dBaseII, Lotus
Database Interface ☐	☐ Window, Door, Lighting

AEC CADD CHARACTERISTICS | | 36-2

Chapter 36—Exam
CADD SOFTWARE

Name _____

Period _____ **Date** _____ **Score** _____

TRUE—FALSE
Circle T is the statement is true or F if the statement is false.

T   F   1. There are many CADD packages available.

T   F   2. Flexibility is one advantage of using a CADD system to generate drawings.

T   F   3. Making drawings on a CADD system reduces creativity.

T   F   4. Plotters produce only one line width.

T   F   5. Selecting a specific software package is probably the single most important decision in putting together a CADD system.

MULTIPLE CHOICE
Choose the answer that correctly completes the statement. Write the corresponding letter in the space provided.

_____ 1. Drawings produced on a CADD system possess a high degree of _____ regardless of who makes the drawings.
A. staleness
B. ambiguity
C. uniformity
D. inaccuracy

_____ 2. Standard symbols, such as trees, can be added to a CADD drawing in seconds from the CADD _____.
A. resource guide
B. library
C. reference manual
D. None of the above

_____ 3. Which of the following is an example of a CADD package designed for a specific field?
A. Andersen's CADD-1.
B. AutoCAD's AEC.
C. CADKEY.
D. AutoSketch.

_____ 4. Three-dimensional CADD programs store a(n) _____ for each point on an object.
A. X,Y coordinate
B. attribute
C. three-dimensional database
D. None of the above

_____ 5. An example of an entity is a _____.
A. line
B. circle
C. box
D. All of the above

SHORT ANSWER
Answer each of the questions using short answers.

1. What are the three dimensions that are commonly referred to in CADD software packages?

   A. _____

   B. _____

   C. _____

2. What is a compound entity?

   _____

3. Identify five common linear units.

   A. _____

   B. _____

   C. _____

   D. _____

   E. _____

4. How can an existing drawing be entered into the computer without having to redraw it?

   _____

5. Identify the three ways that architectural packages generally provide for generating a wall thickness.

   A. _____

   B. _____

   C. _____

MATCHING
Select the answer that correctly matches each term. Place your answer in the space provided.

GENERAL CADD PACKAGES

_____ 1. Entities

_____ 2. Entity editing

_____ 3. Layers

_____ 4. Standard linetypes

_____ 5. Angular units

_____ 6. Display controls

_____ 7. Drawing aids

_____ 8. Text

_____ 9. Geometric analysis

_____ 10. 3D shading

_____ 11. Drawing interchanges

_____ 12. Program customization

_____ 13. 3D primitives

A. Similar to transparent drawing sheets.
B. Decimal degrees.
C. Grid, snap, axis.
D. Font.
E. Copy, erase, move, rotate.
F. Zoom, pan, view.
G. Macros, directories, system variables.
H. Basic elements used to create objects.
I. True-to-life appearance.
J. Continuous, dashed, phantom.
K. IGES, DXF, DXB.
L. Moment, centroid.
M. Cones, spheres, cylinders.

AEC CADD PACKAGES

_____ 14. Database dimensions

_____ 15. Space diagram generation

_____ 16. Drawing walls

_____ 17. 3D viewing

_____ 18. Structural symbols

_____ 19. Plumbing symbols

_____ 20. HVAC

_____ 21. Tree and plant symbols

_____ 22. Site symbols

_____ 23. Schedule generation

_____ 24. Database interface

A. Intersection cleanup, wall thickness.
B. Needed more for commercial work than residential work.
C. 2D, 2.5D, 3D.
D. Bidet, valves.
E. Landscaping.
F. Libraries for mapping.
G. Automatic floor plan.
H. Heating, ventilation, air conditioning.
I. Top, front, rear, right, left side.
J. Lotus, dBase IV.
K. Window schedule.

CADD Commands and Functions

■ OBJECTIVES

After studying this chapter, the student will be able to:

☐ Explain the difference between CADD commands and functions.

☐ List several typical drawing commands used in popular CADD programs.

☐ Describe how ZOOM and PAN commands are used when making a drawing on a CADD system.

☐ Sketch an example of each of the following basic forms of dimensioning—linear, angular, and leader.

☐ Discuss the purpose of layers in typical CADD programs.

☐ List several drawing aids that are provided by most CADD programs.

■ DISPLAYS

1. Commands and Functions. Prepare a bulletin board display which consists of CADD commands and functions. List each command or function and show an example as related to architecture or construction drawing.

2. 3D Functions. Prepare a bulletin board display of 3D functions. Provide a written description as well as an illustration.

■ INSTRUCTIONAL MATERIALS

Text: Pages 539-554
   Review Questions, Suggested Activities
Workbook: Pages 267-276
   Review Questions, Problems/Activities
Teacher's Resource Guide:
   Chapter 37—Teaching Strategy
   Chapter 37—Exam

■ TEACHING STRATEGY

• Prepare Display #1.
• Review chapter objectives.
• Introduce CADD commands and functions.
• Discuss and illustrate drawing commands.
• Assign workbook Problem 37-1.
• Discuss editing and inquiry commands.
• Assign workbook Problem 37-2.
• Present display control commands.
• Discuss dimensioning commands.
• Assign workbook Problem 37-3.
• Discuss layers, colors, and linetypes.
• Cover drawing aids.
• Assign workbook Problem 37-4.
• Prepare Display #2.
• Discuss 3D functions.
• Present utility commands and functions.
• Assign one or more of the Suggested Activities in the text.
• Chapter Review
   —Assign Review Questions in the text. Discuss the correct answers.
   —Assign Review Questions in the workbook. Have students check their own answers.
   —Make a transparency of 37-1 and use for review.
• Evaluation
   —Administer the Chapter 37—Exam. Correct exam and return.
   —Return graded problems with comments.

■ ANSWERS TO REVIEW QUESTIONS, TEXT Pages 552-553

1. entity
2. function
3. d. Drawing.

4. a. Linetype.
   b. Width.
   c. Color.
5. b. Starting point, end point, and radius.
6. Walls on a floor plan.
7. a. HATCH.
8. ROTATE
9. fillet
10. DISTANCE.
11. monitor.
12. PAN
13. ANGULAR.
14. as many as the software provides for.
15. 2 — Yellow.
    6 — Magenta.
16. Linetype
17. d. Symbol template.
18. three
19. 2
20. c. Shaded solids model.

■ ANSWERS TO REVIEW QUESTIONS, WORKBOOK

PART I: SHORT ANSWER/LISTING

1. They tell the computer which entity to draw.
2. They may be typed from a keyboard, selected from a menu screen, picked from a digitizing tablet overlay, or entered using a multibutton pointing device.
3. A. LINE.
   B. ARC.
   C. CIRCLE.
   D. POLYGON.
   E. RECTANGLE.
   Also: Double line, text, drag, and hatch.
4. SKETCH.
5. When drawings need to be modified.
6. ERASE.
7. The COPY command makes copies of the original and places them in certain locations without moving the original. The MOVE command moves the original to a different location while maintaining its size and orientation.
8. It computes the distance around any space indicated on the drawing.
9. A. Control the position and magnification of the window screen.
   B. Indicate the degree to which time-consuming entities are drawn.
   C. Request the screen to be redrawn.
10. A. ZOOM.
    B. PAN.
    C. VIEW.
    D. REDRAW.
    E. REGENERATE.
11. A. HORIZONTAL.
    B. VERTICAL.

C. ALIGNED.
D. ROTATED.
E. BASELINE.
F. CONTINUE.
12. They allow the operator to group associated objects in a drawing, control the visibility of those groups, and provide added visual information through color and linetypes.
13. Provides a reference grid of dots to appear on the screen.
14. Packages for 2.5D store X and Y data points and simple 3D visuals for objects where the thickness was stored earlier. Packages for 3D store data for the X, Y, and Z coordinates of each data point and provide full 3D capabilities from the 3D data base.
15. HELP.
16. A. The screen menu.
    B. The pointer device button menu.
    C. An auxiliary function box menu.
    D. Various digitizer menus.

PART II: MULTIPLE CHOICE

1. A. COPY.
2. C. Arc.
3. B. Rectangle.
4. D. DRAG.
5. A. MOVE.
6. B. Alter the orientation of entities on a drawing.
7. B. CHAMFER.
8. A. Examine the data stored for an entity.
9. A. ZOOM.
10. C. Dimensioning.
11. C. Add specific or local note.
12. D. Drawing entities may be placed on one or more layers.
13. C. SNAP.
14. A. Vertical, 30 degrees, and 150 degrees.
15. C. Shaded solids modeling.
16. B. STOP.
17. D. SAVE.

PART III: COMPLETION

1. line
2. circle.
3. DOUBLE LINE
4. is
5. INQUIRY
6. STRETCH
7. EXTEND
8. ARRAY
9. VIEW
10. REDRAW
11. dimensioning
12. linetype.
13. OBJECT SNAP

14. 3D
15. END.
16. TIME

PART IV: MATCHING

1. K. PLOT.
2. H. Line.
3. B. ARC.
4. L. Polygon.
5. G. HATCH.
6. N. SCALE.
7. E. FILLET.
8. Q. Window.
9. J. PAN.
10. A. ANGULAR.
11. D. DIAMETER.
12. F. Green.
13. C. Blue.
14. I. OBJECT SNAP.
15. O. Surface modeling.
16. M. QUIT.
17. P. System variables.

PART V: PROBLEMS/ACTIVITIES

1. Solution on page 328.
2. Solution on page 329.
3. Solution on page 330.

■ ANSWERS TO CHAPTER 37 — EXAM

TRUE — FALSE

1. T   4. T
2. T   5. T
3. F

MULTIPLE CHOICE

1. A   5. D
2. D   6. A
3. B   7. C
4. B   8. B

SHORT ANSWER

1. A. Keyboard.
   B. Select from a screen menu.
   C. Pick from a digitizing tablet overlay.
   D. Entered using a multibutton pointing device.

2. The location of the entity.
3. A. Starting point, center, and end point.
   B. Starting point, center, and included angle.
   C. Starting point, center, and length of chord.
   D. Starting point, end point, and radius.
   E. Starting point, end point, and included angle.
   F. Starting point, end point, and starting direction.
   G. Continuation of a previous line or arc.
4. A. Specifying the width and height.
   B. Specifying a corner and dragging the opposite corner to the desired location.
5. It cleans up the display by removing marker blips, etc.
6. A. LINEAR.
   B. ANGULAR.
   C. DIAMETER.
   D. RADIUS.
   E. LEADER.
7. To provide a specific or local note.
8. As many as the software provides.
9. 1 — Red.
   2 — Yellow.
   3 — Green.
   4 — Cyan.
   5 — Blue.
   6 — Magenta.
   7 — White.
10. A. GRID.
    B. SNAP.
    C. OBJECT SNAP.
    D. ORTHO.
    E. ISOMETRIC.
11. All lines drawn will be vertical or horizontal.
12. Shaded solids modeling.
13. QUIT.

MATCHING

1. F   9. K
2. L   10. O
3. A   11. N
4. J   12. D
5. C   13. G
6. B   14. M
7. I   15. H
8. E

1.

This assignment requires the use of a CADD system.   Using a scale
of 1/4"=1'-0" and an "A", "B", or "C" size drawing sheet, draw a
border line 480" @ 90°, 348" @ 0°, 480" @ 270°, and 348"
@ 180°.   The space enclosed by this border is exactly the same
as this page in your workbook.   The title block is 12" high and the
plate # box is 36" wide.   Use the following drawing commands (or
your program's equivalent) to generate the lines and shapes indicated.

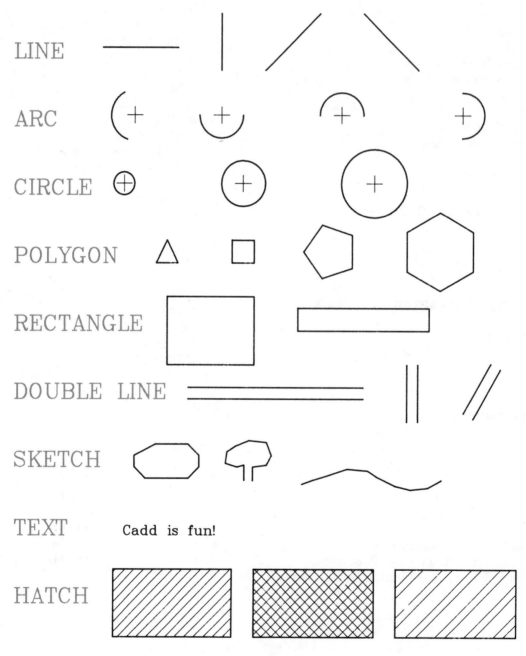

LINE

ARC

CIRCLE

POLYGON

RECTANGLE

DOUBLE LINE

SKETCH

TEXT   Cadd is fun!

HATCH

Add the title, assignment #, and your name to the title block.

DRAWING COMMANDS   37-1

2.

DIRECTIONS:
This assignment requires the use of a CADD system. Set the scale to 1/4"=1'-0" and prepare a drawing sheet identical to the one required for Assignment 37-1. This assignment deals with selected Editing and Inquiry commands. Practice using all of these commands that your program provides, but demonstrate the use of the following:

Draw a circle at one location and MOVE it to another.

○ First Location   ○ Final Position

Draw a rectangle and make two copies of it.

☐ Original   ☐ Copy 1   ☐ Copy 2

Draw one—half of a geometric shape and MIRROR the other side to complete the shape.

Draw a shape and then ROTATE it 15°.

Draw a box and use FILLET to round the corners.

Draw a three—sided figure as shown and EXTEND it to twice its original length.

Use ARRAY to create five circles around a center.

Use SCALE to change the size of a circle to half its original size.

Draw a rectangle and use AREA to determine the area.

16 Sq. Ft.

EDITING & INQUIRY COMMANDS   37-2

3.

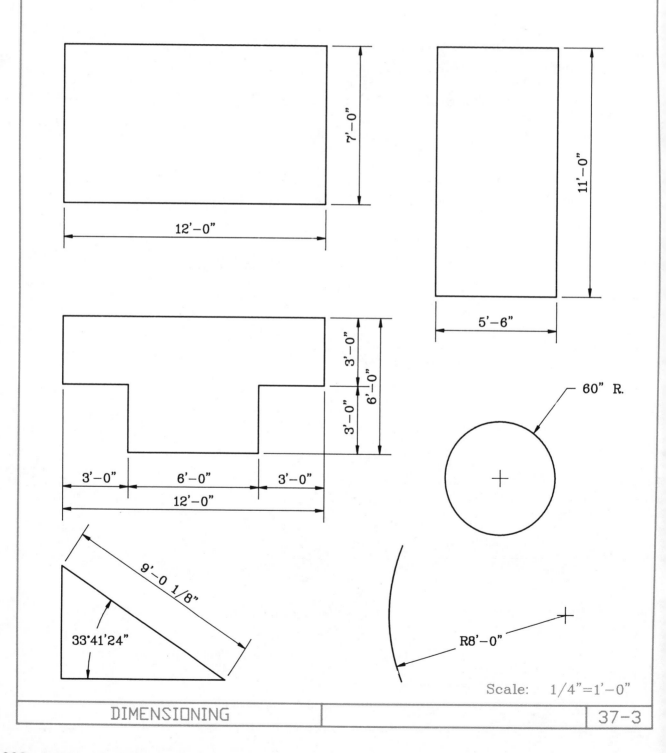

DIRECTIONS:
This assignment requires the use of a CADD system. Draw a border and title block as required for Assignments 37-1 and 37-2. Set the scale to 1/4"=1'-0". Draw a series of rectangles in the space below leaving room for dimensions. Using the DIMENSION command, dimension the length and width of each rectangle. You may wish to add other shapes to show angular, diameter, radius, and leader type dimensions as well.

7'-0"

12'-0"

11'-0"

5'-6"

3'-0"

6'-0"

3'-0"

3'-0"

6'-0"

3'-0"

12'-0"

60" R.

9'-0 1/8"

33°41'24"

R8'-0"

Scale: 1/4"=1'-0"

DIMENSIONING

37-3

Chapter 37—Exam
CADD COMMANDS AND FUNCTIONS

Name _____

Period _____ Date _____ Score _____

TRUE—FALSE
Circle T if the statement is true or F if the statement is false.

T   F   1. Commands tell the computer what entities to draw.

T   F   2. The plot function is used when a hardcopy is desired.

T   F   3. The DRAG command is the most frequently used command in a CADD program.

T   F   4. The LINE command produces lines that remain as separate entities for easy modification.

T   F   5. The POLYGON command enables the construction of a regular polygon.

MULTIPLE CHOICE
Choose the answer that correctly completes the statement. Write the corresponding letter in the space provided.

_____ 1. Functions which provide for the modification of a drawing include_____.
A. ERASE, MOVE, and COPY
B. TEXT, ERASE, and MOVE
C. MOVE, PLOT, and COPY
D. COPY, ERASE, and TEXT

_____ 2. LINE, ARC, and CIRCLE are _____ commands.
A. editing and inquiry
B. display control
C. dimensioning
D. drawing

_____ 3. Which of the following is *not* a method of drawing a circle?
A. Center and radius.
B. Starting point, center, and end point.
C. Center and diameter.
D. Dynamic circle specification by dragging.

_____ 4. Most CADD packages provide several standard text _____.
A. line symbols
B. fonts
C. spacings
D. None of the above

_____ 5. Which of the following is *not* an editing or inquiry command?
A. ERASE.
B. MOVE.
C. LIST.
D. ZOOM.

_____ 6. The _____ command is similar to MOVE except that it places an exact replica of the selected entities at the specified location.
A. COPY
B. ARRAY
C. ROTATE
D. SCALE

_____ 7. The LIST command _____.
    A. displays the files on the hard disk
    B. compiles a list of entities used
    C. permits the examination of data stored for an entity
    D. None of the above

_____ 8. Most CADD packages provide for _____ dimensioning.
    A. automatic
    B. semi-automatic
    C. non-automatic
    D. None of the above

SHORT ANSWER
Answer each of the questions using short answers.

1. List four different ways of entering commands into a CADD system computer.

    A. _____
    B. _____
    C. _____
    D. _____

2. What parameter is always included for each entity?

    _____

3. The ARC command draws partial circles. Several methods of drawing arcs are usually provided. Examples include:

    A. _____
    B. _____
    C. _____
    D. _____
    E. _____
    F. _____
    G. _____

4. What are the two methods generally provided for drawing rectangles?

    A. _____
    B. _____

5. What is the function of the REDRAW command?

    _____

6. List the five basic dimensioning commands generally found in a CADD program.

    A. _____
    B. _____
    C. _____
    D. _____
    E. _____

7. What is the purpose of a leader?

   _____

8. How many layers can be used in a drawing?

   _____

9. What are the standard colors represented by the numbers below?

   1 – _____

   2 – _____

   3 – _____

   4 – _____

   5 – _____

   6 – _____

   7 – _____

10. List five common drawing aid commands.

    A. _____

    B. _____

    C. _____

    D. _____

    E. _____

11. The ORTHO mode ensures that _____.

    _____

12. What are the most sophisticated 3D representations called?

    _____

13. Which command returns to the main menu and discards all changes to the drawing?

    _____

MATCHING

Select the answer that correctly matches each term. Place your answer in the space provided.

_____ 1. Attributes

_____ 2. Regular polygon

_____ 3. DOUBLE LINE

_____ 4. SKETCH

_____ 5. TEXT

_____ 6. DRAG

_____ 7. HATCH

_____ 8. MOVE

_____ 9. ROTATE

_____ 10. FILLET

_____ 11. ARRAY

_____ 12. WINDOW

_____ 13. DISTANCE

_____ 14. ZOOM

_____ 15. PAN

A. Useful in creating walls on a floor plan.
B. Permits moving an image on the screen.
C. Placement can be justified left, right, or centered.
D. Places a box around an object.
E. Relative displacement is the method usually indicated for this operation.
F. Linetype, width, color.
G. Measures the distance and angle between two points.
H. Moves the display window from one location to another.
I. Stipple patterns.
J. Allows a freehand line to be drawn with the pointing device.
K. Can be used to alter the orientation of entities.
L. An object with equal length, sides, and angles.
M. Increases or decreases the apparent size of objects on the screen without changing their actual size.
N. Makes an array.
O. Generates a smoothly fitted arc of specified radius between two lines, arcs, or circles.

Architectural CADD Applications

■ OBJECTIVES

After studying this chapter, the student will be able to:
☐ Understand the major preliminary steps in getting ready to use a CADD package to make drawings.
☐ Explain the advantages of using several layers while making a CADD drawing.
☐ Outline the basic steps in producing floor plans, elevations, foundation plans, plot plans, electrical plans, and details.
☐ Apply the steps for making standard drawings to your own specifications.

■ DISPLAYS

1. Computer-Generated Drawings. Prepare a bulletin board display from computer-generated construction drawings. Select two or three different types of drawings—floor plan, elevation, detail, etc.
2. Student Work. Display examples of student work. Use problems from the workbook.

■ INSTRUCTIONAL MATERIALS

Text: Pages 555-580
   Review Questions, Suggested Activities
Workbook: Pages 277-281
   Review Questions, Problems/Activities
Teacher's Resource Guide:
   Chapter 38—Teaching Strategy
   Chapter 38—Exam

■ TEACHING STRATEGY

• Prepare Display #1.
• Review chapter objectives.
• Introduce architectural CADD applications.

• Discuss getting ready to use a CADD package.
• Present drawing setup.
• Discuss drawing floor plans.
• Assign workbook Problem 38-1.
• Discuss drawing elevations.
• Present drawing foundation/basement plans.
• Discuss drawing electrical plans.
• Prepare Display #2.
• Discuss drawing plot plans.
• Discuss drawing details.
• Assign one or more of the Suggested Activities in the text.
• Chapter Review
   —Assign Review Questions in the text. Discuss the correct answers.
   —Assign Review Questions in the workbook. Have students check their own answers.
• Evaluation
   —Administer the Chapter 38—Exam. Correct exam and return.
   —Return graded problems with comments.

■ ANSWERS TO REVIEW QUESTIONS, TEXT Pages 575-576

1. a. The symbols and conventions used in architecture.
   b. How structures are constructed.
   c. Understand the graphic language.
   d. Working knowledge of computer operation.
2. with the tutorial program.
3. c. Both of the above.
4. "C," or "D"
5. layer
6. b. #0 for door symbols, glazing, and wall cabinets.
7. c. Prepare a space diagram.
8. d. All of the above.
9. TEXT
10. grade

11. Typical wall section.
12. By turning off layers.
13. Different linetype.
14. underlay
15. The floor plans shows the opposite end of the stairs.
16. a. Foundation walls are dimensioned to the outside of the wall instead of to the outside of the rough stud wall.
    b. Windows are dimensioned to the side of the opening of a masonry wall and to the center in a frame wall.
17. a. COPY.
18. c. Dashed.
19. contour
20. The "dimension" layer.
21. a. Stairs.
    b. Fireplace.
    c. Kitchen cabinets.
    d. Windows.
    e. Doors.
    f. Foundation wall details.
    g. Roof.
22. Hatch symbol.

■ ANSWERS TO REVIEW QUESTIONS, WORKBOOK

PART I: MULTIPLE CHOICE

1. A. Size of the drawing.
2. C. Designated colors and layers for certain drawing characteristics.
3. B. Space diagram.
4. A. The outside of the rough frame wall.
5. D. All of the above.
6. C. Symbols library.
7. B. Wall section.
8. A. Hidden.
9. B. The line widths and symbols are different.
10. C. Long dashed line.
11. D. All of the above.
12. B. Circle.
13. A. Actual.
14. C. Grade line.

PART II: SHORT ANSWER/LISTING

1. A. Know the symbols and conventions to communicate.
   B. Know how structures are constructed so that your designs will be functional.
   C. Be prepared to provide the information required by various professionals.
   D. Understand the graphic language to communicate your ideas.
   E. Possess a working knowledge of the computer.
2. A. Standard architectural form (feet and inches).
   B. Feet in decimal form used for lengths on plot plans.
3. Architectural sizes are based on 9" x 12" multiples, while engineering sizes are based on 8 1/2" x 11" multiples.
4. So that the drawings can be merged with other drawings, have the proper line symbols, be easily modified, and permit different versions to be plotted.
5. Automatic conversion of the space diagram into a floor plan.
6. A. Stair treads.
   B. Handrails.
   C. Direction of travel.
7. Yes.
8. A. Will the house have a basement, crawl space, or slab foundation?
   B. How will the house relate to the present grade?
   C. Must the grade be modified to accommodate the structure?
   D. What are the finished floor to finished ceiling heights?
   E. How thick is the floor(s)?
   F. What type of roof construction is planned?
   G. Will standard rough opening heights be used for windows and doors?
   H. What kind of exterior materials will be used?
   I. What type of soffit will be used?
9. A. Dimensions.
   B. Notes.
   C. Scale.
   D. Title.
10. A. Are any special footings required inside the foundation perimeter to support columns, chimneys, as well as their location and sizes?
    B. Are any beam supports (pilasters) needed?
    C. Are any stepped footings or retaining walls needed?
    D. Are there any problems with the grade?
11. Yes.
12. Basement electrical plan.
13. Surveyor.
14. Details.
15. To allow sufficient room for the features to fit in the plans.
16. A. Finished floor to ceiling.
    B. Thickness of the floor system.
    C. Thickness and width of footing.
    D. Height of foundation wall.
    E. Overhang length.

PART III: COMPLETION

1. manual
2. "C"
3. pen
4. multipen
5. 1/2

6. floor
7. TEXT
8. layer
9. symbols
10. DIMENSION
11. paper.
12. dashed
13. colors.
14. tutorial.

■ ANSWERS TO CHAPTER 38—EXAM

TRUE—FALSE
1. T	4. T
2. T	5. F
3. T	

MULTIPLE CHOICE
1. B	9. C
2. B	10. D
3. D	11. B
4. A	12. A
5. C	13. B
6. C	14. D
7. B	15. D
8. D	

SHORT ANSWER
1. A. Knowing the symbols and conventions used in architecture are necessary to communicate precisely and accurately.
   B. Knowing how structures are constructed is necessary so that the designs will be sound and efficient.
   C. Knowing the graphic language so that ideas can be presented in a form that communicates well and is familiar to those who use drawings is also necessary.
2. A. Size of drawing sheet.
   B. Scale of the drawing.
   C. Orientation of the drawing.
   D. Borders.
   E. Title block.
3. A. Standard architectural form (feet and inches).
   B. Feet in decimal form (feet and tenths of feet).
4. A. Use different pen sizes.
   B. Specify the line width and let the plotter repeatedly trace the line.
5. A. Convert a space diagram into a floor plan.
   B. Use the DOUBLE LINE command to draw the walls.
6. To provide height measurements.
7. So they can be discarded when the drawing is complete.
8. Hidden line symbol.
9. Because they use different line symbols that will be drawn at different widths.
10. When locating interior stud walls or other features inside the foundation perimeter.
11. A curved, long-dashed line.
12. At a reference corner.

Chapter 38—Exam
ARCHITECTURAL CADD APPLICATIONS

Name _____

Period _____ **Date** _____ **Score** _____

TRUE—FALSE
Circle T if the statement is true or F if the statement is false.

T F 1. Architectural CADD is a field in its own right.

T F 2. A basic course in computer operation is useful before trying to use a CADD package.

T F 3. Configuring a microcomputer to run a CADD program can be difficult.

T F 4. Most residential plans are drawn on "C" or "D" size paper.

T F 5. The CADD package manual will tell you the effective plotting area for a sheet.

MULTIPLE CHOICE
Choose the answer that correctly completes the statement. Write the corresponding letter in the space provided.

_____ 1. A _____ program is a brief lesson on how the CADD program works and a demonstration of some of its primary capabilities.
A. test
B. tutorial
C. trial
D. None of the above

_____ 2. Most residential plans are drawn at 1/4" = 1'-0" scale. Which two construction drawings are frequently drawn at some other scale?
A. Plumbing plan and plot plan.
B. Plot plan and details.
C. Details and elevations.
D. Elevation and foundation plan.

_____ 3. Using several layers when making a CADD drawing will allow you to _____.
A. plot several versions of the final drawing
B. assign pen sizes or colors more easily
C. turn on or off certain features while constructing a drawing
D. All of the above

_____ 4. What pen width is most appropriate for dimension lines?
A. 0.25 mm (extra fine).
B. 0.35 mm (fine).
C. 0.50 mm (medium).
D. 0.70 mm (broad).

_____ 5. What is the purpose of a space diagram?
A. To show how furniture would fit into a room.
B. To show how the house would fit on a site.
C. To determine how the various areas of the house fit together.
D. To show how a drawing would fit on a drawing sheet.

_____ 6. The first step in drawing a floor plan with a CADD system is to _____.
    A. draw interior walls
    B. locate doors and windows
    C. create a space diagram
    D. None of the above

_____ 7. All construction features on the floor plan should be dimensioned unless _____.
    A. you don't know the dimension
    B. the location or size is obvious
    C. you plan to show it on another plan
    D. it is mentioned in the specifications

_____ 8. An exterior elevation is usually drawn for _____.
    A. the front and rear of the house only
    B. the front, rear, and one side
    C. the front, rear, and both sides
    D. all sides of the house

_____ 9. The reference point of most elevations is the _____ line.
    A. frost
    B. first floor
    C. grade
    D. footing

_____ 10. The _____ is generally used as an underlay when constructing the foundation plan.
    A. elevation
    B. plot plan
    C. typical wall section
    D. floor plan

_____ 11. The _____ plan is usually copied for a first floor electrical plan.
    A. foundation/basement
    B. first floor
    C. second floor
    D. None of the above

_____ 12. The _____ lines are frequently drawn as freehand lines on a plot plan.
    A. contour
    B. property
    C. building perimeter
    D. driveway

_____ 13. Which of the following is an appropriate contour interval for a one-acre building site for a residence?
    A. 1"
    B. 1'
    C. 10'
    D. 100'

_____ 14. Which of the following features of a residential structure would most likely require a detail?
    A. Fireplace.
    B. Stairs.
    C. Foundation wall.
    D. All of the above.

_____ 15. Which of the following is an appropriate scale for a detail?
    A. 1/16" = 1'-0"
    B. 1/8" = 1'-0"
    C. 1/4" = 1'-0"
    D. 1/2" = 1'-0"

Name _____

SHORT ANSWER
Answer each of the questions using short answers.

1. Describe three broad areas of skill/knowledge that are required to produce well-designed and properly communnicated residential plans.

   A. _____

   _____

   B. _____

   _____

   C. _____

   _____

2. Name five variables that are generally set during the drawing setup sequence.

   A. _____

   B. _____

   C. _____

   D. _____

   E. _____

3. What two basic forms of drawing units are commonly used when drawing residential house plans?

   A. _____

   B. _____

4. What two methods may be used to generate different line widths?

   A. _____

   B. _____

   _____

5. What two methods are commonly used to draw exterior and interior walls on a floor plan?

   A. _____

   B. _____

6. Why is a typical wall section generally used when constructing an elevation?

   _____

7. Why should projection lines be placed on a layer by themselves?

   _____

8. What line symbol is usually used for elements of the foundation that are below grade?

   _____

9. Why would the footings and foundation walls be placed on different layers?

   _____

   _____

10. When would you dimension to the inside of a foundation wall?

_____

_____

11. What type of line symbol is used to show the connection between a switch and lighting fixture on the electrical plan?

_____

12. Where is the most logical place to start when laying out a property boundary on a plot plan?

_____

39
CHAPTER

Career Opportunities

■ OBJECTIVES

After studying this chapter, the student will be able to:
☐ List various career options in architecture and residential construction.
☐ Compare the duties and educational requirements of various occupations in architecture and construction.

■ DISPLAYS

1. Careers in Architecture and Construction. Create a bulletin board display of typical career opportunities in architecture and construction. Use photos or descriptions of various careers.

■ INSTRUCTIONAL MATERIALS

Text: Pages 581-586
Review Questions, Suggested Activities
Workbook: Pages 283-286
Review Questions, Problems/Activities
Teacher's Resource Guide:
Chapter 39—Teaching Strategy
Chapter 39—Exam

■ TEACHING STRATEGY

- Prepare Display #1.
- Review chapter objectives.
- Introduce career opportunities.
- Discuss the architect.
- Discuss architectural drafters and illustrators.
- Present information about the specification writer and estimator.
- Discuss the surveyor and construction technologist.
- Discuss teaching architectural drawing.
- Assign workbook Problem 39-1.
- Assign one or more of the Suggested Activities in the text.

- Chapter Review
  - Assign Review Questions in the text. Discuss the correct answers.
  - Assign Review Questions in the workbook. Have students check their own answers.
- Evaluation
  - Administer the Chapter 39—Exam. Correct the exam and return.
  - Return graded problems with comments.

■ ANSWERS TO REVIEW QUESTIONS, TEXT
Pages 585-586

1. the plan is being followed, the materials specified are being used.
2. So the work will meet the standards of safety, health, and property.
3. a. High schools.
   b. Trade or vocational schools.
   c. Community colleges.
   d. Universities.
4. estimator.
5. a. Use of surveying equipment.
   b. Collection of data.
   c. Ability to do mapping.
   d. Knowing the principles of real estate property law.
6. a. Draws the details of working drawings.
   b. Makes tracings from original drawings by the architect.
7. building contractor.
8. specification writer.

■ ANSWERS TO REVIEW QUESTIONS, WORKBOOK

PART I: SHORT ANSWER/LISTING

1. Bachelor's degree from an accredited college or university.
2. Architectural illustrator.
3. Yes.

4. Economics, structural materials, math, and CADD operations.
5. A. Land surveying.
   B. Engineering surveying.
   C. Geodetic surveying.
   D. Cartographic surveying.
6. Requirements for a surveyor generally include a bachelor's degree in surveying or civil engineering. A surveying technician's requirements generally include a two-year program from a community college or technical institute plus practical experience.

PART II: COMPLETION

1. architect
2. architects.
3. estimator.
4. surveyor's
5. teaching
6. construction technologist.

PART III: MULTIPLE CHOICE

1. B. Design structures which meet the standards for health, safety, and property.
2. A. Be familiar with a CADD system.
3. C. Hardware, construction, and building materials.
4. D. All of the above.

PART IV: MATCHING

1. A. Architect.
2. B. Architectural drafter.
3. E. Specification writer.
4. D. Estimator.
5. F. Surveyor.
6. C. Construction technologist.

PART V: PROBLEMS/ACTIVITIES

1. Architect — —
   DUTIES:
   - Work closely with the client in making preliminary drawings, sketches, etc.
   - Prepare working drawings.
   - Assist the client in selecting a contractor.
   - Periodically check on construction.
   EDUCATIONAL REQUIREMENTS:
   - Generally, a bachelor's degree is required, but a two-year degree and several years of practical experience is sometimes acceptable. A license is required.

   Architectural Drafter — —
   DUTIES:
   - Draw details of working drawings and make

tracings from original drawings.
- Often begin as junior drafters.
EDUCATIONAL REQUIREMENTS:
- Usually, several courses in architectural drawing and the use of CAD in high school or community college is sufficient to begin as an architectural drafter.

Architectural Illustrator — —
DUTIES:
- Prepare sketches, drawings, renderings, and illustrations for clients and publications such as commercial catalogs and advertisements.
EDUCATIONAL REQUIREMENTS:
- Similar to those of the architectural drafter or commercial artist.

Specification Writer — —
DUTIES:
- Prepares all the necessary written information needed to describe materials, methods, and fixtures to be used in the structure.
EDUCATIONAL REQUIREMENTS:
- A college degree is usually required with an emphasis on drawings, materials, and building construction.

Estimator — —
DUTIES:
- Calculate the costs of materials and labor for a building.
- Prepare all the paperwork necessary to inform the architect and/or builder of what the costs of the structure will be.
EDUCATIONAL REQUIREMENTS:
- A college degree with emphasis on mathematics and the use of computers is generally required. A background in economics and structural materials is also valuable.

Surveyor — —
DUTIES:
- Establish areas and boundaries of real estate property.
- Involved with the planning and subdivision of land and the preparation of property descriptions.
EDUCATIONAL REQUIREMENTS:
- Normally, a bachelor's degree in surveying or civil engineering is required, but some community colleges and universities offer two year programs for surveying technicians.

Construction Technologist — —
DUTIES:
- Construction technologists are qualified for both technical and supervisory roles in the construction industry. Specializations include estimation and bidding, quality control, site supervision, specifications writing, expediting,

purchasing, and managing construction.
EDUCATIONAL REQUIREMENTS:
- A bachelor's degree in construction technology is required.

Teacher of Architectural Drafting— —
DUTIES:
- Teaching in high schools, trade or vocational schools, community colleges, and universities.

EDUCATIONAL EXPERIENCE:
- A master's degree is required, or at least desired, to teach at most any level, but a doctorate is preferred for teaching at the university level. Practical experience in the field is also a necessity.

■ ANSWERS TO CHAPTER 39—EXAM

TRUE—FALSE
1. T	4. T
2. T	5. T
3. F	

MULTIPLE CHOICE
1. C	5. C
2. B	6. A
3. B	7. D
4. D	8. A

Chapter 39—Exam
CAREER OPPORTUNITIES

Name _____

Period _____ **Date** _____ **Score** _____

TRUE—FALSE
Circle T if the statement is true or F if the statement is false.

T F 1. An architect's job involves a great deal of creativity and sensitivity to form and materials.

T F 2. Architects must pass an examination to obtain a license to practice.

T F 3. Most architects design residential dwellings as part of their work.

T F 4. Architectural illustration is a specialized field that requires a certain amount of art talent.

T F 5. One who calculates the costs of materials and labor for a building is called an estimator.

MULTIPLE CHOICE
Choose the answer that correctly completes the statement. Write the corresponding letter in the space provided.

_____ 1. The academic credentials required for an architect is generally a(n) _____.
   A. few years of work experience
   B. associate degree
   C. baccalaureate degree
   D. master's degree

_____ 2. A(n) _____ generally draws the details of working drawings and makes tracings from original drawings that the architect or designer has prepared.
   A. junior architect
   B. architectural drafter
   C. architectural illustrator
   D. construction technologist

_____ 3. Educational requirements for the architectural drafter usually include _____.
   A. high school graduation
   B. high school graduation with some courses in architectural drawing
   C. two years of community college work
   D. baccalaureate degree

_____ 4. The job of the _____ is to prepare all the necessary written information needed to describe materials, methods, and fixtures to be used in the structure.
   A. architectural illustrator
   B. estimator
   C. construction technologist
   D. specification writer

_____ 5. The educational requirement for an estimator frequently includes _____.
   A. only high school graduation
   B. an associate degree in building construction
   C. baccalaureate degree
   D. None of the above

_____ 6. What professional establishes areas and boundaries of real estate property?
   A. Land surveyor.
   B. Construction technologist.
   C. Architectural drafter.
   D. None of the above

_____ 7. Opportunities to teach architectural drawing exist in _____.
   A. high schools and trade or vocational schools
   B. community colleges
   C. universities
   D. All of the above

_____ 8. What professional is qualified for both supervisory and technical roles in the construction industry?
   A. Construction technologist.
   B. Architectural drafter.
   C. Architectural illustrator.
   D. None of the above